MONEY ORDER

The Money Management Guide for Women

**Womankind Educational
and Resource Center, Inc.**

GAIL R. SHAPIRO, EDITOR

A FIRESIDE BOOK
Published by Simon & Schuster
New York   London   Toronto   Sydney   Singapore

Fireside
Rockefeller Center
1230 Avenue of the Americas
New York, NY 10020

Designed by Christine Weathersbee

Manufactured in the United States of America

10 9 8 7 6 5 4 3 2 1

Library of Congress Cataloging-in-Publication Data

Money order : the money management guide for women / Womankind Educational and Resource Center, Inc.; Gail R. Shapiro.
    p.   cm.
    "A Fireside book."
    Includes bibliographical references and index.
    1. Women—Finance, Personal.   I. Shapiro, Gail R., date.   II. Womankind Educational and Resource Center.
  HG179.M59676   2001
  332.024'042—dc21
                                                                                                00-053821
ISBN 0-684-87098-3

The authors gratefully acknowledge permission from the following source
to reprint material in its control:
Jewish Publication Society, *The TANAKH: The New JPS Translation*
According to the Traditional Hebrew Text. Copyright © 1985.

ACKNOWLEDGMENTS

A very special thanks to Ann Bickford Smith,
president of Womankind Educational and Resource Center,
Inc., and cofounder of the Financial Literacy Project

Our sincere appreciation to the following individuals and organizations, colleagues, family and friends, whose contributions, support, encouragement, criticism, and love made this project possible:

Jill Adomaites, Adelaide Aitken, Anne Bartholomew, Leila Basmajian, Katharine M. Berlin, Boston Women's Health Book Collective, Scott Castle, Carla C. Cataldo, Compago Creative (Marlboro, Massachusetts), Lisa Considine, Crossroads Community Foundation (Natick, Massachusetts), Davis Shapiro & Lewit, LLP (New York City), Anita Diamant, Paige Garrison, Joyce Gordon, Mimi Goss, Greater Worcester Community Foundation, Sylvia Goos Greene, Cathy Gronewold, Joanne Hansen, Nancy A. Haverstock, Nadine Heaps, Karin Hedberg, Helping Our Women (Provincetown, Massachusetts), Barbara Honthumb, Claire Josephs Houston, Janet Jaffe, Suzy Sayle Jimerson, Lynn Klamkin, Ilene Knopping, Cliff Kolovson, Lawrence Kushner, Jennifer Lane, Andrew Maclary, Ed Maclary, Harvey Maclary, Kevin Maclary, Rose Ellen Kohn-McCaig, Tricia Medved, Sue Memhard, Marion Meenan, Middlesex Savings Bank (Natick, Massachusetts), Emily Minty, Steve Moore, Carole Morgan, Michael Murphy, Suzanne Murphy, Judy Norsigian, Peter Oriol, Jane Orr, Martha Frances Patton, Margery Piercy, Sandra Pirie-St. Amour, Nanci Pisani, Pointed Communications (Wayland, Massachusetts), Raytheon Company (Lexington, Massachusetts), Maureen Reilly, Phyll Dondis Ribakoff, Rosie Rosenzweig, Larry Scripp, Arline Shapiro, Dan Shapiro, Danna Shapiro, Hal Shapiro, Jill Shapiro, Rita Shapiro, Steve Shapiro, Alix Kates Shulman, Maddie Sifantus, Barbara Singer, Jenny Smith, Scott Smith, Nancy Stoodt, Sudbury Foundation (Sudbury, Massachusetts), Derry Tanner, Chrisann Taras, Janet Taylor, Jane Titus, Teresa Tobin, Kathleen Usher, Paula Venezia, Gil Wolin, Maxine Wolin, Womankind's current and former board members and friends, Women Supporting Women Center (Exeter, New Hampshire), Women's Center for Wellness (Hopedale, Massachusetts), and more than six hundred Financial Literacy Project alumnae and instructors.

Dedicated to the daughters of Zelophehad—
perhaps the first women in recorded history to stand up
for their economic rights—and all our daughters

The daughters of Zelophehad . . . came forward . . . They stood before Moses . . . and they said, "Our father died in the wilderness . . . and he has left no sons. Let not our father's name be lost to his clan just because he had no son! Give us a holding among our father's kinsmen!"

Moses brought their case before the Lord.

And the Lord said to Moses, "The plea of Zelophehad's daughters is just: you should give them a hereditary holding among their father's kinsmen; transfer their father's share to them."

The Tanakh, NUMBERS 27:1–9

CONTENTS

CONTENTS

MONEY ORDER

INTRODUCTION

IF YOU ARE OLD ENOUGH—AND PARTICULARLY IF you lived in or near a college town—you may remember getting your hands on the first edition of *Our Bodies, Ourselves.* Then titled *Women and Their Bodies,* printed by the New England Free Press and stapled together on newsprint, it sold for 40 cents. Women pored avidly over the chapters: excited, angry, eager to learn, wanting to take more responsibility for our health and our lives.

Now, thirty years and 4 million copies later, *Our Bodies, Ourselves* continues to educate, challenge, and inspire women and health care providers all over the world. Because of the hard work of the brave and brilliant women of the Boston Women's Health Book Collective, a new generation of women is learning to ask questions, and to take responsibility for its own health.

Our goal is to do the same for women's economic well-being. We believe that change begins with education, for education opens women's eyes and broadens our options.

To help you take control of your own financial well-being, Womankind is proud to present *Money Order: The Money Management Guide for Women* as the next step in women's self-advocacy. Topics are presented by women financial experts who love their work and communicate their enthusiasm. In many chapters, you will find "inside tips" by the contributing authors—often, information that financial institutions wish you didn't have.

Collaboratively written by and for women, *Money Order* aims to help readers:

- Become more confident and competent managers of money

- Overcome fear of or aversion to understanding and managing money

- Set and achieve financial goals

- Communicate more effectively with financial professionals

- Become aware of the enormous potential power of women's collective philanthropy and its implications

Illuminated by anecdotes and true stories from Financial Literacy Project students, *Money Order* honors the ancient tradition of women passing along wisdom to other women—in the women's tent, in living rooms, at the playground, and over coffee.

HOW THIS BOOK CAME INTO BEING

Money Order is based on edited transcripts of Womankind Educational and Resource Center's Financial Literacy Project (FLP) introductory six-week financial management classes. Women accountants, attorneys, auto dealers, bankers, financial planners, insurance agents, mortgage specialists, stockbrokers, and other professionals—who adhere to a strict "no selling" policy—present weekly lectures and answer questions.

Women of all ages, income, and educational levels, from different cultural backgrounds and family situations, learn together. Each brings her unique perspective and experience to class. Students' stories and experiences are woven liberally into the text of *Money Order*, as we believe that every student has something to teach as well as to learn.

The FLP is a program of Womankind Educational and Resource Center, Inc., a nonprofit organization incorporated in July 1993 for women in the suburbs west of Boston.

During our first year of operations, Resource Center staff noticed a pattern to the calls that came in: many of the problems for which community women were requesting help had to do, in whole or in part, with money—or, more specifically, with women's lack of financial know-how.

We began to ask ourselves some hard questions: Why are so many women afraid or unwilling to address money issues? What personal and societal factors hold women back from achieving financial independence? What is the basic financial information that every woman needs to know? And how can we teach ourselves or obtain that knowledge? How can women work together to make positive changes not only in our own lives, but also in the lives of all women?

In October 1995, we assembled a team of talented women to examine some of these questions. The group included a teacher/curriculum specialist, financial adviser, attorney, investment broker, accountant, bookkeeper, real estate broker, retired business executive, at-home mother,

development officer, and psychologist. Together, we reviewed existing women's financial education curricula and print materials. Then, in collaboration with a group of target clients, the team designed the content of a core class of financial education and empowerment for women. Womankind's Financial Literacy Project offered the first six-week class in March 1996.

Today, volunteer Womankind board members coordinate the local FLP, with assistance from an advisory board of financial experts and community members. Up to twenty students participate in each class. Scholarships are available for all those unable to pay the full tuition. No woman ever is turned away due to inability to pay.

The twelve hours of instruction time are divided into lectures, small group work, and hands-on problem solving and discussion. Homework is given each week to supplement the classroom time. The course material includes goal setting, assessing net worth, banking, credit, record keeping, major purchases, investing, estate and retirement planning, philanthropy, and topics chosen by the students.

Class graduates are encouraged to continue their financial education by creating new programs. "Designing Your Own Stock Portfolio," a money support group, a group for women going through divorce, two investment clubs, an in-depth class on estate and retirement planning, and a workshop on organizing paperwork are off-shoots of the FLP.

In the spring of 1997, a family self-sufficiency program in a neighboring town requested the FLP course at its site. Clients numbered more than forty single parents receiving welfare and making the transition back to work. With support from a local foundation and a community bank,

Womankind presented the class on-site beginning in October 1997. Two full scholarships and pay differentials enabled two family self-sufficiency clients to be trained as Financial Literacy Project facilitators.

After successfully presenting and evaluating ten six-week classes for 180 women, Womankind offered the first FLP Leaders Training Program in March 1998. Ten women from seven sites in Massachusetts, New Hampshire, Vermont, and Ontario, Canada, attended the three-day session. The Leaders Training prepared these women to develop and teach the Financial Literacy Project classes in their communities.

The Leaders Training Program presented Womankind's successful strategies for organizing, advertising, and teaching the classes, handling registrations, training for speakers, fund-raising, tailoring curriculum to their individual communities, marketing, and generating income for the nonprofit women's centers or groups.

Shortly thereafter, Womankind received the first of many requests for on-site training, and for FLP personnel to speak to groups of women and girls at various sites, including women's centers, high schools and colleges, Girl Scout troops, and various women's organizations.

CHANGES IN OURSELVES, CHANGES IN OUR FAMILIES

As the first Financial Literacy classes got under way, women reported changes not only within themselves, but also within their families. A few partners or children were suspicious or patronizing; many more were encouraging and supportive.

All of a sudden, my teenage son became very interested in what I was doing: "Mom, why are you learning this money stuff? Are you planning to divorce Dad and leave us or what?"

Many women who expected hostility or indifference were surprised.

By happy coincidence, the car-buying class came the week we needed to buy a new car. I went by myself to the dealership—a first in fifty-five years!—and made such a great bargain that my husband, who had been very skeptical, asked me to buy his next car, too.

We began to see an unanticipated benefit: that for women who live with partners or families, the classes helped to open communication around money in a positive, nonconfrontational way. And in older, or "traditional" families where the man is the breadwinner and the woman is the homemaker, many men expressed great relief.

I was so glad when my wife of thirty years suddenly took an interest in our finances. I guess we both thought dealing with money was somehow unfeminine. Being able to discuss the future openly has taken a huge weight off my shoulders, and has created a whole new dimension in our marriage.

Self-supporting women of all ages, as well as those who have been widowed or divorced, have had to deal with money on their own. But many married middle-class women have not. It is particularly common for women who are not working outside the home, who currently are happily married to well-providing men, to avoid thinking about money.

Most women are a missed heartbeat away from financial insecurity. For a woman, there can be no such thing as complacency, and I think that is the most difficult notion to share.

It's not true that women can't deal with money. A lot of us just don't want to!

A woman may come to the FLP class for a variety of reasons. She may be going through or anticipating a life transition: she is about to have a child, or her last child is graduating; she wants to get off welfare, change careers, or get out of an unhappy marriage; she may be saving to buy a house, pay for college, or plan for her own retirement. Some may have a sister or a friend in a difficult situation, and want to help. Some are experiencing problems themselves, such as:

- Sophia, twenty-two, now graduating from college with $125,000 in loans and credit card debt.

- Vicki, a young mother of three, whose husband died suddenly, leaving no life insurance.

- Miriam, who is trying to get back into the workforce after being disabled for seven years.

- Lee, who works two jobs and takes sole care of her elderly father with Alzheimer's disease.

Most students say that they take the class to feel more empowered:

It's our own freedom and welfare we're looking after.

The times I made a lot of money, I always felt guilty. Somehow, I felt I didn't deserve it.

Every woman needs to feel confident she can take care of herself!

MONEY ORDER: WHAT'S IN IT, HOW TO USE IT

Money Order presents information about what we consider to be the most important topics every woman needs to know for a well-ordered financial life.

Interspersed with the text and comments from our students and teachers is advice from women—some famous, some not yet famous—and their responses to the questions "What did you learn about money while growing up?" and "What do you think every woman and girl needs to know about money?"

We open with a historical overview of the question "Why do women have such a hard time dealing with money?" Younger readers may be surprised by the answer, unlike their mothers and grandmothers, who had to face many of the obstacles described.

Money Order tells all women why and how to set goals, how to translate those goals into a viable financial plan, and why good record keeping is so important. You will learn how to establish and manage credit, and how to approach major buying decisions. We discuss how to insure both those major purchases as well as your general financial well-being. An introduction to investing is next, followed by an overview of retirement and estate planning. A "hands-on" lesson in negotiation skills precedes an outline of charitable giving and a discussion of how women working together can make positive changes in our communities.

Much of the information will be useful immediately as you begin or continue to take charge of your financial life. Some of the other, more specific topics will be more useful to you later on, as your financial situation and needs change.

We suggest that you begin by reading through

the entire book to obtain an overview of what constitutes financial literacy. Then, since so many of the important financial decisions you will make in the future will be informed by the choices you make today, go back and study first the chapters pertinent to your current situation.

Making a commitment to become knowledgeable about money—finally—is a lot like getting your annual Pap smear or going to the dentist—no one wants to do it, but you do it anyway because it is good for you, and because even some knowledge can help prevent serious financial, legal, job-related, and domestic problems.

And, like eating well and getting enough physical exercise, reading and doing the exercises in *Money Order* is a way of taking care of yourself. Confronting your anxiety about money is not unlike going on a reducing diet. You may have tried and failed many times before. This time it's going to work. The keys? Your determination and the support and encouragement of other women.

Money Order is different from most books about money in that it is designed to be used by women working and learning together. We strongly encourage you to read the book and do the exercises with a group of women, or at least with one friend. By talking about money with each other, and sharing with each other, you can begin to feel more confident and capable. If you are using the book by yourself, you may find it helpful to share at least some of the exercises with a friend or partner. Our students suggest:

If you think you are going to try to plow through this on your own, stop and think again. It's so much easier with a group. Together you can make goals, challenge yourselves, hold each other accountable. In our group, sometimes we even give each other rewards for work completed!

We also suggest that you share both your experience and your newfound knowledge with a younger woman—perhaps one of high school age. After all, there's a good chance she will listen to you rather than to her own mother! As you yourself learn, you can model for her and teach her to become a prudent money manager, to believe in herself, and to understand the importance of taking herself and her financial life seriously.

WE WANT TO HEAR FROM YOU!

As we begin the next edition of *Money Order*, we really want your feedback. What worked? What did not? What suggestions do you have for improving the book? What would you like other women to know?

We also invite you to bring the Financial Literacy Project to your area. To find out how, please contact us at: Womankind FLP, Box 5365, Wayland, MA 01778, via e-mail to wkerc@ziplink.net, or via our Web site www.womankindflp.org.

Join us on a venture that will change your life—and the lives of women in your community!

—Gail R. Shapiro

Womankind Educational and Resource Center, Inc., is a 501(c)(3) nonprofit organization, incorporated in July 1993, created by and for women. Our mission is to provide access to resources, advocacy, and support to all women, and to promote opportunities for personal and professional development and mutual assistance. Via our Leaders Training Program, the Financial Literacy Project reaches women in all parts of the United States and Canada. Royalties income from the sale of this book is not sufficient to support our work, and we continue to seek funding from individuals, corporations, and foundations. We gratefully encourage your tax-deductible support. Please send gifts to Womankind, Inc., P.O. Box 5365, Wayland, MA 01778. Thank you!

1: Changing the Way Women Think About Money

Contributing Authors:

Barbara R. Honthumb and Gail R. Shapiro

"There is no liberation for women—or anybody else for that matter—without economic independence. If you want control over your life, you have to support yourself."

—ISABEL ALLENDE, WRITER

WHY DO WOMEN HAVE SUCH A HARD TIME BEING comfortable with money? Why is understanding money literally "the next frontier" for women?

We have been asked, "Why a book just for women? Are men and women really so different when it comes to dealing with money?"

Womankind's founder and executive director Gail Shapiro answers, "I know plenty of people—men and women—who cannot balance a checkbook. I have yet to hear a man giggle about it!"

The point is that our culture *expects* men to be knowledgeable about and "good with" money—whether they actually are or not—and does *not* have a similar expectation of women. This societal expectation is not men's fault. It is not necessarily a conspiracy against women, but rather a reflection of a male value system. In our culture, money has not been women's traditional area of expertise—so it is not surprising that many of us have been uncomfortable with or afraid of what we do not understand.

It's about time we got comfortable.

Let's begin with how this value system came to be, why it is prevalent today, and how we can re-spond in a way that benefits both women and men.

THE ROOTS OF THE SYSTEM

From the beginning of time, men's and women's roles were very different. Women bore and raised the children, prepared the food, spun yarn and wove cloth for clothing, tended the elderly and the infirm, and literally kept the home fires burning. Men were the hunters, brought home the food, and, being bigger and stronger, offered security and protection from predators. We could not have survived without each successfully filling our respective roles. This even exchange worked quite well for millennia, until the Industrial Revolution began to blur the biological-based differences between women's and men's work.

In the introductory chapter of her landmark book, *If Women Counted: A New Feminist Economics,*[1] New Zealand economist and former member of Parliament Marilyn Waring explores the basis of Western economics. At the root of our financial system is a very basic bias, indicates

Waring. Work that is done directly to produce things needed for the everyday care and feeding of families, raising children, and so forth generally is *unpaid* work, while work that is done to produce "tokens" that can be used to obtain things needed for the everyday care and feeding of families is generally *paid* work.

Simply put, for centuries, women were not accustomed to being compensated for our work. If compensation was involved, the work then became the province of men. Conversely, if a woman was compensated for her work, it was because she had entered the traditional province of men.

We can look to the economics of health care for an example. Through much of the history of civilization, women took care of the health needs of each other and our families. Wise women and midwives attended to the sick and laboring, and saw to basic preventive care. With the rise of the scientific method and the evolution of Western culture, men became the "owners" of knowledge and the dispensers of scientific medicine. These wise women were then labeled witches, midwives were replaced by obstetricians, and the work that once was simply a part of the fabric of women's life became the source of financial gain—big gain in many cases.

Despite the Oxford English Dictionary's *description of labor as "the pains and effort of childbirth: travail," the woman in labor—the reproducer, sustainer, and nurturer of human life—does not "produce" anything. Similarly, all the other reproductive work that women do is widely viewed as unproductive . . . yet the satisfaction of basic needs to sustain human society is fundamental to the economic system. By this*

failure to acknowledge the primacy of reproduction, the male face of economics is fatally flawed.[2]

The social exchange of services, which is the giving and receiving of services within social networks of relatives, friends, neighbors, and acquaintances, is also regarded as economically unimportant and remains unacknowledged.[3]

Given Waring's examples above, it is easy to see why women might not like, or might be uncomfortable dealing with, money: money has relatively little historical connection to the labor and lives of women. In fact, economic structure pretty much removes women, and the very things women value most, from the financial equation.

Since the Industrial Revolution, we have lost much understanding of our own value to ourselves and to society. By the nineteenth century, as work became more industrialized, women's lives became easier, but at the same time, our work became less critical for basic survival.

We can look at the way women have tried to reclaim meaningful work during the past several decades as a continuum of less-than-successful experiments. We kept house with a vengeance in the fifties, questioned it all in the sixties, tried to do it all in the seventies and eighties, and began reexamining and redefining the meaning of success in the nineties.

Many older women grew up feeling that they had no choices. Their roles were defined: until the middle of the twentieth century, most women either married and had children, or worked in one of the few jobs "appropriate" for women: nurse, teacher, secretary, waitress, or librarian.

The necessity for women in the labor force during World War II lured women out of the kitchen and into factories, munitions plants, and construction crews. Popular opinion and the media gave support and credibility to these strong, patriotic women, who filled in for our brave boys overseas. Writing in 1943, Nell Giles says:

As more men go off to war, more women must take their places. This we all know. The career girl has a better choice of top-of-the-ladder jobs than ever before. She can squeeze into places where position and money, to this time, belonged only to men.[4]

Working gave women not only a new sense of purpose, but also newly found self-esteem. Giles comments:

It is good to see an improvement in the appearance of the girls who are making money for the first time in their lives . . . a pay check of one's own helps.[5]

When the war ended, soldiers returned home, wanting and expecting their jobs back. Suddenly, it became "unfeminine" for women to work outside the home. Women's magazines began publishing articles by experts on the benefits to the family of the stay-at-home wife and mother. "More Babies—More Fun!" and "Find Your Community Work" encouraged women to focus on the domestic front.

Today, as a hundred years ago, a good wife must be a competent homemaker. . . . Just as it remains basically the husband's responsibility to earn the living, it remains basically the wife's responsibility to run the home. It is to be hoped that, as her grandmother did, she recognizes her responsibility.[6]

Some advice on how to be a "good wife," circa 1950:

Do not regard him as a kitchen helper, errand boy or handy man . . . if he offers to dry the dishes, thank him for the favor, rather than regard it as your right. Indulge his whims when possible, even when they seem foolish to you. . . . Bringing up children is never an easy assignment, but the rewards are great. If your situation demands bringing up father, too, the problem is increased—but so are the incentives.[7]

Our models of virtuous womanhood—June Cleaver, Donna Reed, Harriet Nelson—came from television, which began to shape the opinions and beliefs of most American families. We watched TV and saw cleaner floors, lighter cakes, brighter wash, and fresher breath. We saw polite children, handsome husbands, and women content to keep everyone else happy.

Then came Simone de Beauvoir, Betty Friedan, Doris Lessing, Adrienne Rich, and others who wrote about the reality of women's lives, telling the truth as they saw it. We heard that women were being "held down by a patriarchal society," our potential limited by society's beliefs and expectations.

No wonder women—and men—were confused.

The sixties, a tidal wave of change, washed away old values, ideas, and limitations. We raised our consciousness, fought for women's right to control our own lives, entered college and the workforce in record numbers, and delayed or omitted marriage and childbearing.

Nearly forty years later, we still are struggling to find new roles, new beliefs, and new definitions of the most important elements in our lives: work and family, creativity and spirituality. We are testing new models of combining these components in a way that satisfies us and benefits women, men, families, and communities.

Overall, women today have more options. But the reality is that difficult barriers still exist for women, particularly women of color, low-income women, and women with disabilities. The laws and policies created in the past forty years signal a shift in society's beliefs. Behavior change will follow, but it may be slow.

WHERE YOU ARE IN YOUR LIFE INFORMS YOUR CHOICES

A young woman today has a full range of career and family choices. She is growing up seeing mothers who work, mothers who stay home, women on their own. If she is a careful and critical observer, as most young women tend to be, she can see and evaluate the pitfalls and advantages of these options.

I don't want to end up struggling like my mom, who is raising four of us all by herself. Maybe I'll decide to get married, but right now I'm studying hard. I want to get good grades, so I can go to college and become a veterinarian.

A young woman has one advantage over her mother: the evolved societal expectation that she be capable of taking care of herself! She may prefer a single life. Or she may choose a partner with whom she divides the breadwinning/homemaking duties according to the couple's own liking, rather than societal standards. In either case, today's young woman is expected to be self-reliant.

Every one of my friends expects to be able to take care of herself. We want to have the freedom to be independent, and to have a career. But most of us also dream of having the perfect family. Growing up, it never crossed my mind to expect a husband to take care of me. It simply wasn't an option. Not until I got older did I realize that this wasn't always the case for women.

These young women's mothers and grandmothers, born in the first half of the twentieth century, now have more options than ever before. Some are exuberant about this freedom. Some are scared. Some feel unprepared. Many are bewildered: someone changed the rules in the middle of the game.

I grew up thinking, "You finish high school, you marry, you have kids, a man takes care of you, you're set for life." I was not a stupid kid. That was just what I heard. My sister, who's only four years younger, heard a different message: "You get an education, you get a job, you learn to take care of yourself, and then maybe you get married later on." Same background, same parents. What was different? The times.

Somewhere in the back of our heads, even though we know it's not true, we want to believe that someone else—a husband, a father, the government—should be taking care of us. I think maybe it's biological—you know, women are programmed to take care of our young, while someone provides for us. Even if that's true, it isn't too realistic today.

While it's true that younger women have a wider range of options, older women have the self-knowledge and experience to choose their path more wisely. Women at every age and life stage can begin to turn dreams into reality, to create a full and meaningful life. It's not too soon, or too late! As you will read in chapter 2, an important first step is to understand what it is you value.

Which brings us back to the question, "What is it that women value?"

In her important book *Beyond Power,* Marilyn French attempts an answer:

Our morality manifests itself in our choices, how we live, to what we devote our time and money, the kinds of friends we make, the way we spend our leisure.[8]

In *Women's Reality,* Anne Wilson Schaef echoes this thought:

When I am lying on my deathbed, I think I will look back on the relationships I have had and the connections I have made. These will be the things I consider most important. It will not matter whether I have built a bridge, or written a book, or had a university named after me. I will cherish the lives I have touched and those persons whose lives have touched mine.[9]

How powerfully these quotations typify the values of most women!

From talking with our students, and living our lives, we believe that what is most important to most women are our personal relationships with friends and family.

Placing such value on building and maintaining relationships—the "nonproductive" world—is what keeps most women willing to drop in and out of our jobs and careers—the "productive" world—when we perceive that our families need us. Our students speak:

I left my job—only two years from retirement age, when I would have received full pension—because my dear mother needed full-time care, and I was the only one of her children who could give it. I read recently that the value of a long-term caregiver is about $650,000 a year if you add up the cost of all the roles she plays: nurse, cook, housekeeper, personal caregiver. It was hard work, but no amount of money could equal the satisfaction and peace I felt. I am so grateful that I could be the one to comfort Mom and help her through her final months.

Recently, I got divorced and reentered the workforce for the first time in ten years. My main goal was to find a job that would allow me to be home after school for my kids. Working part time means lower salary, no benefits, and giving up my chances for career advancement—at least for now. But I am raising my kids myself, and I want to do it well.

Managing our money is an activity that competes for our "free" or nonpaid time and it competes with the very things that we value—spending time with our families and friends. So we choose to put off learning about the stock market or how much we should be putting away for retirement, and instead spend our time taking the kids to their soccer matches, or going out with friends.

I spend a considerable part of my time producing unpaid work—nurturing my family and relationships. Because this is where I choose to spend my time, it also is a reflection of what I value.

So, the important question is: How can we develop a *women's* system—a system that fits into our lifework—for becoming and remaining financially responsible? While supporting our primary value of relationship, can we develop a way to stay clear and conscious of our need to be fiscally responsible?

We know what can happen if we do not.

Reluctance to think about or take responsibility for our own financial well-being may lead to bad financial decisions, lost opportunities, being taken advantage of at work or at home or during a divorce or other legal action. If we haven't experienced this ourselves, we surely know someone who has been adversely affected.

As thousands of women in this country and worldwide know all too well, economic dependence equals vulnerability. No woman should be stuck in a bad relationship because she has no other viable option for herself or her children. And some women choose to stay in bad relationships because they simply cannot conceive of supporting themselves.

When you have your own money, you can love freely.

The number of women earning our own incomes has tripled in the past thirty years, but we have a lot of catching up to do. Although the wage gap between men and women is closing when we adjust the figures for education and years of work experience, on average, women still earn only 76 cents for every dollar men earn; 55 cents for unskilled workers, and 50 cents for executives. For women past traditional workforce age, the numbers are just as frightening: the average income for U.S. women older than sixty-five is just $8,200—including Social Security!

The problems of gender-based inequity are enormous, and affect women of all backgrounds and income levels. Because so many women drop in and out of the workforce to raise families or care for aging parents, we often are not adequately protected by traditional pension plans or even by Social Security. Women working at low-paying jobs—even those working a full forty-hour week—may not have decent child care and adequate, affordable health care. In more affluent households, most women would find it difficult to maintain the family's economic status on her income alone.

Fully 90 percent of women currently supported by someone else—parents, partner, or the government—will, at some point, be handling finances on their own.

Many women take pleasure in the status that a well-providing husband or partner provides. Even the most independent woman can fall subconsciously into the more-common-than-you-might-think mind-set of marital complacency: "Well, now I have a husband to lean on so I don't have to work as hard."

Writing in 1981, Colette Dowling asserted in *The Cinderella Complex:* "The deep wish to be taken care of by others is the chief force holding women down."[10] This wish may be just as common—although better disguised—among women today. Dreams of the intimacy and protection that marriage brings are not always fully realized: ultimately, you yourself are responsible for your own happiness. Women who have come to this realization the hard way say:

It is a horrible feeling to be financially dependent on someone you neither love nor trust. The fact that he has power over you makes you have to listen to crap even when you know that's all it is. When someone else is paying for your food, your clothes, your rent, and your health care, you are at his mercy.

I'm learning to live in the NOW—and not to blame my partner or anyone else for my "foot dragging."

I took the FLP class to learn to become a "financial grown-up." I no longer expect to be "parented" about money.

I really like having my own money. I never want to have to account to anyone as to how I spend it.

The only way some of us will be able to begin to take charge of our money is to stop thinking about it as a "male thing" and just do it.

My son said to me, "Mom, you manage other people's finances all day long. Why do you have such a hard time doing ours?" That really made me stop and think. It's not interesting to manage your own money. Managing other people's is satisfying, because I'm helping them.

We also need to recognize the possible hidden benefits we may derive from our reluctance to deal with money.

I think we need to give ourselves permission to recognize and accept that reluctance, even as we struggle to grow past it. Whether we want to admit it or not, historically, there has been a premium placed on girls and women looking dumb. What's really behind "If I'm good at math the boys won't like me"? That if we show that we are competent, we will not be able to attract a partner: no one will want us. A pretty reasonable fear—we all want to be loved and wanted. And if we appear to be "too ignorant" to manage the household money—a tedious chore—then someone else will have to do it for us. This ploy is not too different from that of the man who "misses" spots when he washes dishes or vacuums, or who "forgets" to change the baby's diapers.

THE MEANING OF MONEY

For most women, paid work and money itself have to have some meaning beyond just taking care of one's self. Money in and of itself is abstract.

I finally understood that for me, the only reason I wanted to make money was to be able to help others. But to be able to do so, I needed to be financially secure first. It's kind of like being on an airplane, where they tell you to put on your own oxygen mask first before trying to assist anyone else.

Learning how to make intelligent, informed decisions about family finances has set a great example for my child. It's very hard to teach our children about the value of money unless we value it and know how to use it ourselves.

Shared work often is a bond among women, creating a sense of belonging. Today's baby-sitting co-ops and food co-ops mirror the quilting bees of yesterday. Among some groups of women, bartering for their most basic needs is a way of life—and a very concrete way to deal with money.

We have such a wide range of attitudes about money. We may feel that if only we had more or spent more wisely we'd be happier and more fulfilled. Or we may feel that it is somehow "unholy" to make or like money.

My sister and I often wonder how it is that we both have worked in nonprofit organizations our whole lives, while our brothers always have worked in the for-profit world.

For many women, money is just not high enough on the priority list. Men probably value clean clothes, but not enough to do the laundry!

To begin the process of change, we have to "morph" what money means. Money cannot just

25

be a token—an abstract thing that is going to take care of me someday—nor can it be an end in itself, as many men tend to view it. We need to make money relevant to that which we value in life. For many of us, this means we may have to put handling our finances into a relationship context.

One idea that comes to mind is freedom. Freedom from: bad relationships, unnecessary dependency, and abuse. Freedom to: control our own lives, choices, destiny, and so on.

ASSIGNING VALUE TO "WOMEN'S WORK"

Consider all the work we do at home. We carry and care for children; shop for and prepare meals, wash dishes, clothes, and floors; buy clothing and household goods; chauffeur children, care for pets, buy gifts, entertain family and friends, tend the ill, hire repair people, volunteer at school. Whew! My neighbor told me that to hire people to do the work of one homemaker would cost at least $400,000 a year! And we never get to retire!

Women need to be aware that everything we do—not only our jobs, but housework, errands, child rearing—has economic value. If we are part of a couple, for example, both partners should recognize that the one who takes time out from a paid position to care for a child or elderly parent is making a contribution to the family that not only reflects the couple's values, but also has real monetary worth.

And collectively we need to recognize and claim that all of women's work has value. Much of what we do is extraordinarily valuable, but it has

never been assigned a monetary value by our society.

If you ask most men to define "success," as in "So-and-so is very successful," they often mean, "He or she has or makes a lot of money, or has risen to the top of the pyramid."

What is a woman's definition of success? An excellent question!

We already may be wildly successful—in a way that's not recognized now by the culture at large.

Our culture long has fused being successful and being financially wealthy. It is up to women to "defuse" the two, to split them into two separate entities, which may or may not co-exist. To "defuse," we must recognize and claim the financial power and the energy—by first removing the fear and the mystique.

One definition of "successful" is having meaningful interchange with people you care about and love. Having a fat bank account is great. But having someone with whom to share your life, children who are happy and healthy, and/or friends you trust and enjoy—these are what drive most women and what we define as "success."

It is up to each of us to define success for ourselves—and not to be driven by others' expectations or what we perceive to be societal norms.

The women's movement was supposed to give us choices—not demand that we do it all ourselves!

We don't have to have a great career while we are raising kids. We can choose to have kids first, or have a job first, do only one or the other, maybe even balance both—*if* we have a lot of support. Regardless of how we choose to combine work and family, we are making a meaningful economic contribution. We need to think about our economic lives as a continuum. It is common for both men and women nowadays to have three or four separate "careers" throughout the life span. They may be sequential or they may be interwoven.

I love my job, and I have to admit, I'm pretty good at what I do. I love the intellectual stimulation, the way it allows me to grow and develop my talents and skills. Of course I love my kids, but at this stage in their lives, I don't get the same reward as I get from work.

When push came to shove, I left the job of my dreams because my kids couldn't deal with the long hours and the travel. The kids are grown up now, and I have another great job. I'm not one bit sorry for the choice I made.

Some of us bought the idea that being expected, and able, to do everything made us superior to men—definitely not a good way to foster equality or build lasting relationships!

For a while there, self-actualization for women looked a lot like being men. We thought "it" would come from climbing the corporate ladder, getting good jobs, and getting money; then found we weren't satisfied at all.

We didn't have a great time being women, when being a woman was defined by the standards of men.

Women who entered the workplace in the past thirty years are brave women, who, like Joan of Arc, sometimes had to be willing to hide who they are and move in the alien world of men.

During the past thirty or forty years, we have battled through—trying to come up with a new definition of what a successful woman is and does

in both monetary and nonmonetary ways, one that works for us *and* for society.

REDEFINING OURSELVES

As we enter a new century and a new millennium, we have an exciting opportunity to redefine ourselves totally, as long as we continue to give ourselves the right to do so.

As we learn to deal with, understand, honor, and even like managing our money, we are learning that women's route to strength and power is not by becoming men, but by reclaiming our unique feminine strengths. Because we spend so much time nurturing relationships, it is imperative that the time we *do* spend managing our money be spent efficiently and well. We need to understand and respect the importance of getting the most from the financial resources available to us.

And, as we begin to embrace this new way of looking at money, we will begin to demonstrate new confidence. Those of us in relationships with men will find ways to communicate this knowledge to our partners. We expect all men of goodwill to realize that women entering into the financial area—traditionally the territory of men—not only is *not* a threat, it is a relief. We can assure our partners that now "You don't have to do it all, you don't have to be good at it, you don't have to like it, you don't even have to pretend to like it."

Real change will happen only when men begin to cut into "women's work"—when they want to start being more caring and nurturing, when it becomes acceptable and respectable for them to take care of home and hearth. It's beginning to happen.

As our student points out above, as women learn to navigate financial waters, we can invite men to continue to enter what traditionally has been the province of women: to spend time nurturing relationships, caring for children and elders, making our homes peaceful and supportive. We invite men to remember birthdays and anniversaries and their children's teacher's names; to learn to listen empathically without having to fix what's bothering us; to know that if they can use a computer, they can run a washing machine, with no slight to their masculinity.

A more egalitarian approach to money helps build individual relationships, so both partners may prosper economically and spiritually. When we share responsibility for money, our partner's burden is lessened, and both men and women benefit. And such an approach also benefits society.

By learning to move in each other's world, we make room for every person—man, woman, child—to be free to be who they truly are. What a revolutionary idea!

2: Where Do You Want to Be?

Contributing Author:

Gail R. Shapiro

"Learn to evaluate your success by the balance you achieve in your life. Over the years, I have found that everything seems to work out better if you have your personal life priorities in the proper order."
—MARY KAY ASH, FOUNDER, MARY KAY INC.

WHERE DO YOU WANT TO BE? WHAT DO YOU WANT to be doing? And how are you going to get there? Creating a plan for your life means making choices, defining goals, and dreaming dreams. And for those dreams that have a monetary cost, you also must figure out a way to pay for them!

EXPLORING VALUES AND DREAMS

Many of us are not living the life we want because we don't know what it is we want! We may have only a vague notion of what would make us content.

When I was a girl, my heart's desire was to be an actress. I used to round up kids and put on shows for the neighbors. I starred in the senior play, and dreamed of being famous. What happened? Instead of following my bliss, I followed my boyfriend to San Francisco.

We may blame our dissatisfaction on the wrong partner, or the absence of a partner; the wrong job, or not having a job; troubles with chil-

dren, or not being able to conceive a child; our bodies, our family history, economic status, or a physical limitation. Or we may feel guilty, because we think we "have it all," and still are not content.

I used to read those self-help books all the time— you know, the kind that say you can be anything you want. Sometimes they help me to dream a little, but then the baby wakes up cranky, and my toddler turns over the goldfish bowl and my husband comes home hungry. What's the point?

The huge popularity of soap operas, movies, and romance novels underscores the need for so many of us to escape, even for a little while, from the reality of our lives. But once a woman understands that she always has a choice to change that reality, she will begin to feel more powerful.

I lived with a mean man for seven years. I couldn't leave. What turned my life around was a friend who helped me see that I was choosing to stay with him—for right now—because the kids and I depended on his income. At age thirty-two, I finished my GED, then got trained as a paralegal. I was able to get a job right away. By then the kids were in school all day, and I could afford an apartment of my own.

One reason so many of us don't know what we want is that we believe that we don't have a right to want anything for ourselves. We take care of children, partners, parents, bosses, houses, cars, pets, friends—everyone but ourselves. Do we have a right to want? YOU BET WE DO!

Even a woman facing seemingly impossible obstacles can begin to make choices, which will help her design a better life.

I've been legally blind since birth. My parents always told me that I'd just have to try a little harder. Since I can't drive, I will be moving to the city when I graduate. I will be starting my dream job in the fall—as a studio musician, a backup singer for a company that produces commercials. I'm so excited!

Believe it or not, I was seventy-two years old on my last birthday, and I just learned how to write a check! My husband is an accountant, and he always took care of all the money. He had a stroke a while back. While I am lucky to have him at home with me, he cannot write anymore. He wanted me to leave everything to our son and the financial adviser, but I figured, "I can do this." I am learning about our family finances as fast as I can.

After twelve years of trying to have a baby, my partner and I finally decided that it was more important to be parents than it was to have our own biological child. Just last month we brought home our beautiful, seven-month-old daughter. She is the joy of our lives. Now we just long for a little quiet time!

YOUR DREAMS REFLECT YOUR INDIVIDUALITY

For many women, the key missing piece in an otherwise pretty happy life is economic freedom. Others struggle with problems and issues that money can't solve.

My mother always told me, "There are two kinds of problems in the world: the ones you can throw money at, and the ones you can't." That advice still helps to keep things in perspective, even during the times when I've been really blue.

A first step is to sort out what can be accomplished with money, and what can't. You can do this exercise on your own, or work with a partner. Start by thinking about what you value. What is important to you? Who or what gives your life meaning? If you work with someone else, you can interview each other and write down what you say.

Health, family, self-respect, compassion for others, religion, freedom, wisdom, safety, time for myself!

Just my cat and my music.

My family is very important to me, and so is my church. I value honesty and trust, and I always try to do good in the world.

I value:

_____
_____
_____

Next, ask what do you need for survival? What do you need to feel secure?

Food, clothing, shelter, the basics.

I really need a vacation right now.

I need to be able to make a living with my hands. I design and make quilts, and have supported myself for years.

I need:

_____

_____

_____

What do you want? Anything that you strongly desire, but that is not absolutely essential for your basic well-being, is a want.

I want someone to cook meals for me, fashionable new clothes, a house in the mountains.

I need a vacation. I'm totally burned out. I want two weeks in Hawaii, but I'd settle for a week alone in the house.

I want to become a world-famous quilt maker.

I want:

_____

_____

The needs and wants you have just listed are your goals. Describe each one in detail, using complete sentences: "I need . . . ," "I want . . ."

I need _____

I need _____

I need _____

I want _____

I want _____

I want _____

Now imagine yourself attaining these goals. Try one at a time if the exercise is difficult.

I can see myself lying on the beach in Hawaii. The sun is warm, the breeze is gentle. I look great in my bikini, and a cute waiter is bringing me a tray of little sandwiches and a big drink in a pineapple.

Are there any obstacles that are keeping you from meeting your goals? If so, what are they? A very important part of the process is thinking through what may be blocking you. You may be surprised to discover that lack of money, education, or opportunity isn't the only obstacle.

All my friends back home are so jealous! My boss refuses to give me a raise—she thinks I don't need the money if I can afford a Hawaiian vacation. My sister is mad because I was supposed to baby-sit her kids last weekend. My mother is furious because she's always wanted to go to Hawaii and I didn't take her.

Obstacles I face:

_____

_____

_____

Facing imaginary obstacles can help you push past them, or help you decide to make a different choice. Once you are clear about at least one thing you want, the next step is to create objectives and strategies to meet that goal.

When I first separated from my husband, I went to see a financial planner. She asked me, "What are your goals?" I had no idea. I just laughed: "To feed my kids, I guess." She helped me to figure out that I should stay in the house to keep the kids in the same school, and that I had to go back to work. I needed to buy the house from my husband, but didn't have the money. I made a plan. I followed all the steps I mapped out, and amazed myself by accomplishing my goals in less than three years.

Commit yourself to following the plan you have created. Be prepared with new goals when you reach your original targets!

In the same month, I finished my college degree, turned forty, and my divorce became final. After the initial elation, I got so depressed, because I had reached all my goals! It took a while before I could figure out what I wanted to do next!

Following is a list detailing how one young woman plans to reach her goals. If you feel as though you've been "drifting," or that your life has been a series of random events, then using this method may help you gain a measure of control over your life.

CREATING A PLAN TO MEET YOUR GOALS

1. Thinking about your values, desires, responsibilities, and hopes creates a "mission statement" for your life. If you are more of a visual or process-oriented person, perhaps you might try drawing or painting your mission statement first. If you have trouble, try doing this step after Step 2. A mission statement is expressed as a "dream to be made true," or a "pie in the sky" paragraph about your calling or purpose.

Jo, a college senior, says, "My family and friendships are important to me, and I will continue to nurture these relationships. After finishing college, I will use and express my love for travel, languages, and music through my work, which will be meaningful and well-paying. I will become famous, at least in my city, and hope someday to hold a public office."

2. List the goals that, when reached, will make your dreams come true, best reflect your most important values, and fulfill current or anticipated responsibilities. The primary difference between a goal and a mission is that a goal is measurable; that is, you can tell when you have achieved it.

Jo's Goal 1: "To graduate from college in May with honors."

Note the difference between Jo's statement "after finishing college" and the specific and measurable goal just stated. It is, of course, possible to partially reach a goal: she could graduate on time, but not with honors, she could graduate in August, after having to take a summer school class.

Jo's Goal 2: "To find a music-related job located in Paris."

Again, specific and measurable. She either will find a music-related job in Paris or not.

3. Now create the objectives that will enable you to reach your goals. This is easy, and fun. An objective always is stated in terms of who will do what by when.

Objective: "By March 20, I will go to the college library and the local bookstore to see what books are available about jobs overseas." (If you are a very orderly type, you may want to label this "Objective 2.1," i.e., the first objective to meet Goal 2.)

Objective (2.2): "By March 30, I will have read at least two of the books I found."

Objective (2.3): "By April 10, Anna [her roommate] will take me to lunch to meet her uncle, the French ambassador."

Objective (2.4): "I will create and post an e-mail message describing the type of job I want to fifteen different lists by April 10."

4. By now, you may be wondering what all this has to do with Financial Literacy. Each objective can be met by a number of strategies, each of which can be quantified in terms of resources

(time, money, people) needed to achieve the strategy.

Strategy 2.31 (first strategy to reach Objective 3 to reach Goal 2): "By March 1, I will convince Anna to call her uncle, even though she doesn't like him."

Resources needed: three hours to persuade her, $20 to buy her the latest CD.

Strategy 2.32: "By March 15, I will buy a new dress to wear to lunch with Anna's uncle."

Resources needed: Four hours (at least two two-hour trips to the mall), $90 for a two-piece coordinated outfit, Toni to come shopping with her.

5. Don't get discouraged by the level of detail needed. Remember, the more graphically you can picture or describe your goals and the steps to reach them, the easier it will be to do so! You do not have to do this entire exercise in just one session. Take a weekend, a week, or several months. Also, by the time you are done with all of your goals, your first objectives already may be accomplished. You will want to update them. It is *very* helpful to have a "planning buddy," someone with whom you can check in on a regular basis. You can be her "buddy," too, or you may want to start a "success group," at which members help each other review and accomplish their goals.

6. When you have completed your "first pass," you will have the core of a financial plan.

Jo now knows that to meet her objective (2.3) to get Anna to take her to lunch with Anna's uncle, it will cost her $110 and seven hours of her time.

You will have, in writing or in pictures, a record of how much money you need, and when

you need it, as well as how long it will take you to accomplish your goals. Chances are pretty good that you also will have a detailed plan for how to get the resources that you need.

Here's another example. Sarah is forty-five, works as a salesclerk, and is thinking ahead to her retirement:

I've worked hard all my life. I'd like the time to try new things before I get too much older. My partner is five years older, and likely will retire first. We plan to sell our condo and move someplace warm, where we can play tennis and swim as much as we'd like.

Sarah's first goal then might be:

To be able to stop working in fifteen years, when I am sixty.

What does Sarah need to do to accomplish her goal? First, she might set some measurable objectives:

By September 1, I will initiate a discussion with my partner about retirement.
By September 15, I will begin a plan to visit one possible retirement community each year.
By October 30, I will make a financial plan so I know how much money I will need to retire in fifteen years.

Using this last objective as an example, Sarah can now begin to develop a set of strategies:

By September 1, I will call five friends who have used a financial planner, and get their recommendations.
By September 15, I will call and make appointments with three different financial planners.
By October 1, I will interview the three planners

33

and choose one I like.

By October 15, I will meet with the planner, and begin to collaborate on a financial plan.

As Sarah begins the process, she will have a good sense of what resources—time, money, and people—are needed to accomplish her objectives.

We suggest that you set at least one financial goal for yourself, to think about and address, as you read through this book. It may be as simple as: "By [date], I will read the entire book and do the exercises with a group of friends." Or you may be more specific. "By two years from today, I will be debt-free." Other goals set by our students are:

To educate myself about money so I can talk to my partner about our finances.

To start and fund a pension plan for my retirement.

To travel around the world—in style!

To save enough to buy my first home!

To get enough money to start my own business without worrying about living expenses for the first year.

To get off welfare and stay off.

To be able to spend money on myself—without feeling so guilty.

To be able to quit my job and stay home with the kids.

FACING THE PAST—AND THE PRESENT—AND MOVING AHEAD WITH YOUR GOALS

Sometimes, as women engage in the process of goal-setting, we encounter internal resistance. You may find yourself reluctant to move forward, and may or may not know why. If you get stuck, try taking a look at the messages about money you heard while growing up. These messages—from our parents, our teachers, from our society—can have a strong impact on your willingness to take charge of your life. We asked students:

What were some of the messages about money you got from your family while you were growing up?

We encourage you to discuss this question with a group of women. You may be in for some surprises! One group discovered the following:

We learned what money could do for us:

Money is a primary motivator.

Money is a tool used to manipulate behavior.

Everyone needs money to get ahead and to be secure.

We got advice on how to get ahead in the world:

Spend what you don't have (i.e., get credit) so you at least look successful even if you're not.

Best thing I learned? Never spend what you don't have.

Never be without a job. Any job is better than no job.

Being in the right place at the right time can get you money, but a good education is the key to success.

We can get uncomfortable if we don't relate to money the same way as our parents:

I grew up in the forties, in such a traditional family. Dad did it all. And when I went back to work, my mother kept asking, "Well, who's going to stay home and take care of the children?" I wanted to have a career and children, too.

I hear my dad's voice—although Mother worked, Dad seemed to have more opinions: "People who have money have to hurt other people to get it," and "You have to be a kiss-ass to get ahead at work." I don't believe that, but it's hard to shake!

The first time I got a big promotion, I started getting all these intense headaches. I tried everything, but they wouldn't stop. Finally, I saw a therapist, who helped me see that I was really stressed 'cause I was now making more money than my father!

Our mothers taught us what they viewed as survival skills:

I learned that you have to be manipulative around money. When I got married in 1975, my mother was the driving force behind the wedding machine. She took me to get a gown. I asked her, "How much am I allowed to spend?" She said, "Don't worry, we'll work it out." I didn't know what that meant. We had lace sleeves made for $100 each, and the total bill came to $1,200. We went home, and my father said, "How did you do?" She said, "We did pretty well." And he said, "How much is the dress?" And she handed him the receipt for the deposit—$200. He said, "Wow! Expensive—but

not bad." She looked at me and put her finger to her lips, and he said, "Okay—it's worth it for my little girl." So he paid the $200, and she paid the rest. He never knew.

You marry a person because of what his income is.

My message was: Marry someone who's bright and he'll make money.

There are men who don't like the role of provider—stay away from that kind!

In my family, my mother took care of the money. My father was an alcoholic, and he didn't always do his share to keep the household running. She paid all the bills.

We were taught values:

I was raised by my grandparents. My mother was thirteen years old and my father was fifteen when they had me. My grandmother was already retired. She stayed home with the kids, and my granddad was disabled. I had never seen them work. They told me, "Be satisfied and grateful for what you have. You need to get a good education to acquire money and success. Pay everything on time and you'll always get ahead." They had just enough to pay the bills and put food on the table and that was it, but they were really happy.

You should always be generous in giving to those less fortunate than you.

Money is much more important than issues of social justice. Forget about that stuff. Keep your money—you earned it.

We may be afraid that money will distort what's important to us.

Making money is a valid life goal.

**And how money can reflect our worth or
what others think about us:**

Money is power. What you have says who you are.

If you save more, you are worth more.

*Money is clearly man's domain. Men make more,
and control it; we're dependent on men.*

*When my parents were newlyweds, they were out
walking by the ocean. Eleven cents for an ice cream.
All my dad had was nine pennies, so he took the
pennies and pitched them into the ocean. My family story: futility around money. "We're not gonna
get ahead; we're not gonna make it." There was*

*nothing about going back and looking through the
drawers to find a couple more pennies.*

*How much you have determines your human
worth.*

Some of these statements are funny; some are
sobering. As you think about your own family
messages, you will see that the lessons you em-
braced can have a major impact on your ability to
take yourself seriously. By setting goals for yourself, you are beginning to be serious about your
financial life.

The next step is to get organized.

3: Where Are You Now?

Contributing Author:
Margery L. Piercey

"Take charge of your financial self early in life. Do not depend on anyone for your financial health, not your parents, not your partner, not your financial planner, nor your company retirement plan. And beware of anyone who fails to respect your financial self, especially if that someone is a love interest."
—MARGARET MEAD, BUSINESS JET BROKER

IN THIS CHAPTER, YOU WILL LEARN:

- Why good record keeping is the basis for creating an appropriate financial plan

- How to create a record-keeping system that works for you

- How to monitor your financial records

- What records you need to keep

- How to assess your net worth

- How and why to track your income and expenses, and your cash flow

- How to begin translating your personal goals into a viable financial plan

A first step in becoming financially literate is to know where you are. It takes courage to look squarely at yourself—not where you think you should be, or where you would like to be, but where you are, right now. We encourage you to take stock of your current situation—either alone or with your partner. Examining your current financial situation, your spending, savings, and credit habits, can be very frightening. It also can be very satisfying to know where you stand. Often, your situation is not as bad as you think; sometimes, of course, it is worse. Either way, it's important not to let fear hinder you.

Can you relate to any of these thoughts shared by our students?

I threw all my receipts into a drawer and then pulled them out at tax time, hoping to make some sense of the mess.

The idea of budgeting filled me with dread.

I really had no idea how much money was coming in, never mind how much I was spending.

My checkbook was a mess.

I was afraid to put my money into the bank. I was scared that I would write a check for too much.

If you have been ignoring money, worrying about it, or obsessing over it, it is time to take a deep breath, and look in the financial mirror. Consider this exercise like an annual physical exam—a checkup to learn the status of your financial well-being.

Often when we begin an exercise routine or a diet, we look to a friend or family member for support and regular encouragement. Consider doing the same as you begin this process. It may be easier to do with a buddy.

FINANCIAL RECORD KEEPING

As an accountant, I have seen my share of accounting and financial phobias. So I am respectful of anyone who truly is afraid, not just reluctant, to talk about or work with money. Such feelings are not unreal or unrealistic. We will take this record-keeping process step-by-step and make you feel more comfortable. Education is a first step in becoming more at ease with money issues.

You will be reading about mortgages and credit, insurance, retirement and estate planning, planning for education expenses, charitable giving, and spending and investing. An understanding of and commitment to financial record keeping serves as a foundation for these topics, which are the building blocks of your financial plan. For example:

- Going through the process of applying for a loan, you will be asked for certain documents to validate your income. You will be asked for prior years' tax returns and copies of your W-2s or payroll check stubs.

- Maintaining good records is necessary when you want to buy or lease property.

Doris wanted to open a bookstore. She had done her financial research to determine how much cash she was going to need to get started. She had done her market research and picked out the neighborhood in which she wanted to locate her store. Then a great space became available. She approached the lessor, who immediately asked for documentation to support her ability to pay. But her financial records were not all that well organized. During the week it took her to pull together the necessary information, the space was leased to someone else!

- When you are considering the purchase of life and disability insurance, good financial records will be the basis for determining how much coverage you will need to meet your financial obligations in the event of catastrophe.

- In planning for higher education, you must know your living expenses to determine what is available to put aside for higher education. If applying for federal financial aid, you will need to report what your financial resources are.

- For retirement planning, you must know what your expenses are in order to determine what you will need to maintain your desired lifestyle. You also must know how much money you have in pension, IRA, and 401(k) accounts to figure out what other resources you may need.

- For purposes of investing and charitable giving, you must have a good sense of your overall financial picture in order to make wise decisions.

- Everyone is subject to the possibility of an income tax audit. The surest way to expedite an income tax audit is to present the auditor with organized financial records.

HOW TO CREATE A RECORD-KEEPING SYSTEM THAT WORKS FOR YOU

During my fifteen years in public accounting, my clients have included privately and publicly held companies, nonprofit organizations, and individual taxpayers. I have seen the gamut of financial record-keeping systems. I have gleaned some good ideas, translating corporate organizational systems and skills into effective personal systems. In addition, many wonderful ideas have come from FLP participants. We've heard of everything from plastic storage bags to expensive file cabinets.

I have adopted a personal financial record-keeping system not unlike my corporate clients. I keep files by vendor—gas company, telephone company, cable company—in a file drawer. As I pay my bills, I file them in the appropriate vendor file, for future reference. Once or twice a year, I toss out those paid bills that are not relevant to my record-keeping needs. I keep my bank statements and reconciliations in a loose-leaf notebook for easy reference. My filing system also includes a file called "Bills to Pay." As bills arrive, I toss them in the "Bills to Pay" file so that they don't get misplaced. When I sit down to pay bills, I can put my hands on them readily.

I have a tax client who comes to me every year with a shoebox—literally—and this shoebox has been recycled several times. It is labeled "1998" on one side, "1999" on another, and so on. As the envelopes labeled "Important Tax Document" arrive in the mail beginning in late January of each year, this particular client just throws all these documents into the shoebox and always knows where the documents are when it is time to prepare her return.

What system works for you?

- *I have files by topic, not in any order, but I know where everything is.*

- *I file alphabetically.*

- *At the end of the year, I tie all my canceled checks together, so that my working files don't become burdened.*

- *I had the file cabinet system. Now I use an accordion file folder. I put all my financial documents, checks, bank statements, paid bills, and paycheck stubs related to a single month in one section of the folder.*

- *I use a briefcase that was my late husband's to accumulate all of my tax-related documents. When tax records come in, or anything relating to taxes, I put them in the tax briefcase.*

There are three steps to creating a record-keeping system that works for you: cleaning up your old files, along with all those odd piles of papers, figuring out a new system, and implementing the new system. You may have to weed through a lot of nonfinancial "stuff" in the process. Begin by wading through the "paper mess." Here's how:

1. Take a deep breath.

2. Establish a comfortable work surface where you can spread out: a table, an empty bed, or the floor.

3. Gather the following:

- Large trash bag or box (don't panic!)

- Two smaller, shallow boxes (cartons or even pizza boxes will do)

- Marker pen

- File folders (manila or colored)

- Something to hold the file folders (file cabinet, plastic crate, cardboard box)

- Scissors

- Stapler

- Courage and a strong will

- A dedicated period of time

4. Collect all the unopened mail, papers, magazines, and debris from around the house, and put it in one big pile on your work surface.

I found this grueling task much easier to do with a friend. I transported my whole pile to her house.

5. Working from the top, pick up one item at a time. There are only three things you can do with each item. You can:

- Throw it away

- Act on it, or

- File it

6. Evaluate item number one. Into which category does it fit? Is it trash? Throw it away. Do you have to do something with it—answer letter, order from catalog, read magazine, respond to invitation, send donation, pay a bill, discuss with family member, note an appointment in your date book, make yourself a note about it? Mark one box "To do" and put that item in the box. Is it something that requires no action now, but needs to be saved—paid credit card bill, child's diploma, a menu from the local takeout restaurant? Put it in the next box, marked "To file."

The temptation to start interacting with these papers will be enormous. Don't give in. Throw each piece away, or put in the to-do or to-file box.

Once the papers are sorted, dispose of the trash. (Recycle, if possible.)

7. Take the to-do pile. Divide it into things requiring prompt attention (bills to pay, notice of overdue library book, party invitation, sweepstakes you wish to enter, reminder to send medical forms to child's school), and items to do whenever there is time (magazine you want to read, ad for new restaurant you'd like to try, catalog for gifts you might want to purchase). Set aside those coupons you want.

8. Once you've categorized all your items, you are ready to deal with the to-dos. Deal with the most urgent items on the to-do pile. Pay the bills. Return the book. Mail in the sweepstakes. Reply to your host. Bring clippings or other "to-reads" with you to places you are likely to have small bits of time, such as the bathroom, the supermarket checkout line, or commuter rail. In this way, you will reduce the backlog a bit at a time, while keeping up with new incoming papers.

Good job! You are now ready to move on to filing.

FILING IS INFORMATION MANAGEMENT

I dreaded the idea of files—I'm an artist; I like to be spontaneous. But recently, the car I'd had my eye on was on sale—and I couldn't trade in my old car because I couldn't find the title, even after I spent hours going through all my papers. Then and there I decided that having a filing system would free up my time, not cramp my style. I got folders in lots of bright colors, and sorted everything by categories. Why do I file? To be able to find the documents I need, when I need them.

Developing a file system that eases rather than impedes your life is an art and is best when created from within. Certain files will be fixed—ones you will need to keep permanently—while others will change with your needs. Consider filing as a dynamic, imaginative task. What will work for you is very personal—alphabetical, numerical, chronological, color-coded. Do you think in pictures? Do you operate by projects, by people, or by events?

This may sound funny, but I put all my papers in plastic bags—the clear gallon-sized ones with a zip top. I put all my bills in one, my insurance papers in another, and so on. I keep all these plastic bags in a pretty shopping bag. I can see easily what's in each bag.

Some helpful hints:

- Label folders.

- Don't stuff your files to bursting. Divide the biggest files into two or more smaller ones.

- Folders either should be in your file or actively in use.

- File front-to-back or back-to-front, and try to be consistent.

- If a paper can be replaced with minimal effort, consider throwing it away.

- Separate papers into permanent or active files.

- Permanent files are papers you will use approximately once: marriage certificate, title to automobile, mortgage papers. Active files are for things like unpaid bills, tax receipts, and current credit card statements.

Make sure whatever system you choose makes information easily accessible. Can you find what you filed? Don't be afraid to change systems. Your system is likely to evolve.

ONGOING FINANCIAL RECORD KEEPING

Bank Reconciliation

An important part of financial record keeping is bank statement reconciliation. It provides a monthly method of verifying that your cash activity records are complete and accurate.

Early in my career, I did not reconcile my bank statements. But what I have learned in my many years as a CPA and business owner, is that both human and computer errors do occur, and these errors can cost you money.

A while ago, I was reconciling my bank statement. The check number that corresponded to $68.53 in my records was listed as $168.53 in the bank statement. So, I went through the canceled checks that were returned with the bank statement and, sure enough, my check was written for $68.53, but the bank had cleared that check for $168.53. (If you look in the lower-right-hand corner [sometimes on the back] of the canceled check, you will see a number printed when your check goes through bank processing. The number represents the amount that was withdrawn from your account.) I called the bank, and they cleared it up. But that was a hun-

dred dollars I almost lost. The bank might not have caught the error. The point is, you need to look out for yourself.

I got a bank statement, and it reflected $1,200 more than I thought I had. Now, $1,200 is not an amount that I would just miss, or forget about. So I went to the bank and said, "I reconciled my bank statement and there appears to be an extra $1,200 in my account."

They said to me, "Well, you must have made a mistake. I suggest that you go home and check again. If there is a bank error, it will show up as a correction on your statement next month." Next month, same thing. I went to the bank again and said, "Look, you've made a mistake. There is an extra $1,200 in my account." They kept on saying, "No, no, no." So after three months, I closed the account, took my money and the extra $1,200 and put it into a new account at another bank.

Reconciling your bank statement might identify errors in your check register. Sometimes, check register errors are "in your favor," that is, you made a deposit and forgot to record it in your check register. Upon reconciling your register to your bank statement, you discover the error and are pleasantly surprised. But check register errors can be a problem. You may have made a math error. Your register may incorrectly reflect a balance of $1,632, when you only have $632. If you were to write a check for $900 against the erro-

neous $1,632 balance, the $900 check would bounce. The bounced check would cost you a bounced check fee of up to $30, and most likely some embarrassment.

I hesitate to confess, and this is the truth, that I have never balanced my checkbook. To deal with my fear, I keep throwing money into the account and hoping nothing will bounce. It's ridiculous, really.

Not balancing our checkbooks is the great guilty secret of many of us. Although getting started can be a bit onerous, it's not too difficult.

Start now. Don't feel that you have to go back to the beginning of the year or back farther still. Don't make the task overwhelming. Start today and move forward. In doing so, of course, you miss any historical errors the bank or you may have made. However, there's generally a little caveat in small print on the back of the statement that if you don't identify errors within sixty days, the bank is not responsible for making the correction. My advice—pick a day and start.

How to Balance Your Checkbook

The reverse side of most bank statements includes a worksheet to guide you through the reconciliation, including a place to list outstanding checks. Here's an example:

Where Are You Now?

BALANCING YOUR CHECKBOOK

BEFORE YOU START: Please be sure your checkbook contains all automatic transactions shown on this statement (such as automatic deposits, interest additions, credit advances, transfers, payments, service charges, etc.).

THEN: Compare and check off debits and credits on the statement against your checkbook. In the column below, list any checks you have written which do not appear on this statement. Also be sure to include any other deductions recorded in your checkbook but not listed on this statement. In the area below, list any deposits made since the date of the last entry on this statement.

OUTSTANDING CHECKS OR OTHER DEDUCTIONS		
CHECK NO.	AMOUNT	
TOTAL (ENTER LINE 4)		

1. ENTER Ending Balance from front of statement $ _____

2. ADD deposits made since end of statement period   _____

3. TOTAL (1&2) $ _____

4. SUBTRACT outstanding checks (total from left)   _____

5. BALANCE should equal the balance now shown in
    your checkbook $ _____

IF YOUR ACCOUNT DOES NOT BALANCE, check the items below:
1. Are the amounts of all the deposits you have entered in your checkbook the same as those shown on the statement?
2. Are there any checks shown on this statement that are not listed in your checkbook?
3. Is the amount of each check correctly recorded in your checkbook?
4. Is the addition and subtraction in your checkbook correct?
5. Have you checked all automatic transaction involving your account?
6. Is there any interest shown on this statement that is not entered in your checkbook?

THE FOLLOWING APPLIES TO CREDIT LINE CUSTOMERS IN CASE OF ERRORS OR INQUIRIES ABOUT YOUR BILL

Send your inquiry in writing on a separate sheet so that we receive it within **60** days after the bill was mailed to you. Mail your written inquiry to: Middlesex Savings Bank, Loan Servicing Department, P.O. Box 358, Natick, MA 01760. It must include:
1. Your name and account number;
2. A description of the error and why (to the extent you can explain) you believe it is an error; and
3. The dollar amount of the suspected error.

If you have authorized us to automatically pay your bill from your checking or savings account, you can stop or reverse payment on any amount you think is wrong by mailing your notice so that we receive it within **16** days after the bill was sent to you.

You remain obligated to pay the parts of your bill not in dispute, but you do not have to pay any amount in dispute during the time we are resolving the dispute. During that same time we may not take any action to collect disputed amounts or report disputed amounts as delinquent.

OTHER INFORMATION REGARDING YOUR LOAN ACCOUNT

ADVANCES AND PAYMENTS

The **FINANCE CHARGE** is computed on advances from the date of each advance, which may be different from the date of your check or other document requesting the advance. Payments by you will be applied on the day they are received first to the billed **FINANCE CHARGE** and then to your Principal Balance.

FINANCE CHARGE

The amount of the **FINANCE CHARGE** can be computed by multiplying the Daily Periodic Rate by the number of days in the billing cycle and by your Daily Balance, subject to the minimum monthly **FINANCE CHARGE** if such a charge is indicated on the front of this statement. The Daily Periodic Rate is 1/365th of the **ANNUAL PERCENTAGE RATE** printed on the front of this statement. If two **ANNUAL PERCENTAGE RATES** are shown on the front of this statement, the calculations must be made with respect to the range of balances to which each such rate applies. The Daily Balance does not include **FINANCE CHARGE,** either current or as carried over in the Previous Balance from a prior statement period. Although the **FINANCE CHARGE** accrues and is owning daily, it is billed monthly and appears on the front of this statement as of the closing date of the statement period. The Daily Balance can be determined by taking the beginning principal each day, adding any new loans posted that day, and subtracting any principal payments or credits for that day.

LOAN PAYOFF

Your loan balance (Total New Balance plus accrued **FINANCE CHARGE**) may be paid-in-full (assuming no advance is made after the closing date on this statement) by remitting:
a. the Total New Balance as shown on this statement, plus
b. the accrued **FINANCE CHARGE** on the Principal Balance from the closing date of this statement period to the date of the actual payoff.

In the event you remit only the Total New Balance, the accrued **FINANCE CHARGE** mentioned in item (b) above will appear on your next monthly statement.

PLEASE NOTIFY BANK IN WRITING OF CHANGE IN ADDRESS

Enter the ending balance from the front of your statement (statement balance). Then add the deposits you have made since the end of the statement period (deposits in transit), that is, those deposits that you have recorded in your check register but that aren't listed on your bank statement. Add the statement balance to the deposits in transit. Subtract any checks you have written that have not yet cleared the bank (outstanding checks). The balance should equal the current balance of your checkbook. However, if there is any bank activity, such as interest earned on and posted to your account or fees charged against your account, you will need to adjust your register balance by these amounts in order to agree with the reconciliation balance.

If the reconciliation balance doesn't agree with your check register, it means that you didn't write the correct amount in the check register, or the bank made an error. If your balance does not reconcile, try going through the process from the beginning. Check your reconciliation math. Compare the checks listed in the bank statement to those in the check register. Review your list of outstanding checks for completeness and accuracy. If you really are stuck, you can go to the bank and ask to talk to an officer. (Inquire as to whether you will be charged for assistance from the officer.) Generally, they will be very pleased to help you. For those who are comfortable with computers, there are many low-cost check-writing programs, which can facilitate the reconciliation process as well as enhance your record-keeping system.

I decided to print my checks on the computer. I had to ask my kids to teach me. But it's really much easier, and I make far fewer errors!

WHY IS IT SO IMPORTANT TO KEEP THESE RECORDS?

Paid bills supporting income tax deductions are relevant to year-end income tax preparation. Additionally, there may be other reasons to hang on to paid bills for a period of time. For example, if you are planning to sell your house within the next year or so, you should hang on to your heating bills so that you can provide potential buyers with a record of heating costs. It's a good idea to keep your paid credit card bills. If you have a product that breaks, for example, and you take it back to the store and you don't get satisfaction, many credit card companies offer protection.

I bought a camera from what I thought was a reputable electronics store. When I took it out of the package, the shutter button didn't work. I took it back immediately. The store insisted that it was the manufacturer's responsibility. I sent the camera back to the manufacturer. They sent it back to me, and told me to take it back to the store! The store refused to replace it. Fortunately, I had charged it, and I wrote a letter to the credit card company disputing the charge. I paid the whole bill, minus the price of the camera. I'm not sure how it got resolved, but I never did have to pay for it, and I still have the broken camera.

Last October, I bought and planted several bundles of beach grass—worth a couple of hundred dollars. In the spring, it was dead. I went back to the nursery, and they said they would replace it the following fall, when it was again planting season—IF I had my receipt. I hadn't saved the receipt, but I did have the credit card bill showing the nursery transaction. My replacement grass is now thriving!

As you will read in chapter 4, your credit report is your financial life on paper. Sometimes, things can get reported erroneously. The burden of proof will be on you to clear up the error on the credit report. Perhaps a bill was mailed to you late, and so you paid it late. You may have made a note "Lost in the mail, didn't get bill on time." Such records maintained with your paid bills will allow you to correct the problem with the credit-reporting agency.

WHAT RECORDS YOU NEED TO KEEP, WHAT THE IRS REQUIRES

Personal financial records that you should maintain include:

- Federal and state income tax returns and documents supporting income and expense items reported on those returns

- Bank statements and canceled checks

- Investment/brokerage statements

- Deposit receipts

- Mortgage statements

- Credit card statements

- Paid bills

- Charitable contribution receipts

- Payroll stubs

What to keep and for how long is predominantly driven by the statute of limitations on federal and state income tax audits. The IRS has been working to be more responsive to taxpayers in the past few years; however, the burden of proof still remains with the taxpayer.

The volume of records for one individual is really not that great. When I put away these documents, I usually can fit three years of complete sets of records in one relatively small banker's box, a double corrugated cardboard covered box available at most office supply stores.

I keep my historical records in a fireproof file cabinet in the attic.

I've got three years of canceled checks in this one box. The time it would take for me to go through and pull out only the ones that relate to my tax records would not be an equal trade-off for that little bit of extra storage space in my office.

For how long do you need to keep these records? The following general guidelines coincide with the Internal Revenue Service statute of limitations. The Internal Revenue Service could audit your return any time up through three years from the later date that the return was filed or was due. In certain cases, the statute may extend to six years. If you fail to file a return, or if fraud is suspected, the statute of limitations does not close. Since the statute of limitations in some states exceeds the federal statute, your record retention schedule should coincide with the longer of the two statutes. Your state department of revenue can provide you with the applicable statute of limitations.

I often am asked why I recommend keeping deposit receipts supporting deposit activity in my bank account. Specifically for IRS audit purposes, you should keep bank statements and deposit receipts with a notation about the source of the deposit. If you cannot substantiate the difference of what you reported as income on your tax return, and the total deposits in your bank account, the IRS more often than not makes the presumption

FEDERAL RECORD RETENTION GUIDELINES

Bank statements	6 years
Canceled checks	3 years
Bank deposit slips	3 years
Stock, mutual fund, other brokerage transactions	Holding period plus 3 years
Tax returns	Permanent
Real estate records	Permanent
Expense reports	3 years

that you've underreported your income. But if you keep documentation that contains the source of the receipt and evidence of the deposit date, you can substantiate nontaxable deposit activity in your account, such as gift income or reimbursements.

If you deduct for business use of your automobile, you must maintain a record of business mileage and any direct expenses related to business use of your automobile.

Keep your paycheck stubs. When you are going through the mortgage loan process, they will ask you for your three most recent paycheck stubs. I tend to keep them all and then throw them out when I get the end-of-the-year federal tax withholding statement, the Form W-2.

Jamie, a college student working through the summer, kept her paycheck stubs. When she got her W-2 at the end of the year, it reflected that she hadn't had any federal income tax withheld. She looked back at her stubs, which did indeed reflect some federal withholding. This doesn't happen too often in these days of software systems, where the two are integrated, but it can happen.

At a minimum, it is good to keep the last three pay stubs, so that you have your year-to-date current earnings information, at least until you have your Form W-2.

People commonly miss deductible contributions that they make with their credit cards. A lot of organizations allow gifts on credit cards—public television, educational institutions, and national charities. If your credit card statement reflects a deductible contribution, highlight it on the statement and file it in your "charitable contributions" or "tax return documents" file, so that you don't miss it when it's time to file your income tax return. Oftentimes, credit card charitable gifts are acknowledged with a receipt, in which case it is not necessary to retain both the credit card statement and the receipt in your tax files.

A charitable organization is required to give you a receipt for a single gift greater than $250. This law applies only to a single gift of $250 or more: it doesn't apply if, for example, you give $10 to your church every week, totaling $520. Most charities are up to speed on this, but the responsibility is yours, as the taxpayer claiming the charitable deduction, to be sure you get a receipt. The receipt should state whether or not there were any goods or services in return for your contribution and, if so, the fair market value of such goods or services. For example, if while at a charitable fund-raiser, you purchase a weekend in New York City, the receipt should reflect the amount you paid (say it's $800), and the fair market value of the weekend (say it's $550). In this case, your deductible charitable contribution would be $250.

Keep your real estate tax bills, excise tax bills, and business expense receipts. Be aware that in addition to taxable income records, it is a good idea to keep a separate record of any child-support checks you may receive. You should not comingle the deposits if you hope to use the child-support check as part of your income, if you are, for instance, applying for a mortgage. You are not required by law to disclose this income, to avoid discrimination, but if you choose to do so, know that you must be able to document that you actually are receiving the checks each week or month.

ASSESSING YOUR NET WORTH

Net worth is simply a snapshot of your financial condition at any given moment. Calculating net worth is a very basic equation. Simply stated, net worth is what you own minus what you owe. Your net worth is fluid. Next week, when you get your paycheck, your net worth will increase by that amount. You will have brought in more income. If you go out for pizza tonight, your net worth will decrease by, say, $15.

What you own includes cash, investments, retirement accounts, and the current market value of any real estate and personal property you own. These go in the left-hand column, "Assets." In the right-hand column, list your "Liabilities," or money you owe, which may include: home mortgage, car loan, unpaid credit card balance, home equity loan balance, current bills, taxes owed, and student loans.

To find your bank balance and mutual fund assets, simply look at the statements. For the mortgage balance, if it is not on the monthly statement, you can call your mortgage lender. To find the market value of your home, you can ask a real estate broker to come in and provide a complimentary current market analysis (CMA). However, if you keep your eye on real estate transactions and listings in your local paper, you probably can make a pretty good estimate yourself.

For an auto loan, list the amount you owe currently on the liability side, and the market value of your car on the asset side. The market value of cars goes down really fast. You can look in the paper to try to see what your car, in a similar condition, is selling for. For the purpose of this exercise, if you do not know the exact value of an asset—for example, jewelry or artwork or the current resale value of your automobile—you can estimate.

Here's an example:

Six months ago, Alyson graduated from college and began working full-time as a branch manager at a local bank where she had worked part-time to pay her way through college. As a graduation present, Alyson received her late grandmother's valuable cameo ring, which had been appraised two years before for $1,000.

Currently, Alyson is living at home with her parents and driving to work in her newly purchased American car, which she financed through the dealer at 2.9 percent. Alyson charged much of her new business wardrobe. As a result,

47

she is carrying a balance on her credit card at 9.4 percent. She plans to pay off the balance after she replenishes her savings—which she depleted for the down payment on her new car—back to $3,500, a figure she has determined is her "safety net." Now that Alyson is employed full time at the bank, she is entitled to participate in the 401(k) plan, to which she contributes 3.5 percent of her paycheck each pay period. The bank offers a modest matching contribution.

Using the "Assessing Your Net Worth" worksheet, Alyson's net worth assessment is as follows:

ASSESSING ALYSON'S NET WORTH

Assets	Estimated Value	Liabilities	Unpaid Balance
Cash	$50	Current bills	
Checking	$950		
Savings	$3,100	Reserve credit*	
		Credit cards*	$500
Investments		Store credit*	
Money market		(extended payment plans)	
CDs			
U.S. savings bonds	$2,500	Home mortgages	
Treasury bills		Vacation home mortgage	
Mutual funds		Home equity lines	
Stocks		Car loan	$13,500
Other		Student loan	$7,500
		401k loan	
Retirement Accounts			
401(k) plans	$700	Investment margin account	
IRA or Keogh			
SEP		Past taxes owed	
Other pensions			
Annuities		Other	
Real Estate		**Total Liabilities (L)**	**$21,500**
Home			
Vacation home			
Rental property		**Net Worth (A−L)**	**$1,800**
Land			
		Life Insurance Proceeds	
Personal Property			
Furnishings		**Total Estate**	**$ 1,800**
Automobiles	$15,000		
Jewelry	$1,000	* Available but unused credit lines do not get factored into the calculation of net worth.	
Silver			
Art			
Collections			
Boats, planes			
Other Assets			
Business equity			
Loans owed to you			
Other			
Total Assets (A)	**$23,300**		

You can use the chart at the end of the chapter to calculate your own net worth.

Using the worksheet to assess your net worth is a good starting point for taking charge of your financial life. The more often you measure your net worth, the easier it will be to identify trends. If you monitor your net worth monthly for a while, you will see the effect of your current earning and spending habits. If it is going down, you definitely need to make some changes. Is your net worth more than it was six months ago? Good. You are farther along the path of financial independence. Is your net worth less? Try to identify the reason. Did you overspend on your vacation? Did you lose your valuable necklace? These items might cause a temporary downward trend in net worth. If regular monitoring of your net worth reveals consistent downward trends, consider corrective measures: most simply, spend less money!

If tracking shows relatively steady net worth, you may want to adjust your spending and saving to start your net worth on an upward trend.

Your net worth may be negative. A few common reasons for a negative net worth are:

- Excess credit card use—that is, spending more than you bring in

- Underpayment of taxes during the year, resulting in a big tax liability at the end of the year

- Downturn in the housing market, causing your mortgage value to exceed your home value

As you will read in chapter 8, calculating your net worth also is the starting point in estate planning. Your estate—which is of value to your beneficiaries only after you die—is nothing more than your net worth plus any life insurance proceeds.

TRACKING YOUR INCOME AND EXPENSES

To increase your net worth, you must either reduce your liabilities or increase your assets. One way to begin to take charge of your financial future is to take a realistic look at your spending habits.

There are always so many things the kids need, and I want them to have all the "extras" I missed growing up.

I earn a very good salary. But I never have any money at the end of the month. For one thing, I can't stop buying shoes. I'm beginning to think I have a problem.

I spend when I want to get my husband's attention. I wait for him to care about me enough to spend money on me, because money is very important to him. I feel it is a measure of how much he values me. I did the same with my own dad.

Buy a small notebook—bookstores have those miniature spiral books with a hard cover that sell for about $3—or you can just use a notepad from your local drugstore. Get something that can fit easily into your pocket or purse—you will be carrying it around with you for a month.

Write down *everything* you spend. Don't worry, no one is going to see your record but you. If you buy a gumball, write down 10 cents (or 25 cents for the big ones!). If you buy a cup of tea and a muffin, jot down the $2.59. If you give lunch money to your kid out of your pocket in the morning, write that down, too. If you pay your bills by check, they don't need to go into the pocket notebook, but should be added to the following worksheet.

TRACKING EXPENSES

Item	Month	Year

HOUSING

Mortgage/rent

Maintenance

Lawn/garden care

Snow plowing

Cleaning

Repairs

Furnishings, including appliances

Condo fees

Security monitoring fees

Vacation home/time share

UTILITIES

Heat/gas/firewood

Electric

Water

Sewer/dump/trash

COMMUNICATION

Phone—local

Phone—long distance

Calling card

Children's line

Fax

Cell phone

Car phone

On-line service

Postage

Fed Ex/Express Mail

Greeting cards/stationery

FOOD—IN HOME

Grocery store

Specialty shops

Takeout/Home delivery service

Warehouse

Spring water

AUTOMOBILE

Loan

Repairs/maintenance/wash

Equipment

Auto club

Gas/oil

Parking/tolls/tickets

INSURANCE

Home(s)

Auto

Medical/dental

Life

Disability

Umbrella liability

Long-term care

CLOTHING

LOAN REPAYMENTS

TAXES

Federal/state (alimony,

self-employment, capital gains)

Social Security

Local/real estate/personal property

TRACKING EXPENSES

Item	Month	Year
Automobile excise		
CHILD CARE AND EDUCATION		
Nanny/au pair		
Day care center/preschool		
Private school		
Sports/extracurricular fees		
Afterschool care		
Vacation/summer camp		
Lessons		
Religious school		
OTHER DEPENDENT CARE		
Travel		
Home care/facility care		
Alimony, child support		
PROFESSIONALS		
Accountant		
Attorney		
Financial Planner		
Other		
INVESTMENTS AND SAVINGS		
Safe deposit box		
Bank fees		
Broker fees		
HEALTH, WELLNESS, AND PERSONAL CARE		
HMO/insurance copayment		
Bodywork/alternative care		
Uninsured medical/dental		
Medications		
Vitamins/supplements/herbs		
Spa/health club dues		
Hair/nail care		
ADULT EDUCATION		
Tuition/fees		
Books and supplies		
Student loans		
ENTERTAINMENT AND RECREATION		
Vacations		
Movies/videos		
Theater/concerts/ballet		
Cable/pay-per-view		
Restaurants		
Club dues		
Hobbies		
Vices		
Entertaining		
Books/magazines/newspapers		
SERVICES		
Dry cleaning		
Pet care		
Other		
GIFTS		
Family		
Office		
Charitable		
Holiday		
TOTAL		

This worksheet, "Tracking Expenses," was developed by students in the first three FLP classes. They were asked, "What do you spend money on?" Obviously, not all of us can or would choose to spend money on all these items. If there is anything missing from this list that you spend money on, add it!

When I took this list to my financial planner, she laughed. She said, "I've never seen anybody put a line item in their budget for parking tickets." I said, "That's because you don't work in the Harvard Medical Area." It's a fact of life. There are two-hour meters, and they cost a quarter for fifteen minutes. You throw in your eight quarters, then you have to run back two hours later and do it again. If you have a lot of meetings, you get parking tickets at least once or twice a week. That's part of your budget. Period.

When we first made the list, a student asked, "What do you mean by 'vices'?" The speaker said, "Well, that's alcohol, lottery tickets, cigarettes, things like that." "Oh, that's entertainment." She laughed. "Well, you notice it's under recreation, so it's not too judgmental."

Do this exercise for four weeks. At the end of the four weeks, enter onto the middle (month) column of the worksheet: (1) the total of your spending as recorded in the notebook, (2) the total amount from the checks you have written for monthly bills, and (3) any charges you have made on your credit cards that month. Added together, these three amounts should account for all the money you spent in one month. Now enter onto the right-hand (year) column of the worksheet expenses that occur annually, such as auto insurance or holiday gifts.

Now you can review and analyze your entries.

You should have a pretty good idea of where all your money goes. Begin to think about taking some action, if you are not pleased with the results.

This exercise can be pretty painful. The first couple of times I tried to track my expenses, I threw the notebook against the wall!

Ugh! It felt like being on a diet, where you have to write down everything you eat.

At first, I was really reluctant to track my spending. But after a while I began to see that I was making choices—all day long. I began to feel pretty powerful.

I found that it is really okay to care for and take care of my money. I was not being conscious of my daily spending—today I put stuff back at the department store, because I knew I would have to write it down.

INCOME TRACKING

It is surprising how many people do not know their real household income. This may be as true for women who live alone and handle their own finances as it is for women who live with partners. Of course, you probably know the amount of your salary or regular wages. But do you know the exact amount of your take-home pay, that is, your salary less withholdings for taxes, insurance, or retirement contributions? How about bonuses? Have you received money from your folks for your birthday? Did you win a few dollars in the lottery? Did a friend pay back a loan you thought you'd never see again? All of these are income.

Whenever I go grocery shopping, I take what I saved in coupons and put it aside for a new coat. To me, that's earned income.

I never even counted interest income, but it does add up.

As you keep this financial diary over the next month, if you find that you are regularly dipping into your savings or using credit for regular living expenses, you are going to have to determine what changes have to be made in order for you to put aside enough to reach your goals.

TRANSLATING YOUR PERSONAL GOALS INTO A VIABLE FINANCIAL PLAN

If you did the goal-setting exercise in chapter 2 using at least one of your important goals, you should have a pretty good idea of how much time it will take to achieve that goal, and how much money you will need to save. Now the question becomes: Where does that money come from?

We like the concept that Vicki Robin and Joe Dominguez present in *Your Money or Your Life.* They say that every dollar you make represents life energy. If you make $20 an hour, and you go out and buy something worth $20, you've just spent an hour of your life energy. So if you buy a dress for $100, you've just spent five hours of your life. Is it worth it? To you it may be, and to someone else, it may not be. It's a really good way to think about your money.

I'm raising four kids alone, and we don't have a lot of money. But I never, ever say to my kids, "We can't afford that." That's what I heard growing up, and I've always had a "poverty consciousness." I want to send a different message to my kids. When they ask for something out of range, I say, "We choose to spend our money differently."

I am much more likely to spend money that was given to me, as opposed to the money I actually earn.

Some people want to be or have to be extremely frugal: you know, cut coupons, collect rubber bands, save their slivers of soap. But there's an awful lot of time that goes into that. And that's your energy.

I cut coupons and save $20 to $30 a week!

Well, it's personal choice. Some women swear by coupons and others find them a waste of time. Time is money.

I'm an acupuncturist, and all day I counsel people on their energy. I like to think of everything in terms of energy. And when I talk to men, I don't even have to get into it with them: I tell them, "Your energy is just like money," and they understand it instantly. They're programmed to understand money that way. They are not programmed to understand their health that way.

We are so used to spending our energy on other people—we diffuse it.

The original use of paper money was to get rid of the bartering system, and with bartering, you're right there with your energy and it's very obvious how much time you are putting in.

CREATING A CASH FLOW BUDGET

Say the word "budget" and most people shudder. We encourage you to think of a budget as a liberating tool.

You've tracked your expenses now for four weeks. You've stopped—either in disgust or in satisfaction—to take a look at what's before you.

The formula for creating your cash flow budget is pretty simple: the money you have at the start of the month plus the money that comes in during the month, minus the money that goes out during the month, equals the amount that's left at the end of the month. The process is similar to reconciling your bank account. However, with a cash flow budget, you identify the source and nature of the income and expenses.

By "money at the start of the month," we mean your cash on hand, your checking account balance, your savings account balance. We are not talking about other assets or investments now, just the money that comes in and goes out monthly. Add to that money that comes in: your salary, investment income, gift money, child support or alimony, money you find on the street.

Don't laugh. Last calendar year, I made it a project to save every bit of money I found—no matter how gross. By the end of the year, I had nearly $58! Most people would not bend down to pick up a muddy penny—but I did it just to see how much money was lying around! I walk every day, and it's a rare day I don't find at least a coin or two.

Money you have at the start of the month plus money that comes in during the month minus the money you spend that month should equal the money you have left at the end of the month. The total will be either plus or minus; ideally, it will be a plus. Now go back and say to yourself, "Okay, what are my goals?" as you defined them in chapter 2. Look at them all: short-term goals, like buying a new coat; long-term goals, saving up for a house, or putting away money for retirement. Now the challenge is to figure out a way to build in savings for all of your important goals— right in your regular budget.

When we were first married in 1948, we had nothing. We always agreed that we would pay ourselves first. We put $5 a week into a savings account— believe me, many weeks it was hard to take that $5 out first, when there were so many things we needed. But it paid off. You always manage to juggle to pay bills, but you don't always take care of your savings unless you make it a priority. The philosophy is right. You have to plan for a vacation in advance.

If you look at every millionaire out there, the majority of them live within a budget and pay themselves first.

And what happens if you have money left over at the end of the month? What do you do with it?

I put it into savings.

I spend it—it's such a treat to be ahead!

I find that the majority of months, it's a plus. But the minuses take care of it.

For most of us, there's a flow to expenses and income from month to month. Given the fact that some months you will come out positive and some months negative, here is an exercise to try.

You can make a "cash flow" projection. It's kind of an educated guess. For those of you who have run a business, this may be second nature, and for those who have never done this before, it may be a little stretch to think about it. Don't think about living month-to-month. Think about a year. You might do this at the beginning of the year, or you might do this around October for the next year.

Look at your expenses, and as soon as you've tracked a whole month of expenses, you can tell whether that is a typical month for you. December may not be a typical month—a lot of gift giving—same with June—graduations and weddings, school parties and teacher gifts. So you have to look at a whole year to get an overview.

Try making your own cash flow projection using the following chart. Calculate the income you expect to get each month—from your salary, extra work, bonuses, income tax refund, gifts, dividends, child support and/or alimony.

Then, using a typical month of expenses, list that amount under each month. To the typical expenses, add any large disbursements you can anticipate: quarterly real estate taxes, income taxes, and insurance premiums.

Then subtract the expenses from the income for each month. You easily can see where you have extra, and where you might have a shortfall. Ideally, your total expected income for the year would equal or exceed your total anticipated expenses for the year. If so, you are in pretty good shape! You may want to set aside money from the "extra cash" months to make up for the "leaner" months. If you anticipate this ebb and flow of income and expenses, you will have little problem managing. If, however, your estimated annual expenses exceed your planned income, you either will have to cut expenses or increase your income!

Here is an example:

Lucy, a single mother of two, earns $50,000 a year as a speech therapist. Her monthly take-home pay is $3,125, and she expects to be promoted to department supervisor with a pay raise next September. She has calculated her monthly living expenses to be $2,750, a figure that includes one-twelfth of annual expenses, such as insurance premiums, association dues, and an allowance for unanticipated expenses.

Every spring, she helps her sister Sharon, a caterer, and has earned a minimum of $3,000 each spring for the past five years. And each year Lucy's parents give her a generous cash gift for the holidays. Lucy plans to replace her car in October, and to make payments $50 a month higher than her current car payments. Lucy will take one vacation in August, for which she will pay cash. Lucy usually has a tax payment due at the end of the year, because of her freelance income and because she tends to minimize her monthly tax withholdings.

Looking at her cash flow month by month, she can afford to pay her extra tax bill in April, if she reserves cash on hand at the end of the months in January, February, and March. Lucy's freelance work will more than pay for her summer vacation, and her pay raise will cover the increase in car expenses. At the end of the calendar year, the total of Lucy's expected income would be $45,500. Her total expected expenses would be $39,600, leaving her ahead at the end of the year by $5,900. Lucy is in good shape for the upcoming year.

If Lucy did not do a cash flow projection, she might have spent her bonus, then been short of cash in April. Or she might have overspent on a new car, taking on payments higher than she could afford easily. By doing the cash flow projection, Lucy can see that, although she will have greater cash outflow than cash inflow for three months of the year, her overall cash picture is positive. She can now make some decisions regarding monthly savings and even start thinking about the subsequent year when she won't be making the large down payment on a new car.

Lucy's sister Sharon, however, isn't in good shape. This past year, before Lucy introduced her

LUCY'S CASH FLOW PROJECTION

	Jan	Feb	Mar	Apr	May	Jun	Jul	Aug	Sep	Oct	Nov	Dec	Total
Cash In													
Salary or Wages	$3,125	$3,125	$3,125	$3,125	$3,125	$3,125	$3,125	$3,125	$3,300	$3,400	$3,400	$3,400	$38,500
Bonus	$ -	$ -	$1,500	$ -	$ -	$ -	$ -	$ -	$ -	$ -	$ -	$ -	$ 1,500
Seasonal Freelance	$ -	$ -	$ -	$ -	$3,000	$ -	$ -	$ -	$ -	$ -	$ -	$ -	$ 3,000
Gift Income	$ -	$ -	$ -	$ -	$ -	$ -	$ -	$ -	$ -	$ -	$ -	$2,500	$ 2,500
Total Cash In	$3,125	$3,125	$4,625	$3,125	$6,125	$3,125	$3,125	$3,125	$3,300	$3,400	$3,400	$5,900	$45,500
Cash Out													
Expenses:													
Regular Household													
Expenses	$2,750	$2,750	$2,750	$2,750	$2,750	$2,750	$2,750	$2,750	$2,750	$2,750	$2,800	$2,800	$33,100
Gifts	$ -	$ -	$ -	$ -	$ -	$ 150	$ -	$ -	$ -	$ -	$ -	$1,200	$ 1,350
Seasonal Clothing	$ -	$ -	$ -	$ -	$ 200	$ -	$ -	$ -	$ 300	$ -	$ -	$ -	$ 500
Income Taxes	$ -	$ -	$ -	$1,000	$ -	$ -	$ -	$ -	$ -	$ -	$ -	$ -	$ 1,000
Vacation	$ -	$ -	$ -	$ -	$ -	$ -	$ -	$ 850	$ -	$ -	$ -	$ -	$ 850
Other Outflows:													
New Car Down Payment	$ -	$ -	$ -	$ -	$ -	$ -	$ -	$ -	$ -	$2,800	$ -	$ -	$ 2,800
Total Cash Out	$2,750	$2,750	$2,750	$3,750	$2,950	$2,900	$2,750	$3,600	$3,050	$5,550	$2,800	$4,000	$39,600
Net Cash In/(Out)	$ 375	$ 375	$1,875	$(625)	$3,175	$ 225	$ 375	$(475)	$ 250	$(2,150)	$ 600	$1,900	$ 5,900

to Financial Literacy, Sharon was a bit of a spendthrift. Within the previous couple of months, she moved into a new apartment with a much higher rent. Sharon noticed that money was a bit tight and that she might not be able to make her upcoming tax obligation, as advised by her accountant. Lucy helped Sharon do a cash flow forecast, after seeing her through the tedious process of a month's tracking of expenses. Sharon is able to draw about $29,000 from her catering business. She boosts her monthly draw during the months that her quarterly estimated tax payments, related to her self-employment income, are due. She has calculated her monthly living expenses to be $1,500, a figure that includes monthly finance charges on her outstanding credit card balances and one-twelfth of annual expenses.

At the end of the year, the total of Sharon's expected income would be $31,500. Her total expected expenses would be $40,150, resulting in cash outflows in excess of cash inflows for the year of $8,650. Sharon discovered that moving to her new, more-expensive apartment was a bad financial decision. Realizing that she has limited opportunity to expand her self-employment income within the next year, she has decided to look for a roommate for her two-bedroom apartment. She's also decided to go through the goal-setting process in order to determine where she might cut expenses.

I am a graphic artist. I have a couple of busy seasons, spring and fall, in which I earn 80 percent of my income. That has to carry me over the slow midwinter and midsummer periods. But since I can plan for the slack time, I don't panic.

If you need to cut expenses, you will have to make some tough decisions, whether that means giving up your cigarettes or selling your house and moving to an apartment. There are both mi-

SHARON'S CASH FLOW PROJECTION

	Jan	Feb	Mar	Apr	May	Jun	Jul	Aug	Sep	Oct	Nov	Dec	Total
Cash In													
Salary or Wages	$2,100	$2,100	$2,100	$3,000	$2,100	$3,000	$2,100	$2,100	$3,000	$2,200	$2,200	$3,000	$29,000
Gift Income	$ -	$ -	$ -	$ -	$ -	$ -	$ -	$ -	$ -	$ -	$ -	$2,500	$ 2,500
Total Cash In	$2,100	$2,100	$2,100	$3,000	$2,100	$3,000	$2,100	$2,100	$3,000	$2,200	$2,200	$5,500	$31,500
Cash Out													
Expenses:													
Regular Household													
Expenses	$1,500	$1,500	$1,500	$1,500	$1,500	$1,500	$1,500	$1,500	$1,500	$1,500	$1,500	$1,500	$18,000
Gifts	$ -	$ -	$ -	$ -	$ -	$ 150	$ -	$ -	$ -	$ -	$ -	$1,000	$ 1,150
Seasonal Clothing	$ -	$ -	$ -	$ -	$ 200	$ -	$ -	$ -	$ 300	$ -	$ -	$ -	$ 500
Income Taxes	$ -	$ -	$ -	$5,500	$ -	$5,000	$ -	$ -	$5,000	$ -	$ -	$5,000	$20,500
Total Cash Out	$1,500	$1,500	$1,500	$7,000	$1,700	$6,650	$1,500	$1,500	$6,800	$1,500	$1,500	$7,500	$40,150
Net Cash In/(Out)	$ 600	$ 600	$600	$(4,000)	$ 400	$(3,650)	$ 600	$ 600	$(3,800)	$ 700	$ 700	$(2,000)	$(8,650)

nor and major changes you can make, depending on the severity of your situation. If your situation is likely to change soon, or if you've just become unemployed, for example, you will not want to rush out and sell your house!

If you are just a little bit short every month, where can you cut? As you tracked your expenses, did you find some things you wanted to change?

I always used to say, "Oh, I have to save, I'm going to use coupons." Now with the supermarket card, you can just walk in and buy and save an extra $5, $10. They make it easy for you, too—they tell you how much you are saving. I take that cash right out of my wallet and put it in my cashbox.

Your budget should reflect your choices as well as your goals:

In my house, the telephone bills are very high, because I have a child living overseas, and talking to her is a high priority for me. So I chose to cut expenses elsewhere.

If you are just a little bit over budget, you might try cutting back by a percentage. Say you are 10 percent over. Since you can't change the fixed expenses, try cutting each of the variable expenses by 20 percent and see if that does it. Or you might just take out one whole category—"We are going to stop going out to dinner once a week"—and save the money.

My roommate and I did our budgets together. We found we were spending way too much on "entertainment." We decided to find other ways to entertain ourselves. We started renting videos instead of going to a $9 movie—and got museum passes from the public library. We got some cookbooks and tried new recipes—sometimes we invited our friends—instead of getting pizza every other night. We'd been spending close to $160 a month each on concerts! Now we buy the CD instead, and save our money for a few really special bands. We have a lot more cash to put toward our goals, and we feel very good about ourselves!

Making decisions about managing your money in the way that suits you best also can help you to realize your dreams:

_____ 'S CASH FLOW PROJECTION

	Jan	Feb	Mar	Apr	May	Jun	Jul	Aug	Sep	Oct	Nov	Dec	Total
Cash In													
Salary or Wages	___	___	___	___	___	___	___	___	___	___	___	___	___
Bonus	___	___	___	___	___	___	___	___	___	___	___	___	___
Freelance Income	___	___	___	___	___	___	___	___	___	___	___	___	___
Gift Income	___	___	___	___	___	___	___	___	___	___	___	___	___
Other Income	___	___	___	___	___	___	___	___	___	___	___	___	___
Total Cash In	___	___	___	___	___	___	___	___	___	___	___	___	___
Cash Out													
Expenses:	___	___	___	___	___	___	___	___	___	___	___	___	___
Regular Household Expenses	___	___	___	___	___	___	___	___	___	___	___	___	___
Gifts	___	___	___	___	___	___	___	___	___	___	___	___	___
Seasonal Clothing	___	___	___	___	___	___	___	___	___	___	___	___	___
Income Taxes	___	___	___	___	___	___	___	___	___	___	___	___	___
Vacation	___	___	___	___	___	___	___	___	___	___	___	___	___
Other Expenses	___	___	___	___	___	___	___	___	___	___	___	___	___
Other Outflows:													
New Car Down Payment	___	___	___	___	___	___	___	___	___	___	___	___	___
Furnishings & Appliances	___	___	___	___	___	___	___	___	___	___	___	___	___
Other Outflows	___	___	___	___	___	___	___	___	___	___	___	___	___
Total Cash Out	___	___	___	___	___	___	___	___	___	___	___	___	___
Net Cash In/(Out)	___	___	___	___	___	___	___	___	___	___	___	___	___

After doing the goal-setting exercise, I realized that what I wanted more than anything was to own a sailboat—just a little Sunfish, but it might as well have been a yacht. I never had a penny left at the end of the week. I'd even considered financing— but the payments would be $100 a month. We did the tracking income exercise for four weeks, and I noticed that every day, I was spending serious money at Starbucks; a large coffee in the morning, a cappuccino each afternoon. It was my little treat to myself, pocket change, not quite $5 a day. Not until I added it up did I see that I was spending close to $100 each month on coffee! I decided I'd much rather have my boat! I'm on my way!

In creating your budget and managing your cash flow, you may find it necessary to have access to credit. Chapter 4 will describe the process of securing credit and using it wisely.

ASSESSING YOUR NET WORTH

Assets	Estimated Value	Liabilities	Unpaid Balance
Cash	$_____	Current bills	$_____
Checking	$_____		
Savings	$_____	Reserve credit *	$_____
		Credit cards *	$_____
Investments		Store credit *	
Money market	$_____	(extended payment plans)	$_____
CDs	$_____		
U.S. savings bonds	$_____	Home mortgages	$_____
Treasury bills	$_____	Vacation home mortgage	$_____
Mutual funds	$_____	Home equity lines	$_____
Stocks	$_____	Car loan	$_____
Other	$_____	Student loan	$_____
		401 (k) loan	$_____
Retirement Accounts			
401 (k) plans	$_____	Investment margin account	$_____
IRA or Keogh	$_____		
SEP	$_____	Past taxes owed	$_____
Other pensions	$_____		
Annuities	$_____	Other	$_____
Real Estate		**Total Liabilities (L)**	$_____
Home	$_____		
Vacation home	$_____	**Net Worth (A−L)**	$_____
Rental property	$_____		
Land	$_____	**Life Insurance Proceeds**	$_____
Personal Property		**Total Estate**	$_____
Furnishings	$_____		
Automobiles	$_____		
Jewelry	$_____		
Silver	$_____	* Available but unused credit lines do not get factored into the	
Art	$_____	calculation of net worth.	
Collections	$_____		
Boats, planes	$_____		
Other Assets			
Business equity	$_____		
Loans owed to you	$_____		
Other	$_____		
Total Assets (A)	$_____		

4: 'Til Death Do Us Part: You and Your Credit

Contributing Author:

Nanci Pisani

"Guard your credit as you would your virtue. Just like the social currency of reputation, its integrity must be meticulously maintained and shrewdly negotiated."
—CATHERINE W. GRONEWOLD, RESEARCHER ON THE
PSYCHOLOGY OF WOMEN, HARVARD UNIVERSITY

IN THIS CHAPTER, YOU WILL LEARN:

- What credit is and how it works

- How to manage your credit

- How to borrow money wisely to improve your lifestyle without compromising your financial goals

- How to correct mismanaged or erroneous credit

We all have partnerships in our lives. Some we love and some we don't. Some will come and some will go. Your credit will stay with you forever. From the first time that you sign on that dotted line to accept credit from any type of financial institution or retail store, you and your credit are partners for life.

Credit is "permission for a customer to have goods or services that will be paid for at a later date." Having credit allows you to buy that which you cannot or choose not to purchase with cash. Very large purchases such as a home or a car may otherwise be out of reach, unless you are able to take a loan, and pay it back over an extended period of time. Having credit also empowers you to

borrow funds for a variety of reasons, such as renting a car, purchasing a home, paying large medical bills, tuition, or simply to take advantage of a special offer.

Once thought of as a privilege, a credit card is now a staple of American adulthood and independence. Having a credit card is necessary in today's world, as it provides you with the following opportunities:

- To extend buying capacity—as long as two or three weeks without finance charge

- To buy over the phone or via the Internet

- To cash checks and for identification

- To guarantee hotel reservations

- To rent a car

- One bill each month for purchases

- A record of personal and business expenses

THE ORIGIN OF CREDIT

When businesses were small and community-based, the local proprietor knew the customer personally and knew where he or she lived! "Institutional" credit began just before World War I, with department stores issuing small, metal "dog tag" plates to selected customers. Gasoline credit cards followed, with the greater popularity of the automobile and people's increasing mobility. But credit cards as we know them today did not exist until the 1950s. Until then, people either paid cash or had a store account.[1]

Diner's Club became the first national credit card not limited to just gas and oil. Francis McNamara, who owned a loan company in New York, came up with the idea. He issued a cardboard card with the customer's name and account number, good at many different Manhattan restaurants, charging the customer an annual fee of $5. In 1951, the Franklin National Bank in New York issued the first card that could be used at other types of business.[2]

- To buy tickets for concerts, theater and sporting events

- And above all, if used well, to establish a good credit rating to enhance your life

WHAT IS YOUR CURRENT CREDIT SITUATION?

You likely are in one of four situations right now. You may have no credit: either just starting out, or establishing credit on your own for the first time, such as during a divorce. You may have excellent credit and want to make sure it stays that way. You may have had some slow credit in the past and are wondering how to repair it. You may have had to file for bankruptcy due to extenuating circumstances, and you feel that your purchasing power has evaporated.

Or you may be in transition, for a variety of reasons. No matter what your current circum-stance, you can take charge of your credit, and you can educate yourself so you can make the best possible choices at this point in your life. Be assured: everything can be fixed—maybe not exactly as you had hoped, but every financial situation *can* be improved.

STARTING OUT: HOW TO ESTABLISH A CREDIT HISTORY OF YOUR OWN

To begin establishing credit, open a checking and a savings account and make regular deposits and withdrawals. When you have built up some savings, apply for a secured loan—that is, a loan against your savings. Make the payments regularly and on time. Or you can ask a relative to cosign a loan for you. While you are responsible for making the payments, the cosigner guarantees to the lender that she would be responsible if you did not make the payments.

Then, apply for a gasoline or retail department store card, use it, and make payments on time. You need a steady source of income, from a job or from child support or alimony, to be able to get a card. Once you have established that you can make payments responsibly, you can apply for a bank card (MasterCard or Visa). Again, use the card and make all payments on time. The key to obtaining credit is assuring lenders that you are a good risk.

Although you are able to pay off a bank card balance by making a small monthly payment and carrying the rest, it is important to recognize that the longer you carry that balance, the more interest you will have paid.

Here is an example: Say you have a Master-Card with a $1,000 limit and an APR (annual percentage rate) of 19 percent. You spend all $1,000 of credit on your card and pay the minimum amount of $15 back to the credit company every month. Yes, you are decreasing your debt by $15 once a month, but you also are being charged for the balance you still are carrying.

If you paid $15 a month every month for a year, that would be $180 off your $1,000 debt. That would mean you'd be down to $820. Then you have to multiply that figure by the APR of 19 percent and you find that you are being charged $155.80 a year, because you carry that balance on your card. It still might not sound that bad until you realize you have to add that fee to the $820 you have yet to pay. Even though you have been paying a little off every month, you have decreased your debt only by $24.20 in an entire year!

It would take you twelve years to pay off your card at that rate, and you would have paid $2,160 in total to the credit card company—more than twice what you spent originally! And that assumes you do not charge another penny to your card after the original $1,000 of spending.

One tip to reduce credit card debt more quickly and save on interest is by making payments every other week rather than every month, and by not decreasing the payment amounts until the card is paid off.

A credit card is similar to a short-term loan, with no defined payoff term. The issuing bank pays for your purchases and typically charges you from 5 percent to 25 percent interest, depending on how valuable a customer they think you are, until you pay them back. Since you give the bank no collateral in case you default, the credit card loan is an unsecured loan. The bank also charges the retailer—the store or business from which you are purchasing—a service charge, typically 2 percent to 5 percent, for the privilege of accepting the use of their credit card.

Other cards, such as American Express, Diner's Club, and CarteBlanche, offer a short-term extension of credit convenient for travel or entertainment. Generally, these cards have no spending limit, but do require that you pay off the balance in full every month.

In the 1980s, computer technology allowed creditors to obtain access to a credit bureau's databases immediately. These technological advances also facilitated the development of new products to assist creditors with evaluating, analyzing, and monitoring customers' records, as well as highlighting people at high risk of delinquency. Newer technology also means you, the consumer, can be better protected as well.

While I was on vacation in California, my credit card number (but not the card) was stolen. Since I still had the card, I didn't find this out until a day after I got home. I went to the local florist, and *attempted to charge $25 worth of flowers. My card was refused. I was told to contact the issuing bank. I was so embarrassed. This had never happened to me. I knew my payments were on time. What had happened? Turns out, there is a common scam used on vacationers. An unethical employee of a restaurant or retail establishment copies the number of the card. He or she then attempts to use the number to make a small purchase. If it goes through, the crook starts on bigger purchases. In this case, the credit card company's investigation unit monitored my spending: watching the pattern of charges on my whole vacation. When they saw a purchase in a neighborhood unlike the one I'd been visiting, for an item inconsistent with what I'd been buying, they tried to contact me. Since I was traveling, they couldn't reach me. Since they suspected the number was being used fraudulently, they shut off the card. Afterward, they fell all over themselves apologizing, but they were just doing their job. It's kind of scary, though, to realize they know so much about you.*

YOUR CREDIT BUREAU REPORT

Credit reporting agencies gather their information via a tape from the creditors with which you have established credit. Each creditor sends a tape to the credit reporting agency on a monthly basis. The credit bureau report shows information from which a prospective lender can predict your intent and ability to repay. Think of your credit bureau report as your alter ego because, in a sense, it is. It reflects your lifestyle and your spending patterns. It discloses where you shop, how often you use credit, if you pay your creditors as agreed, and how much credit you have outstanding at any one time.

The credit bureau report discloses so much about you: your name, your age, and your current and previous addresses. It details when you first established credit, exactly how you pay your creditors, and even whether you pay or do not pay. It will list all the accounts you currently have, as well as those you have had in the past. The credit report typically shows:

- All opened accounts reported for the period of time that you have credit with an institution

- Bankruptcy information retained for ten years

- Delinquency information retained for seven years

- Inquiries from creditors, whether or not you actually established credit with that institution. Such inquiries remain on your file for two years.

As a consumer, you not only have a right to see your credit report, it is also vitally important that you monitor your report on a regular basis. Usually, the information is accurate, but bureaus do receive or report false information from time to time. It is up to you to make sure that the information on your credit report is true and up-to-date.

Several years ago, I was shopping for an automobile. When I had chosen my new wheels, the next step was to seek a loan from the bank. I never gave it a second thought as I filled out the application, because I assumed that my credit was impeccable. Much to my surprise and chagrin, I was declined! When asked why, the reason for denial was due to the fact that the credit report had somehow erroneously recognized my address as a "prison."

How did that happen? I come from a town so small that there are no numbers on the main street residences. My address was simply West Main Street.

On that street there also was a retreat center. Somehow, the credit reporting agency not only classified this quiet retreat center as a prison, but they incorrectly matched my address to that one. In order for me to correct their error, I had an arduous process of verifying that I was not in prison, that the retreat center was not a prison, and that the credit reporting agency had made a mistake. That took several days, letter writing, copying documents, and mailing things to reporting agencies. I lost the opportunity to buy that particular car. Another came along, but it was not what I originally had wanted. So you see, it's better to manage your credit before you need to make a purchase.

You may be unaware of a blemish on your report:

I recently had a credit bureau report pulled for me because I was in the process of purchasing a house. Though I did not know it, I had a delinquent status on my account on a credit union Master-Card. The mortgage company that was underwriting my application called to question me on the delinquency. "Can you explain the delinquency that's on your report?" I was totally unaware that it had existed and asked for details. They simply gave me the name of the credit union. It was my responsibility to contact the credit union and identify the delinquency. And do you know what the problem was? A balance of two dollars, a finance charge that the credit union had not properly credited. But it showed up as a delinquency, a chronic "thirty day overdue," two years after it had not been "paid." I had made a purchase, and I had

returned the item, and for some reason the credit union didn't fully credit the amount. So for a $2 mistake on their part, I had to write a detailed and lengthy explanation as to why my credit showed up delinquent! I was able to purchase the house, but it was a huge inconvenience.

A credit reporting agency is required to:

- Provide a report to you. You may request in writing at any time that you be sent a copy.

- Verify any information with which you disagree.

- Respond back to you with the results of their investigation.

- Delete any information they cannot verify.

On an annual basis, you should get a merged credit report on yourself from the major credit reporting agencies to verify that:

- Your name, address, Social Security number are correct

- The credit that you have is accurate in terms of the payment history

- The credit listed on your report is yours and not anyone else's

- No credit listed shows up late if you have not paid late

- If you have paid off and closed out accounts, they are listed as such

You can obtain a credit report directly from the reporting agency or on the Internet. Check local listings in the phone book or on the Web for credit reporting agencies. Depending on the state in which you reside, there may be a small fee for you to obtain your report, but it's worth it.

Once you have received the report, take time to review it closely. The reporting agency will provide you with instructions on how to read the report, so you will know what they say. Below is a sample page from a credit bureau report.

experían

	Prepared for		Report date
			(Date report is run)
	Report number		Questions?
			Call 800 583-4080

Page 3 of 10

Credit information about you *continued*

Source/ Account number (except last few digits)	Date opened/ Reported since	Date of status/ Last reported	Type/ Terms/ Monthly payment	Responsibility	Credit limit or original amount/ High balance	Recent balance/ Recent payment	Comments
FIRST USA BK NA 201 NORTH WALNUT ST WILMINGTON DE 19801 (Your account number will appear here)	3-1994/ 10-1996	10-1996/ 10-1996	Revolving/ NA/ $0	Individual	NA/ NA	NA/	Status: paid/never late. This account is scheduled to continue on record until 10-2003. Creditor's statement *"Account closed at credit grantor's request."*
CHASE NA 100 DUFFY AVE HICKSVILLE NY 11801	7-1988/ 5-1999	7-1988/ 6-1999	Revolving/ NA/ $134	Individual	$12,600/ $9,723	$4,959 as of 6-1999/	Status: open/never late.
CITIBANK/BRADLEES 245 OLD COUNTRY RD MELVILLE NY 11747	3-1996/ 4-1996	3-1996/ 5-1996	Revolving/ NA/ $0	Individual	$1,200/ $185	$0/paid as of 5-1996/	Status: inactive/never late.
FILENES 70 FRANKLIN STREET BOSTON MA 02122	6-1989/ 11-1998	6-1989/ 6-1999	Revolving/ NA/ $0	Individual	$1,400/ $463	$0/paid as of 6-1999/	Status: open/never late.

CORRECTING CREDIT BUREAU ERRORS

A good time to look at your credit bureau report is before you're about to make a major purchase, such as a car or a home. Give yourself four to six weeks to correct any problem as well. If you find yourself having to seek assistance from a credit reporting agency or a creditor to repair your credit, always get the name of the person with whom you are speaking, document your conversation in writing, even in an abbreviated fashion, get that person's title, and be sure that person has the level of authority to help you.

If you find what you consider to be an error, consider taking the following steps:

- Verify in detail your perception of the error. If a late payment, provide to the agency a copy of the check used to make the payment, the money order receipt, or the receipt from the bank.

- If your name or Social Security number is wrong, send along a copy of your license or Social Security card. If you have changed your name, send a copy of your marriage license, divorce decree, or court documents relating to the the name change.

- If you cannot verify the mistake in writing with proof, contact the bank that is claiming the error and ask if they will correct the issue on the credit report on your behalf. Ask them to send, in writing, a dispute form to the agency and ask that they send you a copy as well.

It is important to document everything in writing when attempting to resolve a credit situation. Obtain the name of the person(s) with whom you are working to resolve the issue, at both the bank and the reporting agency. Once the situation has been resolved, request that they send you a letter stating so, and keep this for your records.

You have the right to dispute any information that is incorrect on your file. However, if the information is verified to be correct, it will not be removed.

"Credit doctors" and "credit clinics" all claim to be able to erase bad credit. In fact, you are simply being charged fees to have these individuals dispute information you can dispute and correct yourself for free, by following the procedures outlined above.

Once you have established credit, used it responsibly, and paid your bills on time, you should have excellent credit.

WOMEN AND CREDIT

The Equal Credit Opportunity Act of 1974 guarantees, among other things, that women will not be denied access to credit based solely on their gender. This law particularly helps married women to establish credit by requiring creditors to report account payment information in the names of both spouses on any joint accounts as of June 1, 1977. If you were married before this date and have only combined accounts with your husband, it is probable that the credit reporting agencies do not maintain a file in your name. It also is important to know that some creditors may disregard this law. If you suspect this is the case, you can contact the major credit bureaus to be sure a file is kept in your name. If you do have a file, obtain a copy of your credit report as well as your husband's so that you can compare them. Then be sure to contact any creditors who are reporting information only in your husband's name if the account was opened after June 1, 1977.

THE LOAN APPLICATION PROCESS, OR THE *ABCCCC*'S OF CREDIT

Every bank establishes credit guidelines to ensure that standards are applied to each loan applicant in the same manner. Policies are developed to be consistent with the amount of credit risk the bank is willing to assume.

Credit analysis is the process a lender uses to determine the ability of the prospective borrower to repay the debt and also her willingness to do so. Credit analysis often is presented in terms of the C's of Credit.

- *Capacity* refers to the applicant's income relative to her debts and expenses. Debt-to-income parameters are established to minimize the risk of default. Additional factors, which can affect the borrower's capacity, are employment and residence stability. While there is no one standard that banks use, the traditional method of calculating debt-to-income is to allow a percentage of your gross (before tax) income, typically around 35 to 50 percent.

- *Character* is a very important consideration when analyzing an application. Character, as it relates to credit analysis, generally refers to the applicant's willingness and desire to repay obligations as demonstrated by her payment history.

- *Capital* is the amount of liquid assets that easily can be turned into cash, such as savings, securities, or investments that could be relied upon to pay back the loan, if income should decline or if one runs into unexpected expenses.

- *Collateral* is any asset used to secure a loan. The collateral is used only to strengthen the loan. The loan is never made on the strength of the collateral alone, unless the individual is borrowing her own money, such as in a passbook loan.

The shift from most customers paying off their credit card balances every month (convenience users) to more carrying a balance every month has resulted in a lengthier interviewing process when you apply for a loan. It is prudent for any banker to know what's going on with an individual prior to final disposition. After all, she is responsible for dispersing the bank's funds—ultimately, the shareholders' funds! So, if you are in the banker's office and she is asking you some questions about your credit, or your spending habits or history, be assured that asking a lot of questions is a sign of a good banker. She is conducting a needs assessment profile. That enables her to decide what the best product line may be to meet your needs.

The lender is looking at many components as she tries to approve a loan for you—primarily your intent to repay and your ability to repay. In addition to your credit report, she will look at employment, at disclosed income, at your spending habits, at your savings habits. She will want to know what your checking and savings balances are. Do you have savings accounts? If you don't, that's not necessarily a bad thing, but it is a flag. Or she may see: "She has $7,000 worth of credit balance. She has no savings. She has been at the job for only two months."

Given that kind of information, the banker

may reasonably conclude that some changes may have been happening in your life recently. A prudent banker is careful to develop a full picture prior to making a final decision. She will want you to have some savings, so that if you should lose your new job, you will be able to repay your loan.

CREDIT DECISION

Upon receipt of a completed application by a customer, an analysis is performed to:

- Determine if the purpose is sound and legal.

- Verify address, employment, income from place of employment or other means, savings, other assets, as well as review outstanding credit listed on the application.

- Assess value of collateral, if any is to be considered.

- Evaluate applicant's credit history through a credit report.

- Determine applicant's ability to pay through the income stream that she has disclosed.

- On occasion, certain banks also may look to determine a secondary source of repayment.

Sometimes during the credit investigation, it becomes apparent that the individual has too much open credit—that is, credit is available to her that is not now being used, but could be—or too many charge cards, has had credit problems in the past, or has no credit.

THE CHANGING CREDIT CLIMATE

The traditional credit and banking industry has been changing dramatically in recent years. Just a few years ago, my role as a bank officer was to wait in my office for customers to come in requesting loans. Now, due to the fierce competition from nonbank institutions that have grabbed market share, bankers are in the field, actively soliciting business. And as you are well aware, banks and other lending institutions are marketing much more aggressively through a variety of media, including telemarketing and print advertising as well as on the Internet.

I grew up during the Depression. We learned, "If you can't afford it in cash, you are not getting it. You either save for it or you do without." My kids, and now my grandkids, see it quite differently. They want it now. And this need for "now" can come with a heavy price, if we are not disciplined.

Sometimes, we can get in over our heads:

Dottie used to have good credit as well as a good job. She always paid her bills responsibly. And because she did pay her bills well, she was considered a good credit risk by the banks that were purchasing her name for a credit card solicitation effort. Dottie started getting these revolving card offers in the mail and began to say to herself, "You know what, I'm going to fill it out. I'm not going to use it. I'm going to have it just in case." And you know how tempting that can be. So one day Dottie is feeling a little blue, and she gets in her car and she drives to the mall. Next thing you know, she's made a $200 clothing purchase on her credit card. She says to herself, "Oh, I'll pay that off within the month. Not to worry." And the next time she shops, *she uses that credit card again, but chooses not to pay off the balance in full when the bill arrives, leaving her with a balance and a finance charge due. That outfit just became more expensive. The pattern starts. Soon that card with a $2,000 credit line is at its maximum. Another card offer comes along and she signs up. Now Dottie has a $5,000 balance on a couple of different cards. And she gets a third invitation for an introductory offer of 5.9 percent for six months.*

She thinks, "I'm going to take those two cards I have now. I'm going to transfer that balance to the newest 5.9 percent rate with an even higher limit. I'll pay it off within six months. I know I can do that."

Sadly, Dottie has created a nasty spending habit that is spiraling out of control. If the pattern continues, she will be spending more than she is making. Dottie needs to pay off those cards, but, more important, she needs to realign her way of thinking about credit. She needs to break the cycle that she has created for herself. That takes a good deal of courage. Only she can change the pattern. But she can get help.

If you find yourself in a situation similar to Dottie's, it is important that you contact the bank where you have any loans, credit cards, checking or savings accounts. If you have a good banker, she will work with you to correct your dilemma.

She may suggest alternatives to improve your current situation. She will question you to determine how you arrived at this point, whether it seems to be temporary or not, and how she can help you to resolve it, based on your current income, collateral, and/or other sources of repayment.

Sometimes, you may be in credit trouble for reasons other than late payment:

I had a good relationship with my boyfriend, until he lost his job. I let him use my credit card to get some cash. Things were okay for a while, but then he got depressed and stopped even looking for work. I was upset and starting really getting on his case. Finally, he just stopped speaking to me. I was out three thousand bucks. I mean, I was in love. I didn't make him sign an IOU or anything. How stupid of me! I could take him to small claims court, but what's the point? He still doesn't have any money to pay me. Believe me, I get really frosted each month when I make that payment!

We live on Harvey Hill. Our neighbors around the corner, who have a similar last name, live on Harvey Hill Road. They went to Florida for three months, and had all their mail forwarded. Unfortunately, a lot of our mail went to Florida, too. We started getting many overdue and shut-off notices. It wasn't our fault, but it made a mess of our credit rating.

In 1998, credit card charges in the United States for Visa, MasterCard, American Express, and Discover were more than $1 trillion, according to CardWeb, a credit research organization in Frederick, Maryland. In 1998, customers owed $440 billion to Visa, MasterCard, Discover, and Optima. And there was $518 billion outstanding in revolving credit balances.[3]

Shortly before my mother was diagnosed with Alzheimer's disease, she gave all her credit card numbers over the phone to this guy who called selling "credit card insurance." Of course, he went on a spending spree at her expense. We denied the charges, and ended up not having to pay for his theft. But it was a nightmare to straighten out! The credit card companies all were very helpful, but her credit was essentially ruined.

There are several federal regulations in place to protect you, the consumer. The Fair Credit Reporting Act is one. It prohibits a company from disclosing false information about you. The Equal Credit Opportunity Act prohibits banks from denying credit to you based on your race, creed, color, religion, or marital status.

Also by law, your banker cannot require that you have your spouse cosign a loan. If you apply for a loan and you are declined because of insufficient income, the banker has the right to counter your initial request by asking for proof of additional income, possibly in the form of a cosigner, but it cannot specify that the cosigner be your spouse.

I wish that I'd had lectures on these subjects in school. If I knew then what I know now, it could have saved a lot of trouble early in my marriage. When we first were married and went to buy a house, my husband's credit history was impeccable. Mine, however, had several late payments for credit cards. I used to pay bills only once a month, when I got my paychecks. It never occurred to me that the companies really cared if the payment was a few days late. I just thought that was why they charged interest. I had never thought to mention this old habit to my husband—it never came up in conversation—and he found out in the banker's office. I had to write a long letter explaining why these long-

ago payments were late. We did get the loan, but unfortunately the stage was set for a marriage full of mistrust about money.

At some point, you will be requested to fill out a loan application. As part of the underwriting process, the lender will pull a credit report. That will help her to be able to instruct you as to how you can improve your credit, perhaps suggesting that you take a consolidation loan to help pay off all debt.

A consolidation loan is a new loan, for an amount sufficient to cover all the other loans a customer may have. The advantage of a consolidation loan is that the customer then has only one payment to make each month, instead of several. It is a way of "starting fresh," although the total amount of debt is the same. Typically, these loans require some kind of security to approve the request—maybe a car, maybe savings.

Or the banker may help you draft a letter to the creditors that you owe, asking for some type of forbearance on the credit balance. She may give you the number of a credit counseling service in your area. And she should tell you those advertisements telling you that you can "get rid of your bad credit" for only $69.95 are hogwash!

What is considered poor credit or a high credit risk report? Poor credit results from sporadic or no payments on a loan or credit card, with no extenuating circumstances such as illness, death, or loss of employment.

If you find yourself with one or more bills you are not able to pay, take action now. By all means contact the institution to let them know that you might not be paying on time. Call them and speak either to the branch manager or to the manager of the collection department. Advise them of your current financial status. They may even ask you to come in and talk with them face-to-face. They may ask you to bring recent income verification. They are not trying to humiliate you. They need to find out what the situation is and make some arrangement, so it's a win-win situation.

It's a win for you because you've confronted the situation. And it's a win for the bank because they will work with you to resolve your financial dilemma, prevent a loan foreclosure, get their money, and preserve a customer relationship. No reputable financial institution wants to repossess your car or foreclose on your home.

Sometimes you think the financial difficulty is only short term and will pass in a month or two. You may be embarrassed to call the lender, and decide to make the payments as best you can. If the situation does not resolve itself as quickly as you had hoped, you then may start missing payments. Those late payments will show up on your credit bureau report. So it's a good idea to position yourself financially, if you know of an impending layoff, a divorce, a need to help out a sick relative, or any other situation which may have or which already has had an impact on your finances.

You also can contact your bank for help if you have credit trouble not related to credit cards; for example, if you are carrying some old medical bills, and then lose your job.

To determine whether you may have overextended yourself with credit card debt, you can ask yourself the following questions. Do you now charge goods or services you used to pay for with cash? Are your expenses increasing faster than your income? Do you often make only the minimum monthly payments on cards? Have you ever taken a cash advance on one card to pay off an-

other, or to pay day-to-day expenses? Are you worried about your credit card debt?

If you feel you need help, and your banker does not suggest it, you may wish to contact the Consumer Credit Counseling Service on your own.

CCCS counselors will work with you on budgeting, reestablishing a good credit rating, creating a savings plan, as well as working on your behalf with your creditors to establish a payment plan that meets your budget and the needs of your creditors. CCCS is a nonprofit service, for which you may pay a small fee. The national phone number for CCCS is 800-388-2227. When you dial that number, it will identify the area code from which you are calling and connect you to a local office.

WHEN A YOUNG PERSON HAS CREDIT TROUBLE

What happens to youngsters who get in over their heads with student loans? Are you, as a parent, required to help them? And how can you help your son or daughter without actually paying off his or her debts yourself?

If your child is of legal age, you are not responsible legally, although, as a mother, you may be very tempted to want to "rescue" your son or daughter. Banks are seeing a rise in younger clients acquiring a great deal of credit. At college, students are introduced to many different products, especially revolving lines of credit. Understandably, they are entranced by the offers and take one, two, maybe three card offers. And they use those cards. Before they know it, they are feeling strapped, with an inability to repay the balances they acquired. We need to educate ourselves

---

Take a younger woman under your wing by introducing her to your personal banker.

---

and our children about the consequences of overspending.

A good banker may spend a lot of time counseling young people about fiscal responsibility. She may seek ways to help them repair their excessive credit balances, often with consolidation loans. Since not many young people have the in-come or collateral sufficient to obtain a consolidation loan, the banker may ask for a cosigner. By law, she cannot dictate who may or may not be a cosigner.

Sometimes, a recent graduate may come in with $40,000 worth of student loans. She is now at a new job and trying to get ahead. But she has this

---

"SEDUCTION BY PLASTIC": TEENAGE WOMEN AND CREDIT CARD COMPANIES

When I was eighteen and going off to college, I discovered an amazing thing: preap-proved, no-annual-fee credit cards. So easy to get, with applications posted on class-room bulletin boards and representatives stationed outside the dining halls nearly all the time.

At first, I thought I'd just sign up for one or two. I didn't think I'd end up using them that much. I thought they might be handy in case of an emergency or if I didn't want to carry cash. I signed up for my first MasterCard the beginning of freshman year. It took the credit company only two weeks to send me the card in the mail—a lit-tle silver card with a $1,000 limit. I was delighted!

Having the card made me feel independent and important. Finally, I wasn't de-pending on my parents' money and credit anymore. I was on my own and they didn't have to know about this if I didn't want. The first thing I did when I got my new credit card was to go out shopping with my best friend "just to try it out." We went to the lo-cal mall and I ended up spending $500 that day. It wasn't like "real" money. I knew I would have to pay it off eventually, but that's the whole point of credit cards, right? They're like a loan and you're required to pay just the minimum balance every month.

Well, that was only the beginning for me. I got another card two months later, this one with a $500 limit. And then another one for $1,000. I had a part-time job, so I could easily pay off the minimum $15 every month. I was on top of the world. I'd

---

grown up in a single-parent household, and I always felt guilty asking for money. Finally, I could have all the little luxuries I wanted without having to beg my parents for an extra twenty bucks. I bought clothes, jewelry, compact disks, pretty much anything I wanted. I kept spending and went through my "free" $2,500 in less than three months.

I started to worry. I'd become so used to spending on a whim and now I didn't have any more room on the cards. I felt desperate. Shortly after, I got sent a Discover card with a $1,000 limit. When I had used up that entire card, I applied for my last card at the end of freshman year. I was given a credit limit of only $300 on that Visa card because I "had a minimal income and a lot of credit already."

Now it's a full year later and I am slowly trying to pay off that $3,800 in debt. I finally sat down one day to try and figure out some of my finances and realized that I was in way over my head with a lot more debt than I could handle. I went to buy a used car this summer and almost wasn't approved for the loan because I never paid off more than the minimum payment on my cards each month. I also had a large amount of debt compared to my monthly income.

I was told my dad might have to cosign for my loan. I was really ashamed and felt not so grown up anymore. Eventually, I was able to get the loan only if I paid the dealership "a few thousand dollars in advance," which I had to borrow.

I had never stopped to read about the finance rates on the cards I owned. My rates for the different cards ranged from 17 percent to 20 percent yearly! That means I was charged an average of about 18.5 percent on the balance I carried every month on each card. I never knew this would add up so quickly.

I would pay off three months of minimum payments and think, "Great. I've paid $45 of my debt, which means I have $45 of open credit on my card again," and I would spend all of that, reversing all my progress. Remember, I'm talking about only one of my cards here—not all four! It's really scary when you analyze your spending that closely. And can you imagine if I'd had $10,000 of credit—or more? I'd be paying the credit card companies for the rest of my life, would never be able to charge anything else on the cards I did have, and probably would not be able to take out loans of other sorts, because the creditors wouldn't think I was responsible enough to pay them back, based on my payment history.

No wonder credit card companies make so much money. There are a lot of people who only pay their minimum balances every month and end up paying so much more money because of the incredibly high interest percentage rates.

Don't be fooled by the introductory rates of 3.9 percent for the first six months. Eventually, the rate is going to be back up to that 19 percent again and you'll be in

> **more debt than ever. I'm out of school and working now, and faced with paying off not only my credit card bills, but also student loans, car payments, car insurance bills, rent, and a lot of other monthly expenses.**
>
> **This "seduction by credit card" is the horrible trap I fell into by being an uninformed consumer. I am really paying for it now—literally and figuratively. My advice? Save some cash and splurge a little sometimes, even go so low as to beg your parents for money, but don't start out like I did. It's just not worth it.**

huge payment to make every month. Often the student loan servicing agency will be able to consolidate the loans, which should shrink payments dramatically.

Some banks don't actually consolidate student loans because the federal student loan rates are quite low in the student loan industry. If the student has the capacity to consolidate and refinance, it's a good idea to do it through the loan services. They have alternatives available to you to ease the burden. You may be able to get a forbearance for six months or so, which means that you do not have to make payments during that time, though interest does continue to accumulate.

Student loans generally are set up at low interest rates and with long payback schedules, so that new graduates can handle the payments once they begin working.

FACING BANKRUPTCY

As recently as twenty years ago, bankruptcy was considered taboo. The 1982 edition of the *American Heritage Dictionary* defined bankrupt as: "A debtor, who upon voluntary petition or one invoked by his creditors, is judged legally insolvent and whose remaining property is administered for his creditors or distributed among them."

This definition underscores the seriousness of bankruptcy—before a time when credit was so free-flowing, when anyone could get credit.

Bankruptcy is an enormous problem right now for consumers as well as for lenders, precisely *because* it is so accepted. In 1998, there were more than 1 million cases of bankruptcy recorded—an astonishing number.

I'm sure if you listen to any talk radio shows, you'll hear a lot of commercials "soliciting" bankruptcy: "If you can't handle your debts, don't worry about it, I'm Attorney So-and-so, and I can get all those annoying creditors off your back, even the IRS." I'm surprised that commercials like that are allowed on the air. But they are. Some folks are so heavily in debt, and so very scared. Often, they don't even know how to figure out what their true debt structure is, and what they can do to get out from under.

If you are in deep financial trouble, the first step is to figure out your budget. Then, on a monthly basis, identify what your income is and what your expenses are, including your debt load, using the charts in chapter 3. And figure out what is left every month after the bills are paid. Then you can work with your banker to determine a reasonable monthly payment to pay off the debt over time. Finding the right personal banker, and

In 1997, 1.3 million people filed for personal bankruptcy, a 300 percent increase over 1981. The most common reason? Not having enough income to pay their bills.[4]

the right bank, may be a big plus in helping you prevent bankruptcy.

HOW TO CHOOSE A BANK

All banks claim that they want your business. With all the mergers and acquisitions, the big banks are getting bigger. You may begin to feel less of an individual and more of a number, unless you take the initiative to seek out a local bank, a community bank, or to establish a personal relationship with a branch officer of a larger bank. Because, as in many areas of life, relationships can make all the difference. Whether or not you are happy with your bank depends on what your objectives are. Some possible criteria for choosing a bank are:

- Alternative delivery systems. How do you prefer to do your banking? Banking at a branch, ATM, home banking from your PC? Internet banking?

- Convenience. Do you care if the bank is not in your backyard? How often do you go to the bank?

- Products available. Do you need a full-service bank, which offers investment and insurance products or car, credit cards, home, and student loans?

- Early morning, late afternoon, or weekend hours.

- Relationship. Do you want a bank that knows its customers personally?

- Good deposit rates.

- The bank is in good shape financially, and doesn't appear to be a takeover target.

Key to evaluating a bank is to look past the promises it makes in good times, and consider whether it will help you when times are not so good. Will it be there for you if you lose your job, get divorced, or if you overextend your credit? Can you consider it one-stop shopping for all of your banking needs?

Being able to evaluate a bank or other lender, and to establish a good working relationship, will be helpful when you are ready to buy a new car, a new home, or finance a college education.

5: Getting the Most for Your Money: Major Purchases

Buying and Leasing an Automobile

Contributing Author:

Jill Mirak

"Remember, following SALE signs is not a financial plan!"
—CARLA C. CATALDO, GRANT WRITER

IN THIS SECTION, YOU WILL LEARN:

- What you need to know before buying a car

- How to make car buying a positive experience

- How to choose a dealership

- How to make a fair offer for an automobile

- To evaluate whether to buy or to lease

While it's true that buying a car can be a very emotional experience, buying a car should be a positive emotional experience in which you have fun! Believe it or not, you can buy a car that you love from a person with whom you enjoy doing business. You can be happy and excited throughout the purchase and ownership experience.

Unfortunately, this is not always the case for women. Buying a car seems to be one of the last real bastions of male power. And we need to get over that. We're serious. We're good shoppers. We can shop for a car just as we can shop for anything else. Think about it like this: there is really no difference between spending $20,000 or $200 or $20. You're just buying something. You want to get a good deal, you want good service, you want good value.

Although 65 percent of car-buying decisions are made by women, only 7 percent of car salespersons are women. Most men don't want to talk to women car salespeople. But women are used to talking to men. And sometimes to being ignored:

You go into an auto showroom and you're invisible. That's the way it's been. When I went to buy a new car, I brought my sixteen-year-old son. The salesman looked at and talked directly to him!

To become confident about the car-buying process, it is important to educate yourself. Before going out to buy a car, ask yourself some questions:

What does owning a car mean to you? Is it mere transportation? Status? An extension of your personality? How long do you expect to keep the car? Do you have a car that you want to trade in or sell privately?

What are you looking for in a car? Do you want a sedan, sports car, wagon, minivan, SUV?

Automatic or manual transmission? Import or domestic? Front-wheel drive, rear-wheel drive, or four-wheel drive? What options do you prefer, and which do you require? Stereo, cassette, CD player, power windows and locks, air-conditioning, global positioning system (GPS)? Which safety features are important to you: anti-lock braking system (ABS), airbags, automatic seat belts, security systems?

How will you pay for the car—cash, monthly payment, financing through dealer or through bank? If you are financing, how much down payment can you afford, and how much can you afford monthly? Consider sales tax, excise tax, insurance. For how long do you want to make payments?

Can the car be used as a business vehicle? Will it be used to transport clients? Is leasing a good option for you? How many miles each year do you drive? Your car should be a friend, but, remember, it is only a car.

RESEARCH

After you have determined what you want in a car, you will need to do some research. You can start by driving down the road and looking at all the cars. "Gee, that looks pretty to me, that one looks kind of sporty." And then you might visit some dealerships. You can go in and say, "Just looking." Don't let yourself become intimidated. This first phase could last six months. You might look at the brochures, you might get some consumer magazines and see how the cars are rated, go to the library, or ask friends or even people you see driving the car you are considering, "How do you like your car?" Then you might want to test-drive.

After a while, you'll narrow down your choices

again. And soon you'll have an idea of what you want. Then you can look in *Consumer Reports* or a price guide, or do an Internet search. You just can type in the key words "Car buying" in any browser. Or you can get an *Auto Week* magazine; it has the Internet addresses for all the major car information sites. There are now about twenty-five different car-buying sites on the Internet. Reports show that nearly half of all car buyers use the Internet at some point in their research.

Most of the car-buying sites are alike. They offer prices, options, reviews of the make and model. The information is fairly standard, since much of it comes from the car manufacturers themselves.

Enter the name, the make, the model of the car, the year (assuming it's a new car), what part of the country you live in (some cities are more expensive than others), whether it's a standard or automatic. The sites will show you every single option for every single car that's made. And they will come back with a suggested retail price and the dealer's price.

After you have identified the kind of car you want, and have a pretty good idea of options and how you will pay for the car, the next step is to go shopping.

FINDING A DEALER AND NEGOTIATING A PRICE

The next step is to find a dealer you can trust and with whom you feel comfortable. Along with insurance salespeople and lawyers, car dealers get a bum reputation. How can you find a reputable dealer? The same way you should get all referrals—from friends or colleagues who have had positive and fair experiences. Let the dealer know that you were recommended by a friend, mention her name, and likely the dealer will be even more anxious to please you.

We firmly believe that where you buy your car is as important if not more important than what you pay for your car. Buying from a reputable dealer gives you recourse if something should go wrong and affords you expert advice on servicing the vehicle in the future.

When you go to a dealership, you are creating a relationship. Tell the dealer the information you have gathered, the options you want. If the dealer's cost, or invoice, is $20,000, you can't go in and expect to get that car for $19,995, because then she couldn't stay in business. She needs to make a profit.

The "list price" or "sticker price" is the manufacturer's suggested retail price, or MSRP. The dealer's cost or invoice is what you want to know. This is how much the dealer paid to the factory to purchase the car. To find out what the dealer paid for the car, you can ask the dealer to show you the invoice, or you can get the same information from car-buying magazines (try *Edmonds*). The many car-buying sites on the Internet also will provide this information.

People—especially guys—go into dealers thinking, "I want to get the rock-bottom price." And there are things you can do, like going in at the end of the month, when the sales force has to make its quota. You'll get a better deal than if you go at the beginning of the month. In fact, the very best time to buy a car is when you are not in a hurry—you will make the best deal!

And you can go in and say, "I know how much you paid for this car. This is what I think is a fair profit. Deal or not?" You're going to do better

than if you go in all hesitant and unsure. For lower-end cars, a profit of $300 to $600 or more, depending on the make and model of the car, is reasonable. This figure applies to cars readily available in dealer stock. If you are buying a very "hot" car, one that is in high demand, this strategy will not apply. You likely will have to pay what the dealer is asking.

If you are buying a higher-end car, say, for about $30,000, you may make a slightly higher offer. Remember that dealers must make some profit, in addition to having to pay for the showroom, for their salespeople, and for their overhead.

When I went in, I had done my homework. I had driven a similar car for two years, so I knew I wanted the next model up. The first one didn't have intermittent windshield wipers. That did it for me. I didn't have them for two years. What a pain! And it didn't have a trunk light. So I thought, "I need a little bit better car." So I went to the dealer and said, "This is the car I want. The only options I want are air-conditioning and intermittent windshield wipers." He told me it only comes with power windows—that's the package. Well, I didn't want power windows, but I had to get them if I wanted the air-conditioning. Okay. I said, "This is the car I want, these are the options I want, this is how much profit I think you should make. Can you sell me the car for this amount?" And he said, "Ah, ah . . ." and he started to talk about all the other options. I stopped him and I said, "I just want to know: if I pay you $500 or $600 over your cost, which I think is a fair profit, will you sell me the car?" And again he started with a pitch. I said, "I don't want to hear all your salesman talk. There is an offer on the table here.

Do you want to deal or not?" At that point he just sort of closed his mouth, and said meekly, "Okay."

I did the same thing once with a woman salesperson. She said, "Five hundred dollars if I have it on the lot, six hundred if I have to get it somewhere else." I said, "Fair."

As a guideline, you can offer the invoice price, less the wholesale price of your trade-in, plus a small profit. Keep in mind that the same car may be priced differently by different dealers, because they may have different overhead costs.

Whether or not you are paying cash, you negotiate the price first. If you finance, the dealer may be making more money. You can try to negotiate the interest rate, or you can shop rates at your local bank. It's often easier and quicker to finance through the dealer and may be worth the extra bit of interest.

If you're buying a car off a lot—and they have billions and billions—it's costing them money every single day that car sits on the lot and goes unsold. You often can save by buying off the lot rather than having them find your car at another dealer.

And make sure you are not paying for options you don't want:

You can get prices off the Internet, so when you walk into the dealer, you're knowledgeable. I went in and told the dealer, "Look, I don't want that pinstripe." He said, "It's already on the car." I told him, "I don't want to pay for a feature I don't need." And he wanted to move the car, so the pinstripe was free.

When you are discussing price, be sure to ask about the cost of "dealer prep." "Dealer prep" is what the dealer does to ready the car for delivery: washing, removing stickers, checking for scratches, and the paperwork involved. It is usually not negotiable; however, you can ask the dealer what was or will be done to "prep" your vehicle.

PROTECT YOURSELF AND YOUR CREDIT

Sometimes, when you go into a showroom and are just looking, they may say, "Oh, we need your driver's license." Don't give it to them. They can be running a credit check while you're still on the showroom floor. It's one thing if you take a car off the lot, and out for a drive. Then you have to give your license to them. But if you're just looking, don't do it. You may hear, "Oh I need your driver's license so I can run this price by the sales manager." He's in there checking your credit rating and seeing if they even want to deal with you. You simply can refuse, or you can say, "Gee, since I wasn't planning to test-drive today, I don't have it with me."

Remember that several credit checks in a short period can have a negative impact on your credit rating, even if you are not buying anything.

Similarly, when you go to renew your driver's license, don't put your Social Security number on the license or on anything else. Don't put it on checks when you make a purchase. Why? Because with Social Security access, others can find out all sorts of information about you.

REBATES AND TRADE-INS

Rebates are offered on many models and makes, to sell them quickly and reduce dealer inventory. They are usually higher in value and more frequent at the end of a model year (often August to November). Rebates are like a coupon that you can apply to the purchase price, thereby lowering it, or, in some cases, you can take the rebate in the form of cash. Rebates are offered by the manufacturer to the customer.

If you have a car that you would like to trade in at the dealer's, make sure that you take it with you at the time of negotiation. The dealer needs to see it and drive it to determine its value. Understand that if you trade in your car at a dealer's, the dealer will give you the wholesale value for your car, which you then can apply toward the purchase price of a new car. The wholesale price is, on average, 20 to 40 percent less than the retail price, or the price you could get for your car if you sold it privately. The dealer needs to do work to your car, warranty it, add a profit, and then sell it. The dealer can sell the car for the same price that you can sell your car, so the dealer cannot buy the car from you for that price. It has to be less.

> *We've gone to places and they wouldn't even tell us exactly what they were giving us for a trade-in. I kept saying, "What are you giving us for a trade-in?" And when they tried to talk about monthly payments and stuff, I said, "If you can't tell me exactly what you are giving us for a trade-in, then I'll just go somewhere else."*

The advantage to trading in to a dealer is that you avoid the aggravation and potential liability involved in selling your car. Potential buyers will be calling you and coming to your home to see your car. In some states, you may be liable if you sell a car that turns out to have defects, even months after the sale.

If you decide to trade in, you can ask the dealer to itemize the price that he is giving you

for your car. Again, remember that the wholesale price is going to be a lot less than the price for which you may see your car advertised in the newspaper classifieds. But also keep in mind that if the dealer is giving you a significant discount off the MSRP of the new car, then he only can give you the wholesale price for your trade-in. If you paid the full MSRP for the new car, then the dealer could give you a retail price for your used car. You can have one or the other, not both.

ADD-ONS AND AFTERSELL ITEMS

What else will you need or want to make the car purchase complete? You may want to think about extra features, and extended warranties.

There's always a big debate about whether you should pay extra for undercoating. Although it's unnecessary, most cars already have it.

I firmly believe in extended warranties and security systems. They both are forms of insurance for your personal safety and your pocketbook. If you intend to keep the vehicle for longer than the manufacturer's warranty, look into extended warranties. A security system will always save you money on your insurance (between 20 and 35 percent off the comprehensive portion in Massachusetts) and will give you some peace of mind. You can negotiate alarm prices and warranty prices.

If you decide to purchase a warranty, it's a good idea to get a manufacturer's warranty as opposed to an aftermarket warranty (also known as a reseller's warranty). They are much more comprehensive and well worth the small additional cost.

As you negotiate the purchase of your new car, keep in mind the seven ways a dealer makes money: sale of a new car, sale of a trade-in, financing, accessories, insurance, warranties, and security devices.

LEASING

A lease is a long-term rental agreement between you and a bank or other financial institution. According to AAA, about 30 percent of all new cars will be leased, not purchased.

With the average price of a new car now greater than $20,000, many consumers would have to take a loan for five or six years in order to be able to afford the monthly payments. At the end of that period, the car might be long overdue for replacement! A lease enables you to make a reasonable monthly payment, and to turn in your vehicle every three or so years for a newer model.

Because there are so many additional fees connected to leasing an automobile, it is important for you to find out exactly what is—and what is not—covered by your lease agreement.

The advantages of leasing are:

- The monthly payment is lower than if you buy.

- There may be little or no down payment.

- You get to drive a new car every two to three years.

- You can drive a more expensive car, if that is important to you.

- You can avoid the issue of trade-in when the lease expires.

- As of this writing, you can take a tax write-off for business use of a leased vehicle.

The disadvantages of leasing are:

- You do not own the car; you have no equity, and have nothing to trade in.

- You may have to pay for the extra mileage.

- You still are responsible for repairs and you must follow the recommended manufacturer's maintenance schedule.

- Ending the lease early can be very costly.

Look at the lease before you sign! When you are given a price for the monthly payment, ask whether it includes (if applicable in your state) sales tax and/or excise tax. Also be sure you know how many miles you are allowed to drive each year—ten thousand, twelve thousand, fifteen thousand—and what is the cost per mile if you drive more than the allotment. Be clear on the term of the lease—two years, three years—and whether or not there is a disposition fee. If you don't lease another car from the same dealer, you may have to pay a "drop-off" charge.

DONATING YOUR AUTOMOBILE

Something you may wish to consider when you are buying or leasing a new car is to donate your old car to charity. You will benefit the organization of your choice, and perhaps get a tax deduction as well. For more information on how to donate your car, you can contact local charities directly or ask your local community foundation (see page 206) for ideas.

Financing an Education

Contributing Author:

Paula Mogan

IN THIS SECTION, YOU WILL LEARN:

- Elements of the financial aid package

- Paying and saving for higher education

- Matching the college or program to the student

- Traditional and unexpected sources of loans, scholarships, and grants

- How to avoid common financial planning mistakes

For many middle-class families, higher education for their children is a given. For some working-class families, and families new to the country, a college education is an all-but-impossible dream. Whether or not parents should work hard to be able to finance an education for their children is a very personal choice:

Personally, if I had $300,000 tucked away, I'd rather buy each of my kids a starter home, and let them put themselves through college!

We would do anything—anything—to give our daughters the best possible education. After all, it's

at college you make lifetime friendships and connections that will serve you for the rest of your life! With a degree from the right college, doors open to you.

Is a college education really worth the high price? Many think so, citing reasons ranging from the general benefits of a more literate society to the networking opportunities college can provide, to the personal benefit one derives from being exposed both to new ideas and to fellow students from a wide variety of backgrounds.

In terms of dollars and cents, however, there is no question that a college education can pay off in higher future earnings. College graduates earn on average substantially more than those with only a high school diploma: 44 percent more for young men; 51 percent for women.

The U.S. Bureau of the Census reports that median earnings for full-time, year-round workers age twenty-five or older are as follows:

Education	Female	Male
Less than ninth grade	$14,132	$18,553
High school diploma	$21,963	$30,868
Bachelor's degree	$35,408	$49,982
Master's degree	$42,002	$60,168
Professional degree	$55,460	$90,653

Fortunately, the old adage "Where there's a will, there's a way" applies to college education, with the availability of financial aid. According to the College Board, financial aid awarded last year totaled more than $64 billion.

The financial aid system is shrouded in mystery, intimidates everybody, and can be an overwhelming process for most families. There are so many myths and fallacies about financial aid, and so much misunderstanding, that many families don't bother to apply. They may think they do not qualify. Regardless of your income level or your assets, if you feel you need financial aid—in other words, if you cannot just take out your checkbook and painlessly write a check for $20,000 or $30,000 each year for four years—then you ought to apply.

ELEMENTS OF THE FINANCIAL AID PACKAGE

Since the financial aid situation seems to change every couple of years, it is best to check with the financial aid office at the college and with your bank, to be sure that you have access to all sources of aid. There are several types of aid, each with its own set of qualifying factors, and dollar limits.

Financial aid has four components. *Grants* demonstrate need and *scholarships* can be tied to athletic or academic performance and do not have to be repaid. *Loans* count as financial aid when they have favorable repayment terms and low interest rates. *Work-study* is money the student works for in a school-sponsored job. Work-study is not counted as income in determining eligibility for other financial aid.

At this writing, forms of financial aid include: federal Pell grants, state grants, federal Stafford loans, campus-based aid, Supplemental Educational Opportunity Grants, the Federal Work-Study program, federal Perkins loans, collegiate scholarships, unsubsidized federal loans, unsubsidized Stafford loans, supplemental loans to students, and PLUS loans. Also, some states have special savings programs for college.

The two most popular student loans are the subsidized and unsubsidized Stafford loans. A subsidized Stafford loan is awarded on the basis of financial need. The federal government pays interest on ("subsidizes") the loan until you begin repayment and during authorized periods of deferment. An unsubsidized Stafford loan is not awarded on the basis of need. You'll be charged interest from the time the loan is disbursed until you have completely repaid it. If you allow the interest to accumulate, it will be "capitalized"—that is, the interest will be added to the principal amount of the loan and will increase the amount you have to repay. If you choose to pay the interest as it accumulates, you'll repay less in the long run. The interest rate on Stafford loans is set by the federal government on July 1 of each year, and as of this writing is currently 6.32 percent. The maximum amount that an undergraduate can borrow for both the subsidized and unsubsidized Stafford loans is $2,625 in the student's freshman year, $3,500 for the sophomore year, and $5,500 for junior and senior year in college.

To keep an academic scholarship, the student must maintain a certain grade average. For most middle-income families, student loans will be the largest component of the financial aid package.

And everyone has a different philosophy about student loans.

My kids will take all the loans they can get, all the way through school. I want them to take responsibility by working for their education.

I'm thirty-three and I just finished paying off my student loans. It was incredibly painful. I wouldn't want my son or daughter to have loans.

My husband and I worked our way through college. We expect our children to do the same. They will appreciate their education so much more. We will help each of them through the first year, then they are on their own.

If you need to borrow at all, take advantage of any available student loans. Generally, the rates are lower than a bank loan. However, there may be instances when a home equity loan makes sense. The interest that you pay on the home equity loan is usually tax deductible, so you may want to discuss this option with your tax planning adviser. The rates are much better than what parents can borrow from a bank.

Parents always have the option of paying off the loan for the student. When the student graduates from college, the family can assess what kind of career she will have, what her employment opportunities will be. Will she be doing social work and earning $22,000 a year, or going into corporate law, starting out at $60,000? The family can decide together who is going to pay what.

Say my son goofs around for four years and does not study. He's on his own. But if he works really hard, when he graduates, we probably will assume part of the repayment. 'Til then, he is going to think that he has the loan.

If a student is lucky enough to get work-study, she should take it. The money earned through the work-study program is not reportable as income for purposes of her financial aid next year. She may have to claim it for taxes, but it is not going to work against her. Another benefit of campus employment is that the student often has the opportunity to study while working, particularly if he or she is fortunate enough to obtain a job in the library or an athletic facility.

I was eligible for work-study, but turned it down because I liked my job at Blockbuster so much. When I applied for next year's financial aid, I realized I'd made a big mistake. I was losing aid money by working there.

My son got a $5-an-hour work-study job in the library at his college. He said, "But, Ma, I can make $10 delivering pizza for Papa Gino's." You need to weigh the choices and to show your child the benefits from a financial aid point of view of taking work-study as opposed to working off campus.

It is very important to involve students in those kinds of decision making. They need to know that college costs money. They need to know that you trust them to take responsibility for themselves, no matter who is paying the bills.

Most college students are dependent on their parents, while some, because of family situation, might qualify as independent. There may have been a death. They may have an ill parent. They might have been working full time and actually supporting the parent. Those kids get special consideration.

Madeleine left an abusive home at the age of sixteen and lived on the streets, doing drugs and panhandling. At age eighteen, she went into detox and decided to clean up her life. With the help of a caring adult who wrote letters of recommendation about the challenges she had overcome in her personal life, she got accepted to a state community college. She earned straight A's for two years. She is now at a large private university on a full scholarship.

Establishing student independence is tricky. If you have a child who says, "I am just going to go off and do it all on my own and I do not need you guys," it will be very hard to reestablish dependent status should he fail. A student who really is independent should get all the benefits, including increased financial aid. But for people who are just trying to find a way around the system, it is not a good idea.

Financial aid is available for older students who are entering college for the first time, or who are returning to college after a long absence. Many older women may not have had the opportunity for education.

I could see the divorce coming down the road. I married at twenty, had only two years of college under my belt. I had four kids. I wasn't trained for any kind of work outside the house. I figured I'd better go back to college now and finish my degree. I went nights and in the early morning when my youngest was in kindergarten. By the last year, the situation at home was intolerable. I filed for divorce. Suddenly, I had 50 percent less income. The college financial aid office was great, and helped me to get enough loans to graduate.

The same financial aid regulations apply to older women, and the processors cannot discriminate because of the applicant's age. Many colleges and universities now have special programs designed for women returning to college at a later age. (See the "Resources and Readings" section for more information.) Many programs offer evening courses, and distance learning is increasing, making a college education within just about everyone's reach.

HOW FINANCIAL AID IS DETERMINED

The financial aid process is governed by something called the *Congressional Methodology,* a government document of rules and regulations an inch thick. The *Congressional Methodology* determines what a family can afford to contribute to college expenses. The process has gone through many permutations, and lately has become increasingly complex.

There used to be one document called the Financial Aid Form, the FAF. After that, people had to fill out three different forms with a variety of deadlines, in order to apply for financial aid. The latest version of the federal form is called the FAFSA (Free Application for Federal Student Aid), which every applicant for financial aid fills out, no matter whether they plan to attend a state college or university or a private one. There is another form called the Profile, which is even more intrusive than the FAFSA. Some private colleges require the Profile, whereas state colleges and universities require only the FAFSA.

The forms can be so intimidating that a lot of people say, "I am not even going to bother filling it out." And they hear horror stories that one college or another doesn't give any money, so they may limit their choices based solely on rumor.

The Higher Education Bill that was reauthorized in 1992 broadened the eligibility for aid for all families. Unfortunately, the bill did not add any more federal funds to the higher education pot, but it did ease the restrictions so that more middle-class families can afford college.

The way the system works is that a student has to fill out the FAFSA form to be eligible for either the subsidized or unsubsidized Stafford loan, as well as for any grants. All students who apply are eligible for a Stafford loan.

Certainly, if a family has any extenuating circumstances—a death, a loss of income—those will be taken into consideration.

The chief breadwinner in the Engle family was disabled, and the family had very little income for three years. Now that she has returned to work, the family has a good income, but still has a mountain of back debt. They need to be able to explain the situation to the financial aid director.

Apply if you think you have need just so you can gain access to loan programs, because the government has special loan programs that carry lower interest rates than what anyone can get at the bank.

Also, be sure to send in the FAFSA form as soon as you can. You cannot apply before January 1, but you can at least get your records in order. You can do an estimated tax return and have that form in the mail as early in January as possible.

Since the restructuring of the system, it is more important than ever to apply early and apply accurately. We think the government does a real disservice to people by having the deadline for filing in May. Since they distribute funds on a rolling basis as the applications come in, you can still apply for aid in late April or May, but you'll have greatly reduced your chances of getting some money.

Filing an estimated tax return is well worth the effort. Then fill out all the financial aid forms, including copies of your estimated tax return, and send the forms to a processing center. They will send the forms back, but in a computer printout. When the forms come back, you will have the opportunity to make corrections and adjustments. But, in the meantime, the college financial aid office has all your financial data.

The process works like this: once you fill out the financial aid forms, the *Congressional Methodology,* or the needs analysis system, measures you as a family, and determines how much your family can afford to pay. There are many, many different variables, and some definitions with which you will want to be familiar.

The estimated family contribution, or EFC, is the amount the family is expected to contribute out-of-pocket toward the tuition bill each year. Dependent students are dependent on parents for support. Both the parents' and the students' income and assets are evaluated when determining EFC. Independent students are not dependent on parents for support. In general, single undergraduates must be twenty-four years of age to qualify as independent.

Here is an overview of the formulas used to calculate the family contribution. Contribution from parents' income = (parents' income − income protection allowance − taxes − employment expense allowance) × 22% to 47%. Contribution from parents' assets = (parents' assets − asset protection allowance) x 5.6%. Contribution from student's income = (student's income − taxes − $1,750) × 50%. Contribution from student's assets = (student's assets) × 35%.

PARENTS' CONTRIBUTION

The financial aid processor measures the parents' assets and the parents' income to come up with the parents' contribution. Whatever is on the parents' federal income tax return will be looked at by the schools. And there are serious consequences, like imprisonment and a $10,000 fine, should one be dishonest.

Unfortunately, I've come across a couple of gentlemen with significant incomes who asked, "How do they know that what you are putting on the forms is right?" And I said, "You have to provide them with your 1040." And one said, "What's to keep me from giving them a phony 1040?" I felt terrible thinking that I had just helped a crook. I wanted to take back everything I had told him! Here's a person who earns all kinds of money but was trying to beat the system. What I didn't tell him is that 30 percent of the financial aid forms are audited, just like when you pay your taxes.

In determining the contribution from parents' income, the processor gives certain allowances for the size of the family, for the taxes it must pay, and for how many wage earners there are. Those allowances are subtracted out, and the result is then multiplied by between 22 percent and 47 percent, based on a sliding scale.

A family of four with an income of about $45,000 would be expected to contribute about $2,100 from the parents' income.

Next, they look at parents' assets: stocks, bonds, mutual funds, savings, money markets. The equity in the parents' home is not considered in the federal formula, but will be considered by the individual private college or university.

When the Higher Education Bill was reauthorized, home equity was excluded from the formula at the federal level. If the student is applying to a state college or university, you will fill out only the federal form, the FAFSA. You do not have to list the equity in your home as an asset. At the institutional level, on the profile required by many private colleges, they are going to want to know everything about your house: when you bought it, what you paid for it, how much equity is in it.

In determining parents' contribution from assets, including home equity, the family is given an asset protection allowance. This figure is based on the age of the older parent.

For example, the Martinez family has $100,000 in assets, including equity in the house, some stocks, and cash. Mr. Martinez is forty-five years old and his wife is forty. The family would get an asset protection allowance based on Mr. Martinez's age, since he is the older parent. And at age forty-five, this figure might be $42,300. So $42,300 would be shielded out of their $100,000. The asset contribution would be based on only $57,700, not $100,000.

Next, the family's assets are multiplied by about 6 percent. So if a family had $50,000 in assets, the expected family asset contribution would be $3,000.

For those whose children will be entering college as they near retirement age, the asset protection will be very useful. If one parent is not working, they will get a huge asset protection allowance. About the only thing that the federal financial aid system protects is money set aside for retirement, such as that invested in IRAs and 401(k) plans, which is another good reason to sock away money in those areas.

But on the private college and university profile, money set aside for retirement each year is added back in.

Jane Davis, a single mother, earns $40,000, but her adjusted gross income is $36,000 because she put $4,000 away for retirement. She now has $20,000 total in her retirement account. The profile will not look at the $20,000 total, but will add back in the $4,000 she set aside from her pay that year.

Some colleges strongly encourage parents to borrow from their retirement funds. Considering the fluctuations of the economy, corporate downsizing, and unforeseen events, borrowing heavily from a 401(k) to finance a child's education could be a major mistake, as you may not be able to replace the money by your planned retirement age.

The Ivies and the pricier schools are very aggressive about wanting to tap into your retirement plans. We suggest you take a hard stand on that. The money you have set aside for retirement is yours, and to use it for your child's education, quite frankly, is risky. You may choose to borrow small amounts from a 401(k). We're not saying that you shouldn't even consider it. But be very careful. Do not let the financial aid office pressure you if it is not what you want.

Two special, but certainly not uncommon, situations are worth noting. If the parents are divorced or separated, the processor uses the income and assets of the parent with whom the student lived for the greater part of the twelve months preceding the date of the financial aid application.

If two family members are in college at the same time, each student has a separate family contribution figure, consisting of half the parents' contribution from income and assets plus the student's own contribution from income and assets.

STUDENT CONTRIBUTION

In the opening paragraphs of the *Congressional Methodology*, it says that all moneys saved and invested in the child's name are earmarked for education. The system can be incredibly unfair to children.

The processor looks at student assets plus student income. They expect 35 percent of the student's own assets to be used toward education. For those who know that they are never going to qualify for financial aid, this may not matter.

For example, Chris Franklin and Pat Regan have saved their pennies for seventeen years, and have $10,000 in their daughter's name. Their daughter is entering college, and will be required to contribute $3,500, or 35 percent of her assets. If they had saved that same $10,000 in the parents' names, the expected contribution would be only 6 percent, or $600. So you can see the inequity.

Some people ask, "Should we take out any money that we have in children's accounts? Is there a record of it? How far back might someone check? Six months? One year? Two years? Should we be taking her money out of the savings account immediately?"

It depends on each family's situation, but, generally, the sooner you transfer any money, the better. For example, if your child applies for early decision in November of her senior year, you will be required to provide the prior year's tax return. You also will provide the current year's return, once it is filed. Optimally, assets should be moved to the parent's name prior to the child's high school years.

Any financial decision has to make sense. Very careful consideration is required before you make any shift in assets.

For example, even though parents' assets are assessed at 6 percent and students' at 35 percent, you really have to look at the whole picture before you make a determination to shift everything out of Janie's name and put it in yours. What if you bump yourself up into another tax bracket?

Some parents set up a trust for the benefit of the child. Some use the Uniform Gifts to Minors Act (UGMA). It's important to know that this kind of account cannot be changed later on. (See chapter 8 for more information on the UGMA.) Educational planners often see folks who have money in the student's name and then want to shift it around. People have done it, but it's tough. Just don't assume that the IRS isn't watching.

Grandparents' assets and income are not counted toward the family contribution. So if your family is lucky enough to have grandparents who can help with college expenses, they can fund some or all of the education. The assets that they give the student or the parents should not have a negative impact on eligibility for the next year because they will not show on the financial aid form. Be sure that any gifts are given to you after you receive your financial aid award letter.

As for student income, the first $1,750 earned each year by the student is protected. The balance is multiplied by 50 percent.

Elizabeth, for example, worked hard at two jobs during the summer between her freshman and sophomore years, and worked in the mail room during the school year. She earned $6,500 last year. She will be expected to contribute $2,375 toward her tuition bill this year.

The total of the parents' income contribution and the parents' asset contribution plus the student's income contribution and the student's asset contribution equals expected family contribution, or EFC. The EFC is the starting point for the financial aid director. Special financial circumstances that don't show up on paper need to be explained individually to the financial aid office.

NEGOTIATING FINANCIAL AID

The Changs' daughter is a junior at a small private college. They are paying full tuition for her. Their second child just got accepted to Stanford, but didn't get very much financial aid because the family has a good income. Even so, they can't afford $50,000 a year for college. So they will go back to Stanford to discuss their case.

Financial aid is almost always negotiable. If a college really wants a particular student, she has a good chance of getting more aid. Outstanding scholars, athletes, musicians, or those with other special talents have a bargaining chip. Find the school that wants the special talent your student possesses, and you will find a financial aid director most willing to meet and talk with you.

Some of the pricier, well-endowed schools are better prepared to offer a good financial aid package. One common misconception of many families is that their child cannot afford to apply to the expensive private colleges. In fact, the lower the income of the family, the better chance it has of getting the most financial aid, assuming the school wants the student.

Mary, a nationally recognized cellist, just got accepted to Harvard University. Between her parents' contribution and her summer earnings, the EFC is $8,000. Right now Harvard costs more than $33,000 a year. The truth is, Harvard is so well endowed that it could pay for every single kid to go there forever for free. If Mary can demonstrate need, there is a pretty good chance she will get a $25,000 financial aid package.

State colleges and universities provide an excellent education, but just do not have the same resources. A family has to be incredibly needy in order to get awarded significant financial aid from a state college or university.

MATCHING THE COLLEGE, THE STUDENT, AND THE FAMILY'S RESOURCES

Choosing a college that is a good fit for the student is a time-consuming process, even before considering financial aid. A student who is willing to go out of state has a much better chance of getting accepted to a school, because she is rounding out the demographics. She also has a much better chance of getting some financial aid. Also, certain regions of the country are far more expensive than others.

For instance, Greta, a high school junior, lives in Connecticut. She doesn't want to be very far from home, and is looking at colleges in Maryland, Delaware, Virginia, and North Carolina. Many fine schools in the mid-Atlantic states and the South cost between $12,000 and $15,000 a year. A comparable school in New England might cost closer to $30,000.

CASH FLOW HELP

We believe that if you truly want a college education for your child or for yourself, and are willing to work hard and to be flexible and creative, you can have it. Some colleges offer free or reduced tuition to employees and their families. If you've got kids on their way to college, and you've been thinking about a job change, maybe now is the time to consider that change!

At Harvard University, for example, if you work as a part-time employee—and since many jobs are based on a thirty-five-hour week, part-time could mean as few as seventeen and a half hours—after a few months, you are entitled to take one course for 10 percent of the tuition cost. After several more months, you can take two courses per semester for 10 percent tuition. The catch is, you have to come in as an employee first, not as a student. But if you are determined and patient, you can do it. Many of the larger universities have similar programs.

While the following tips to help with the family's cash flow may not work for all students, some of them may be right for you:

- Ask questions about financial aid offerings.

- Position the student for a good aid package.

- Try for an academic scholarship.

- Look for athletic scholarships.

- Stay in state.

- Consider cooperative education.

- Check the military offerings.

- Accelerate, that is, take as many courses per semester as allowed.

- Mix work and study.

- Understand needs analysis.

- Borrow against the house.

- Increase deposits to retirement accounts, thus decreasing expected parent contribution.

- Take advantage of in-demand professions.

- Negotiate the aid package.

- Investigate commercial payment plans.

- Invest in EE savings bonds.

- Sacrifice.

COMMON FINANCIAL PLANNING MISTAKES

At the thought of planning for education expenses, many families tend to panic. Some make expensive mistakes. Some of the more common financial planning mistakes are:

Spending your life savings, money you really need to preserve for your own retirement

Look at it the other way around. You would not steal from your children's education fund to pay for your retirement. Both are important, but they are not meant to serve the same purpose.

Borrowing money at unnecessarily high interest rates

If you can tap into the student loan programs, do so rather than borrowing from a bank. Usu-

ally, the loan programs will be more favorable. Also, the college that your child attends will give you a lot of information about ways to borrow.

Timing investments incorrectly, paying penalties, and losing out on earning potential

Avoid paying penalties by having to cash in term certificates early. When children are really young, go for a long stock portfolio. But as your child is getting closer to attending college, then you need to start shifting your assets so that you have more liquidity.

Spending energy looking for special scholarships in the false hope the scholarship will ease the tuition burden

A whole industry has sprung up around scholarship searches. Some cost only $45, but others cost $500 or even $1,600. For instance, if you are blue-eyed, left-handed, of Polish descent, and you play the tuba and you think there may be a special scholarship for you, subscribe to the database, but do not spend $500. All these companies subscribe to the same database. They will give lists of scholarships to you based on your special talent, ethnic background, or other criteria. But you still have to do all the work to apply for the scholarship.

Asking children to consider colleges that are not right for them because you think you'll save some money

You may have your heart set on having your child attend your alma mater, a large in-state university. But she may want something very different. The small, private out-of-state college she has her heart set on may cost a lot more than you had planned. But if she is going to be miserable, you may want to reconsider.

Neglecting to file for financial aid because you assume you don't qualify

If you and your partner both work, you may think you are not eligible for aid. But the cost of college has increased at such a clip, that even a family with an adjusted gross income of $100,000 might be eligible for some help.

THREE CERTAINTIES REGARDING COLLEGE COSTS

There are three certainties regarding college costs. First, college costs will continue to increase at a rate nearly double that of inflation. They have risen 6 to 8 percent during the past twenty-five years. Second, grant and scholarship aid is not going to keep pace, and, third, many families will tend to panic and make needless financial planning mistakes.

Learn more about the process, educate yourself as much as you can, and know that an affordable college education is possible for you and for your children.

Home Buying and Refinancing

Contributing Authors:

Maureen Reilly, Gail R. Shapiro,
and Maxine Wolin

BEFORE YOU BUY: THINKING ABOUT BUYING A HOUSE

Sixty-seven million American families now own a home. Owning your own home can be an emotionally satisfying, very positive experience. Many women find a great deal of pleasure in being part of what traditionally has been "the American dream," whether they are buying a house on their own or with a partner. In addition to the tax incentives for home ownership offered by the federal government, paying off a mortgage each month, with the goal of eventually owning your home free and clear, is a way of investing in yourself.

To finally have a house of one's own, perhaps after years of living with parents or renting, can offer great satisfaction:

It's all mine: house, decor, garden—the whole works.

It's something tangible to leave to my kids.

Buying a home is expensive and also can be emotionally challenging:

To a woman who is considering buying a house, I would tell her how important it is to become comfortable with writing checks for LARGE sums of money!

Buying a home is an investment risk, ties up much of your cash, not to mention your weekends, and is definitely not *for the faint-of-heart!*

It's a myth that homes always go up in value. In the Northeast in '88 and '89, home values went down as much as 50 percent.

When you rent an apartment and the refrigerator breaks, you call the landlord. When it's your own house, you have to repair the refrigerator—or buy a new one.

We've owned our home for twenty years. In that time, we've installed a hot water heater, two new tanks, and a complete septic system. We've painted the house—three times inside and twice outside. We've needed new shingles, a new roof, and to have the driveway paved. In hurricane season, trees fell on and damaged the deck, a tree fell on the shed and smashed it, and the next year, a tree fell on the new shed, too. We've had four plumbing emergencies: five including the Barbie doll hat my kid flushed down our only toilet—on Christmas Eve! We've installed two new kitchen floors, one complete new heating system, bought a new clothes dryer and refrigerator. Twice we had an ant invasion in the bathroom; once they ate through the floor! We've had to retile the kitchen counter, repair countless holes in the walls from kids slamming doors and throwing footballs, and replace a couple of windows. New screens, new carpet, storm windows—there's never money or time to spare when you own your own home!

As you consider buying a home, you may want to consider the following: How does home ownership fit into your personal financial goals? (See chapter 2.) What is your current income? What is your debt? How will you save for the down payment and closing costs? (See chapter 3.) How much will it cost each year to own and maintain a home? Is your credit excellent? If not, how long will it take to clear it? (See chapter 4.)

Where do you want to live? What size house will you need in five years? Ten years? Also consider "quality of life" issues: neighbors, distance from work, a good school system, whether there is a yard.

Sometimes circumstances can prompt a home purchase:

After we'd been living in the same two-family for ten years, our landlady suddenly wanted our apartment for her aged mother. We couldn't afford anything nearly as big, and ended up buying a little condo on a side street. But it's all ours.

We thought we'd wait to start a family. But there I was, pregnant, only a year after we married. We'd dreamed of raising a family on a quiet street with a yard—so decided to "go for it" right away. That was nearly thirty years ago. The kids are grown and gone now, but we're still here, and we've never had any regrets.

MORTGAGES AND OTHER HOUSING COSTS

In the past ten to twelve years, lenders have greatly reduced the cash needed for down payments, making home ownership more feasible than ever before. If you are like most Americans, you will need to take a mortgage to buy a house.

A mortgage is a long-term loan, made to you by a bank or other lender, for the difference between the purchase price of your home and the down payment you are able to make. A mortgage generally is paid back in monthly installments of principal and interest. In the first several years of a mortgage, most of the monthly payment goes toward interest. The amount of the payment applied to the principal—and thus your "equity" in the house—increases over time.

In addition to paying principal and interest on the mortgage loan, the homeowner also must pay real estate taxes and homeowner's insurance. These four expenses connected to home ownership often are expressed as "PITI" (principal, interest, taxes, and insurance). Every mortgage holder must pay PITI expenses, and some towns also charge the homeowner for water and sewer or septic. Then there are home repairs and maintenance: roof, furnace, hot water heater, electric system, plumbing; interior and exterior painting, landscaping, and mechanical systems; and appliance purchase, repair, and maintenance: stove, refrigerator, microwave, washer, dryer, lawn mower, snowblower, tools.

When I first moved to the suburbs from the city twenty years ago, I was shocked at how isolated everyone was. No one shared. Each house had its own washer and dryer, a lawn mower that was used maybe an hour a week, weed whackers, edgers, power tools. . . .

The day we moved in, we were flat broke. We realized that we needed so much right away: curtains, shades, cleaning supplies. The basic things you need really add up fast.

Is owning always better than renting? It may be more feasible to rent if you don't know where you want to live, if you prefer not to tie up all your cash, if you prefer not to tie up all your weekends, or if you know you are due for a job transfer in the near future.

PLANNING AND SAVING FOR YOUR FIRST HOME

Long before you are ready to buy your first home, there are several steps you can take to make the process easier.

It may be a very good idea to visit a mortgage broker to find out what to do and what not to do.

A lot of times people come to me having paid off all of their debts. But now they have no money in savings. And they come in and they sit down and they are very proud of themselves. "I don't have any debt; I'm just going to have my mortgage." Then I say, "Well, how much money do you have to put down?" "I don't have any. I just paid off my debt." That's like putting the cart before the horse. You should come to a mortgage person prior to making a decision on a house to get this information. Do you need to pay off something to qualify? If you don't, don't do it. Keep the money for your down payment. But there's a misperception that you've got to come in without any debt. That's just not correct.

You can and should start saving for a down payment. Begin by creating a separate house fund, and adding to it on a regular basis.

Find out about special state and federal programs for which you might be eligible. Through Community Development Block Grants to states and larger cities, the federal government offers several programs for first-time and low-to-moderate-income home buyers. Programs include homeowner education classes, low-interest mortgage rates, and low-down-payment loans.

Sometimes, these programs can be difficult to find. Every state has different rules, and may call the program by a different name—even areas within the same state may have different programs. Often your local bank won't tell you about all the programs available to you—after all, they may be competition. You can try calling the local office of HUD, the federal Department of Housing and Urban Development, which administers these programs.

In New England states, you would ask for the Office of Community Planning. Tell them you are interested in learning about programs for first-time and low-income home buyers and ask what's available. In other states, you may try the local housing rehab program, often listed under "Housing and Community Development."

One such program is the shared appreciated mortgage. Your local Federal Housing Administration (FHA) lender may offer you a below-market rate in exchange for a share of the profit when you sell. You get all the tax benefits, and the lender doesn't make a profit unless you do.

The Federal Housing Administration (FHA), a wholly owned government corporation, was established under the National Housing Act of 1934 to improve housing standards and conditions; to provide an adequate home-financing system through insurance of mortgages; and to stabilize the mortgage market. The FHA was consolidated into the newly established Department of Housing and Urban Development (HUD) in 1965.

The FHA continues to exist to serve public purposes that would otherwise go unserved. Its mission today is to:

- contribute to the building and preservation of healthy neighborhoods and communities;
- maintain and expand home ownership, rental housing, and health care opportunities;
- stabilize credit markets in times of economic disruption;
- operate with a high degree of public and fiscal accountability, and
- recognize and value its customers, staff, constituents and partners.

Thanks to the mortgage insurance products the FHA helped to pioneer, such as the long-term amortizing loan, the nation's home ownership rate has soared to an all-time high.

With the National Homeownership Strategy in place since 1995, the FHA has placed a great deal of emphasis on marketing and outreach to minorities and first-time home buyers. Loan originations for minority home buyers are increasing, with the result that this group constituted 29 percent of all new homeowners in the past few years.

The FHA expanded its Home Equity Conversion Mortgage (HECM) Program, which allows elderly homeowners in need of income to draw on the equity of their home while remaining in place. This is sometimes called a "reverse mortgage."

If you or your spouse is a veteran, you may be eligible for a Veteran's Administration loan, which offers mortgages through its VA Loan Guaranty Service, with 0 percent down. You pay only closing costs. For more information, visit the Web site at www.homeloans.va.gov.

Other ways women can enter the housing market:

- Borrow for a down payment from family members. Nearly one-quarter of all first-time buyers get help from their families.
- Buy with a partner: you can team up and buy a three- or four-family house; each will occupy one of the units, and you rent the other(s).
- Buy and renovate a property in distress or bid on a foreclosure.
- Make a one-time withdrawal of up to $10,000 from your IRA, at any age, to help with the down payment for a first home. The money will be fully taxed, but there is no early-withdrawal penalty.
- Find a family member to cosign the mortgage with you. The coborrower's name does not need to appear on the deed; he or she need only sign the mortgage note. If the down payment is less than 10 percent, however, then the coborrower must intend to occupy the home.

In addition to the federal programs for low-income home buyers, there are several independent-sector programs. One of the best known is Habitat for Humanity. Habitat builds homes for low-income families, using volunteer labor, including that of the new homeowners. Habitat offers a no-interest mortgage, with an average down payment of about $500, and an investment of three hundred to five hundred hours of "sweat equity." Habitat sells each house at no profit, and aims to help more families settle in their own homes. Contact: www.habitat.org.

To find out more about alternative housing programs in your community, you can contact your local community foundation (see chapter 10).

OBSTACLES TO HOME OWNERSHIP

Difficult obstacles can stand in the way of home ownership. Women, racially mixed couples, unmarried couples, couples with young children, lesbians, seniors, disabled individuals, and those who have been on welfare may find themselves subject to discrimination when shopping for a new home. Discrimination is illegal but too often is prevalent. If you feel you have been denied opportunity illegally, you may bring your complaint to a Multiple Listing Service (MLS) broker, your state Justice Department, or your state's attorney general. Everyone who wants to own a home deserves an equal chance to do so.

As we said, home ownership long has been a pivotal part of the "American dream," yet 11 million American families either are homeless, live in substandard housing, or can pay for housing only by giving up medical care, adequate food, or clothing. Two-thirds of these families live on incomes below 30 percent of the area median. Two-thirds either are elderly or are families with children. In most communities today, workers earning minimum wage cannot afford to rent a two-bedroom apartment with utilities, even by working a full forty hours per week.

READY TO BUY

When you are planning to buy (or sell) a home, you can do it yourself, or you can choose to work with a Realtor. To complete a sale, a willing buyer and a willing seller must come to agreement. And because real estate transactions can be fraught with so much emotion and potential legal complications, and because so much money is involved, almost all people choose to work with a knowledgeable professional to guide them through the process. "Realtor" is a copyrighted designation, used only by brokers who qualify as members in good standing of the National Association of Realtors (NAR) state and local boards, and who agree to abide by a prescribed code of ethics.

Many first-time buyers think buying directly from the homeowner saves money. The perceived advantage of "do-it-yourself" home buying is that you may save the 5 to 6 percent commission typically charged by a Realtor. In fact, many "do-it-yourself" sellers add the commission to the listed price and do not know the comparable market prices for their neighborhood, and so may overprice their home. An impartial third party often is better suited to negotiate for a successful sale. Personal feelings do not enter into the transaction, and some unpleasant situations can be avoided.

HOW TO CHOOSE A REALTOR

When you start to interview Realtors, look for someone whose disposition and work habits seem to fit yours, someone who has empathy for the trauma of moving to a strange place, be it across town or across the country. You will want someone you feel you can trust. It is helpful to find someone in the neighborhood where you are looking to buy, as he or she will have inside information you likely will find helpful.

Do you feel comfortable talking with the Realtor? Is he or she listening to and respectful of your needs? If you feel you are being rushed, speak up! You can slow down the process and not lose out on the house you want.

Choose a full-time, experienced agent who tries to meet the majority of your requirements within your price range—someone who does not limit the number of houses he or she will show you. Your agent should be flexible enough to try to show you homes on your schedule, not on the agent's. Be sure the agent loves his or her work, for work it is, even though friends will say, "How much fun it is to show pretty houses."

Look for a Realtor whose firm is connected to a network of top national real estate companies that can make appropriate referrals when necessary. Your agent's firm should have access to the latest technology, especially if you are moving long-distance. A computer may help in your search, but not even "virtual reality" can replace the feeling of an actual physical tour of the house you are considering making your home.

Also, be sure that your Realtor's firm subscribes to Multiple Listing Service (MLS). MLS is a compilation of the homes for sale in a designated area. It allows your agent to search for all the homes for sale fitting your criteria, listed by brokers who subscribe. Using MLS saves time for you and for the agent. It allows a more complete picture of homes available in your price range and area. Brokers must pay a fee to belong to MLS, as well as a fee to list a property for sale.

Make sure you choose a buyer's broker (or buyer's agent)—one who will write protections into your contract such as, but not limited to, contingent on appraisal, home inspection, and termite inspection. A buyer's broker is an agent who agrees to represent *only* the buyer during the real estate transaction. To the buyer, a buyer's broker has the duties of loyalty, obedience, disclosure, and confidentiality and to treat both the buyer and the seller with honesty and fair dealing.

In some circumstances, the same broker may represent both buyer and seller. If acting directly through one or more Realtors within the same real estate firm, and with the knowledge and consent of both the buyer and the seller, the agent may do so. Of course, the agent still is obligated to disclose the facts that may have an impact on either party to the sale. She is required to deal honestly and fairly with both parties.

WORKING EFFECTIVELY WITH A REALTOR

Just as your Realtor is responsible for treating you honestly and fairly, you will enter into the partnership with certain obligations. From the Realtor's point of view, you will be expected to be loyal to your agent and not call a second or third agent while you are working actively with the first. To be a "dream client," you will describe your wants, needs, and financial conditions truthfully, and will be open to seeing all properties your agent thinks are suitable for you, including new construction. And, most important, you should trust the agent to search diligently and well on your behalf.

Should you have a problem with your Realtor, the first thing to do is to talk with him or her. The next step would be to contact the owner of the firm for which the Realtor works. If you have a dispute that cannot be settled by the firm, a mediation conference, composed of a panel of Realtors, is the next step. Most disputes are settled there, but small claims court can be pursued. Very few disputes reach this stage.

SELLING YOUR HOME

When you are ready to sell your home, your Realtor can show you the sale prices of comparable homes in your neighborhood. The Realtor is able to point out the pluses or minuses of these homes versus yours. As the seller, you should choose a Realtor for much the same reasons as a buyer: for MLS exposure, for safety in opening your home to strangers, and to bring in potential buyers who are prequalified for the appropriate price range. Also, you are not obligated to be home for showings, and the price of major advertising and promotions is paid by the listing agent. You only have to deal with one person—the listing agent. The same qualities you look for when choosing an agent to buy a home are the ones to look for when you plan to sell your home.

To have a successful home-buying experience, choose your Realtor carefully, as you would any other financial professional—use recommendations and referrals from friends, and, most important, trust your instincts!

BEGINNING THE HOME-FINANCING PROCESS

Being financially prepared makes you a more desirable buyer. Just as in other financial arenas, use personal referrals to put you in touch with a lender. Before beginning to work with a Realtor, or making an offer on a house, it is a good idea to get preapproved for a mortgage. Make sure you are comfortable with and have confidence in the person who is preapproving you.

"Preapproved" means that you have submitted all the documents needed to verify your ability to carry a home mortgage and that the lender has run a credit check on you. A buyer who is "preapproved" has a firm commitment from a specific lender.

You also may hear the term "prequalified." At an early stage in the process, a Realtor, mortgage broker, or bank officer can "prequalify" a potential buyer by examining financial data and suggesting the maximum amount of a mortgage, and therefore the maximum price of the house. Since no documents are submitted, there is no commitment on either side. Prequalification simply gives you, the buyer, an idea of what you could afford as you begin to shop.

Typical preapproval questions might include: How much in savings do you have available for a down payment? What work do you do? How long have you been on the job/in business? What is your current salary? Do you have any commission, bonus, or overtime income? For how long have you been receiving it? If you are paid hourly, how many hours do you work per week? Do you

have any debts, such as car loans, student loans, credit cards, or personal loans? Do you own other real estate?

In preparation for a preapproval, you should gather the following documents: two years of W-2 forms, two years of tax returns if self-employed, commissioned, or claiming bonus income, your most recent pay stubs to reflect a thirty-day period, three months of bank and investment statements, proof of alimony or child-support payments, if these are to be considered, and monthly coupons for long-term debt, such as car or student loans.

QUALIFYING FOR A MORTGAGE

Four factors are used to determine your qualifications for mortgage potential. They are: credit, assets, appraisal, and ratios.

An assessment of your credit will determine: How well do you pay your bills? Are payments made on time? Are you current on all or just some of your past or present loans? Sometimes, you will be asked for a written explanation for certain items on the credit report. Or you may be buying a first home and have no credit. Then you would be asked for at least three forms of credit references, such as a rental reference and utility accounts.

Key credit issues are: Have you any prior late mortgage payments? Any bankruptcy? Bankruptcy does not necessarily disqualify you from getting a mortgage. But any judgments, collections, or liens must be explained in writing and paid in full prior to the closing. Also, the credit bureaus now score every application, and most lenders have a predetermined minimum acceptable score.

In looking at your assets, the general rule is that at least 5 percent of the down payment must be from the borrower's own funds. Money for a down payment cannot be borrowed in the form of an unsecured loan, although it could be borrowed and secured by real property, stocks, or other assets, such as a 401(k) plan.

If you are lucky enough to get a gift that is 20 percent or more of the down payment, the whole payment can be from the gift. But new products are being developed all the time. There is now available a 3-percent-down mortgage, all of which can be from a gift, so it pays to ask!

Gift funds must come from a blood relative. A friend or roommate may not be the donor of gift funds. If the funds for the closing are coming from the sale of another home, then the HUD 1 Settlement Statement will be needed to verify these funds. In all cases, the lender will look for enough funds for the down payment and closing costs. If you have less than a 20 percent down payment, you will be required to have private mortgage insurance (PMI), an additional monthly charge that protects the lender, not you. However, if you are putting 10 percent down, you can avoid paying the PMI this way: you would take a combination of a first mortgage for 80 percent, thus avoiding the insurance, and a second mortgage for the remaining 10 percent.

APPRAISAL OF PROPERTY

An appraisal will be done on the home you wish to buy, in order to assess the market value. Most residential lenders will give mortgages for only one- to four-family properties. These can be owner-occupied or they can be investor units.

Single-family second or vacation homes also are acceptable to most residential lenders.

An appraisal of the property is very important to determine exactly how much the property is worth. The lender is actually securing that mortgage against the home that you're buying, with the home being the collateral for the lender. So they ask for an appraisal, independent of the lender.

What the appraiser does is not an exact science; while there are guidelines, the process is somewhat subjective. She may look at a house and say, "Okay, I see that this house has a two-car garage and a finished basement. The one next door does not." And she'll make adjustments. She will try to find a house as similar as possible, in the same neighborhood, to the one you are buying. The previous selling price of the house is not an accurate appraisal guide because market value changes so much with time.

A few years ago, the market was so heated up that many houses were selling for more than the asking price. It was crazy: multiple bidders, a buying frenzy! They were in a bidding war to buy these houses. A year before, the market was much calmer. So home values may change, depending on the circumstances of the timing of the transaction.

The lender will lend based either on the appraised value or the purchase price, whichever is less.

A couple came in recently and said to me, "Gee, we got a steal on this house. We're buying it for $140,000." And the appraisal came in at $150,000. So now they wanted a mortgage—90 percent of $150,000. Couldn't do it. It's the appraised value or the purchase price, whichever is less.

In the Boston area, as well as in other parts of the country, appraised values seldom are really a big issue. Properties appraise out quite nicely. But in other states, the situation is different. If you're buying a house for $200,000 and it appraises out at $180,000, there may be adjustments to the loan amount. Or you may go back to the seller displeased and say, "Hey, this is not appraising out—what's the problem here?"

RATIOS

Ratios are guidelines: the landmark for all borrowers qualifying to buy a home. The "first ratio," also called the "housing ratio," is the total housing cost to the buyer's monthly gross income, or net income if self-employed. The total monthly housing cost is the total of the monthly principal and interest payments on the mortgage, plus the monthly costs of property taxes and homeowner's insurance, or "PITI." This monthly housing payment generally should equal no more than 28 to 33 percent of your monthly gross income.

For example, Janet earns $40,000 a year. She plans to buy her first home, and is concerned that her housing payment be in line with her income. Using the formula at 33 percent, we take 40,000 and divide it by 12; 3333.33 times 33 percent. This equals $1,100, so Janet would qualify for a $1,100-a-month housing payment.

The second ratio, or "back ratio" or "total debt ratio," includes the housing payment plus any other monthly payments. This ratio should be no more than 36 to 38 percent of your gross monthly income. There always will be exceptions to the ratios. Some factors that could offset a higher ratio are: a large down payment, excellent credit, a high net worth, strong potential for increased

earnings, a higher first ratio with no debt, a demonstrated ability to save, and/or substantial reserves after closing.

You should consider your total housing costs in the context of your own budget, and make choices that will allow you to maintain a comfortable lifestyle. It would not make sense to buy a house so expensive that you could not afford to heat it, or to buy groceries or other basic necessities.

Sometimes, your ratios may seem to be in line with the guidelines, but you may not have shown an ability to save, and, with the home purchase, your housing expenses will be increased substantially. If, for example, you currently are paying $500 a month for rent, and you wish to purchase a home for which the monthly costs will be $1,200, you should look very carefully at your current and past spending habits. Have you been saving on a regular basis? Do you have too much credit card debt? Do you feel capable of handling such a big increase? Strong credit, abundant reserve cash, and a solid work record are important, especially for the low-down-payment buyer.

Your income is key to figuring the ratios. In determining income, the numbers just have to make sense.

For example, if you're self-employed, you may write off a lot of your income because you don't want to be taxed on it. But when it comes to selling the mortgage, the lender has to look at net income. For self-employed people and others who may not fit a "traditional" model, there are special mortgage programs available.

A woman who runs a home-based day-care center literally writes off all of her income. That's what her accountant advises, that's legal, and it's fine. We're not going to tell her differently. But she could not qualify for a mortgage under the standard process. She did, however, have a lot of cash from an inheritance—enough to be able to afford 20 percent down. So we found her a "no-income/no-ratio" program. The fact that she had 20 percent down made her eligible, even without income. The lender also wanted to verify that she had six months' mortgage payments in reserve—in a savings account or in an investment account, that she had excellent credit, and that the property appraised out. So instead of looking at the income as carrying the mortgage, they're looking at all the other things. Her interest rate is a little higher. She is penalized because she's not going through the standard process, the standard guidelines. But, hey, it got her into a house. She was happy.

Here's another story:

Ruth just got out of graduate school, and takes her first job in high-tech. She's been on the job only two months, and wants to buy a house—absolutely fine. She has to be on the job only one paycheck and we'd lend to her, if everything else makes sense. If she had bad credit and other things popped up, we'd take a second look. But assuming everything looks okay, she doesn't need a two-year history.

When looking at ratios, know that everything is figured in months: mortgage payments, income, bonuses. Now bonus, commission, part-time work, Schedule C (if you're freelancing or running a business)—anything that's variable over time—typically needs a two-year average. And you can't just dash out and pick up a part-time job in order to be able to afford the mortgage. You need at least a one-year history, preferably a two-year history.

Child support and alimony are very common sources of income for women seeking to qualify for a mortgage. The most important thing is to make sure you are documenting the income. It's very important to keep that income separate. If you get an alimony or a child-support check, you should photocopy the check and deposit the money by itself. You don't want to commingle it with whatever other funds you might get. By law, you do not have to disclose that income to the lender if you are not planning to use it to make your housing payments. But if you need to count it in order to qualify for a mortgage, you want to separate that deposit. You will be asked for a six- to twelve-month history of receipt, and for a divorce decree that shows that the payments will continue for at least three years. Make sure that you are keeping very good records of the receipt of that income.

Normally, the lender will ask to see your bank statements for the last twelve months. And they need to see that deposit. The fact of the matter is, a lot of people do not pay child support and alimony on time. Nationally, only 30 percent of all mandated child support actually is paid.

Here is an example of ratios. If you can see the numbers, you may get a better feel for it. Let's look five years into Ruth's future. She is still at that high-tech firm, making $60,000, plus an end-of-the-year bonus. Her base income is $5,000 a month. Last year, she received a $10,000 bonus. And then this year, she received $15,000; $25,000 divided by two is $12,500, divided by twelve would be $1,041. We add that to her base income ($5,000) for a total of $6,041.

Now, let's say she wants to buy a $250,000 house. She has some of her own savings, but she's also getting a gift, say, 20 percent down, so she will need a $200,000 mortgage.

So at 7¾ percent, her principal and interest

payment (you have to use a special calculator) would be $1,432 and change. Now you must add in two other components: real estate taxes, say, $250 a month, and homeowner's insurance, say, $50 a month. So her total housing payment is going to be $1,732.

The first ratio is housing ($1,732) to income ($6,041), which is 28.7 percent. So she's spending roughly 29 percent of her income on her mortgage payment. That's within the acceptable range of 28 to 33 percent. Whether it's your first time or your twentieth time buying a house, you have got to make the numbers fit your own life. The ratios provide guidelines so that you and the lender can be confident that the numbers will work.

Personally, I would not want to be up at the 33 percent end. I would feel squeezed. But people live so differently. Some people want to travel. Some people want expensive clothes. Some people have children. Some people are on their own. You have to decide what works for you.

There's one more qualifying ratio that comes into play because people have debts for things other than their homes. They have car loans. They have school loans. They have credit cards. So let's say our Ruth has a car loan of $250 a month, and student loans of $200 a month. And let's say she's got $1,000 on credit cards, for which she makes the minimum payment of $50 a month.

A common question is, "Do you use what I have outstanding on my credit card or what I could have outstanding on my credit cards? I have available credit of $10,000." We use the outstanding balance and payment shown on your credit report at the time we pull your credit. The fact is, we could

grant a mortgage and you could lose your job three months later. We can't possibly foresee those kinds of things. We take a snapshot. And that's the way we underwrite.

So Ruth has $500 a month in long-term debt. We take $1,732, the housing cost, plus her other long-term debt, which totals $500 per month, and divide that by her income. This is what's called the "second ratio" or the "overall debt-to-income ratio." Ruth is at 36.9 percent. She could go as high as 38 percent, a figure the lender finds acceptable and that is unlikely to overtax her budget. Her case is pretty clear.

Where the creativity comes in is with people who don't fall directly within the guidelines. It still may make sense to do the loan. We may have a situation where somebody is high on the first ratio—the housing-to-income ratio—but she has very little long-term debt. That could make sense. We serve a lot of people in the computer industry who have decided to become consultants, who feel that consulting is a lot more lucrative than working for some of these big companies. Normally, we look for a two-year history of self-employed income, but we'll look at as little as one year if the person is working in the same field. We don't want to see somebody being a baker one year, an engineer the next, and a dancer the year after that.

What about when a couple is relocating? The spouse who is being relocated has a firm job offer and a known salary. But the spouse who's coming along may not have a job yet. If that spouse is presently working, we can use a percentage of that income to get them qualified for a new house. It's called "trailing spouse income." The lender is counting on the likelihood that he or she is employable. They won't use the full income; they'll use a percentage. So there's an outlet for just about anybody.

Even people with bankruptcies can get a mortgage. The big factor there is time. Are the problems that caused the bankruptcy over and not likely to reoccur? Has the person reestablished credit? Most people who want to buy a house can.

FIXED- AND VARIABLE-RATE MORTGAGES

With a fixed-rate mortgage, the interest rate on the loan remains the same for the entire life of the loan. You, the borrower, pay the same total amount each month, with more of the payment going toward the principal and less toward the interest as the loan matures. For years, there were only a few mortgage products on the market: a thirty-year fixed-rate, a twenty-five-year fixed-rate, and a fifteen-year fixed-rate. Now, with the advent of the variable-rate mortgage, or adjustable-rate mortgage (ARM), there are many more choices.

Variable-rate mortgages are useful for many different situations. You may think you're going to be transferred down the road. Or you may simply grow out of this house in a couple of years. So you are not really in a position to need a thirty-year fixed-rate mortgage. You are in a situation where you are willing to accept some risk.

Here's how a variable-rate mortgage works. Let's say you look for a "five-one" ARM program. This means that the interest rate is fixed for the first five years of the mortgage and then for the remaining years, six through thirty, it can change every single year. The initial rate is lower than the rate for a fixed-rate mortgage, and there are caps to the changes after the first five years. There's a 2 percent annual cap and a 6 percent lifetime cap, which means that the interest rate cannot go up or down more than 2 percent a year, nor more than 6 percent over the life of the loan. The caps come into play after the initial fixed term. So if you are not planning to stay in one house for very long, you may get a better deal, and of course you can refinance at any time.

My youngest child will graduate high school in two years, and then . . . I'm outta here! I just refinanced to a three-year adjustable mortgage with a very low introductory interest rate. Before it goes up, I plan to have sold my house.

Here's an idea of the possible difference in interest rates. At a time when interest rates on a thirty-year fixed are, say, 8⅝ percent, on a "five-one" they might be running at about 8 percent. So you can see there's quite a bit of a spread between 8 percent and 8⅝ percent. The difference in monthly payments on a $150,000 mortgage would be about $67 a month.

An ARM can be very attractive, as long as you are aware of the risk: that the interest rate can go up. Is it worth it for you to take an ARM? Your mortgage broker can advise you on what factors you should consider. But you have to go back and fit the numbers into your own life.

I have a thirty-year fixed-rate mortgage because, first of all, we're in a house where I think we are going to be for quite some time, but we have two children, and I wanted to know the worst-case scenario we could face with the mortgage payment. Even though I think I could have refinanced within five years, I did not want to take the risk. For me, it didn't make sense.

The challenge with any adjustable mortgage is to watch it closely each year. You need to have some concept of how it works and when it may make sense to refinance.

My advice for refinancing would be to look for a "no-point, no-closing-cost" product. A "point" is 1 percent of your mortgage amount. So if you are getting a $200,000 mortgage, one point would equal $2,000. Most banks and many mortgage companies give you the option to pay or not to pay points.

"Closing costs" are the costs often charged in connection with executing a new loan: title search, attorneys' fees, a copy of the plot plan, an appraisal, and credit reports.

Whether or not an ARM is right for you comes down to your own personal comfort level, remembering that you always have the option to refinance.

REFINANCING

Once most people get a mortgage, they are apt to forget about it. That's why a good mortgage broker will try to be proactive, monitor her customers' interest rates, and call them if interest rates are down and say, "Here's a refinance opportunity." Because as much as you might say, "Oh, I'll keep an eye on interest rates," often people don't. They just keep on making that mortgage payment and don't necessarily think, "Gee, could I be doing something better with that mortgage?" Or they fear they may have to incur closing costs again. Generally, refinancing your mortgage can save you from $50 to more than $100 a month, which really can add up over time.

Much of the refinancing we are doing today is done on a no-point, no-closing basis. With a no-point, no-closing-cost mortgage, all the fees are built into the interest rate. But if that interest rate is lower than the one you have presently, you will be saving money from day one.

Recently, I heard a speaker on a major daytime TV talk show. He was some financial guy, and I couldn't believe he was still spouting these old rules! He said, "Not until the current interest rate is a full two percentage points lower than your rate should you consider refinancing." He's absolutely wrong. If you can get an interest rate, assuming a no-cost, no-point program, of a quarter percent better, you'll be saving money, at no cost to you.

If you have both a mortgage and a home equity loan, you can refinance one without the other. If your first mortgage wasn't very competitive, you can refinance your first mortgage and still keep your equity line open. Look for a no-prepayment-penalty clause, and look for refinance opportunities. But look for them on a no-point, no-close basis.

In the opinion of most mortgage brokers, if you're refinancing, do not pay fees. You also want to make sure that you always have the option to prepay or to refinance. You've got to be careful. Most mortgages will have no prepayment penalties. With a prepayment penalty, what they're saying is, "We'll give you this mortgage, but if you refinance out of this mortgage within, say, three years, we are going to hit you up with a three-month interest penalty." It's expensive. It's ridiculous. Think twice before taking a mortgage with a prepayment penalty. You want to be able to refinance at any time.

We bought our house in August. We refinanced under a no-point, no-close. I took a thirty-year fixed. Then we refinanced two months later, back into another no-point, no-close. And we probably saved three-quarters of a percent on the interest rate. We'd just had a dip in interest rates.

Interest rates tend to travel in cycles. A few years ago, you could get a no-point, no-close thirty-year fixed at about 7 percent. Then the rates went up. Tomorrow, they'll be someplace else. You just have to keep some perspective. Remember, interest rates have been as high as 18 and 19 percent.

You may think you are going to be in a house forever, but it is likely you will end up refinancing. This allows you to take advantage of the interest rate cycles. Staying flexible in the mortgage market is a valuable tool these days; more so than it was years ago, because today there are so many more options.

Here's the way to analyze the difference between a no-point, no-close product and one for which you pay points and closing costs. Assume a rate of 8⅜ percent, for a no-point, no-close mortgage. If you did pay closing costs, they would be roughly $1,800. Then if you paid one point plus closing costs, your rate typically would be ½ percent lower than with a no-point, no-close product. So, with a $200,000 loan, at 8⅜ percent, your principal and interest payment would be $1,555.58. Now, assume the one point with closing cost rate is 8⅛ percent. At that rate, your principal and interest would be $1,485. So the difference between those two is $70.58 a month. That sounds good until you realize you have paid $2,000 for the one point, plus the $1,800 for the closing costs. So your total initial cost is $3,800. At that rate, it would take you fifty-four months just to break even. And you may not stay in the house or hold on to that mortgage long enough to recoup your cost.

You may plan to stay in the house, but you may get relocated. You may lose your job, get married, get divorced. A lot can happen in three years that you can't anticipate.

BEFORE YOU OBTAIN A JOINT MORTGAGE

It is very important for you to know that if you are married, or if you are buying a house with someone else, when you sign on to a mortgage you are 100 percent liable for that mortgage. It's not a fifty-fifty partnership. You are each 100 percent responsible. We strongly urge that both you and your home-buying partner—spouse, significant other, or roommate—be present at the closing and that both understand what's going on. Because if you're left, you're left with the whole mortgage—not half of it.

FINDING A MORTGAGE LENDER

To find a good mortgage lender, you usually will do well depending on referrals. Ask friends who have just bought a house. Or ask your financial planner or a real estate broker for the name of a reputable lender. Find out from the potential lender how long it has been in business. And then check a couple of different banks or mortgage companies to get rates and to see how competitive they are. Don't automatically assume that the bank where you have your savings and checking accounts necessarily will be the best mortgage lender. Quite often it will not. As long as you are comfortable with the lender and feel it is trustworthy, the rates offered are primary.

Just as in every other profession, there are unscrupulous lenders. We have seen some who, to get your business, will suggest that you lie on the application to get prequalified. Then there is the story about the guy who was refinancing over the Internet and was in for a big surprise at the closing: the broker had lied about the interest rate!

Every mortgage lender must be licensed by the state. If you run into a problem with a mortgage lender, you can turn to the banking commission or attorney general in your state, both of which should keep a record of complaints to which you may have access.

We talk to many people "on spec." We haven't written their mortgage, we've just given them advice. The idea is for us to provide good service to our customers and to potential customers. Even if we don't do your mortgage, you may say, "Gee, she spent an hour with me and she didn't get paid." And you might tell a friend.

A good mortgage lender will shop around many sources to get you the best available deal, and will find the product that best meets your needs. She will help you with the plentiful paperwork that surrounds the mortgage process, and will be easily available to talk with you and to answer your questions throughout the process.

Having read about how to choose a new car, finance higher education, obtain a mortgage for your new home, it is time to look at how to protect your major purchases with insurance. The next chapter will show you how.

6: Insurance: Protecting Yourself, Protecting What You Have

Contributing Authors:

Jill Zupan Adomaitis, Adelaide Aitken, Nadine Heaps

"No woman should marry until she is able to support herself financially, because one day she may have to—and her children as well."

—ABIGAIL VAN BUREN ("DEAR ABBY"), COLUMNIST

IN THIS CHAPTER, YOU WILL LEARN:

- Why insurance should be the base of your financial plan

- Seven types of insurance you should consider

- How to determine what insurance you need

- What to look for when you buy insurance

When you hear the word "insurance," what comes to mind?

Expensive.

Complicated.

Fear.

Necessary.

Usually you need your insurance when something bad happens. You use it when you are in a car accident, there's a flood, somebody dies. There is trauma associated with it.

Many of us have a negative attitude about insurance and often about insurance agents, partly because there is so much confusion about the subject, partly because there has been a lot of publicity about a few unethical companies and practitioners, but mostly because no one wants to think about a disaster affecting themselves or their loved ones.

Because it is frightening and uncomfortable to think about illness or accident or theft or disability, many women just refuse to think about it. To educate ourselves, and then choose insurance coverage to meet our needs and our budget, is liberating. Changing our attitude to one of prevention rather than fear, we can look at insurance as protecting us, our families, and the things we have worked hard to acquire.

We will be discussing the seven most common types of insurance: health, disability, life, long-term care, auto, homeowner's, and liability.

- Health insurance pays for doctors' visits and hospitalization, and sometimes prescription medication.

- Disability insurance pays you a fixed percentage of your salary for a fixed amount of time, if you are unable to work due to accident or illness.

- Life insurance pays cash to your survivors when you die, to pay off your debts and possibly provide them with some income.

- The newest kind of insurance—long-term care—addresses the biggest financial vulnerability for women older than sixty-five. Even six months in a nursing home can wipe out the life savings of the average woman.

- Most states require car owners to buy some auto insurance—to cover damage to persons and property in case you or a driver of your car is involved in a crash. If your car is new, you also will want to buy insurance to repair or replace your own vehicle.

- Homeowner's—and renter's—insurance covers damage to your property, theft of your belongings, and pays for medical expenses and damages should you be legally liable, for example, if someone injures themselves on your property. Homeowner's insurance generally also pays for flooding from broken pipes, fires, storm damage, and any property damage that you did not cause.

- In the current legal climate, where everyone is open to the possibility of a lawsuit, liability insurance supplements your auto and homeowner's insurance, providing extra coverage. If, for example, you have a teenage driver in residence, or you serve on the board of a nonprofit organization, or operate a home-based business, liability insurance may be a good choice for you.

Not all women need all kinds of insurance. And we don't always have to pay for it all ourselves. Many employers offer health, disability, and life insurance. Some even will contribute to long-term-care insurance.

Auto insurance and homeowner's insurance are almost always purchased by individuals, not provided by employers. You can save money buying insurance through a group. An automobile club, a credit union, or an association to which you belong may have discounts for members.

What kind of insurance—and how much—is right for you? Educate yourself *before* you talk to an adviser. Talk to more than one salesperson. Remember, you are the consumer. Compare prices and policies. Don't buy more, or less, insurance than you need.

Financial planners often refer to insurance as the "bottom of your financial pyramid," topped by cash reserves, enough to see you through an emergency; then accessible investments, such as money market funds; then tax-sheltered plans such as those you create for retirement (IRAs, SEPs, 401[k]s). At the top of the pyramid are exotic investments such as pork belly futures or collecting antique cars.

You wouldn't believe how many people planners see who are experts on ancient Persian rugs and don't have disability coverage.

My husband is obsessed with the top of the pyramid. We don't even have any savings, and this scares me.

HEALTH INSURANCE

The easiest, least-expensive, and most effective form of health insurance is, of course, to take good care of yourself. Women are so good at taking care of others; sometimes we neglect to take proper care of ourselves. You know the basics: eat and drink wisely, exercise regularly, get sufficient rest, get regular checkups and appropriate screening tests, avoid toxins, maintain a balance between work and play, engage in some form of regular stress-reducing practice, continue to seek opportunities to grow your intellect, your spirit, your creativity, and be sure to give and get lots of hugs!

Despite our best efforts at self-care, many of us do become ill or injured at some point in our lives. The most important kind of insurance you can have is some kind of health coverage An unforeseen disaster can wipe you out financially. Even a broken arm can cost several thousand dollars, if you do not have insurance.

You may be covered by one of these ways:

I have medical insurance through work, but I have to pay half.

I'm self-employed. My husband has health, life, and disability insurance through his company. So, as long as I am with him, that is not a problem.

I'm still covered on my parents' policy because I'm in school.

Medicare picked up my coverage when I turned sixty-five.

I have insurance for myself and my son. Not through my job—I work at a temp agency—but through the state from my previous job.

Both my partner and I are self-employed, so all of our insurance is individually purchased.

There are different kinds of providers: the HMO, or health maintenance organization, the PPO, which stands for preferred provider organization, and Medicare. The difference is that with an HMO, you pay a premium and then you pay a little bit per visit—a "copayment"—and that covers your visit. HMOs provide a range of services, from routine checkups to emergency hospitalization.

A PPO is a network of health care providers who offer services at reduced rates, predetermined by its contract. With a PPO, you, the consumer, usually pay the whole bill, on a fee-for-service basis, and then you file a claim for reimbursement. It's a bit more work on your part. Medicare, for which we are all taxed, is the federal government's program to cover some medical expenses when you get to be sixty-five and are eligible for Social Security.

Most insurance plans are step-rated, which means that the premiums are based on the insured person's sex and age. The older you are the higher your premium will be. Generally, females between the ages of nineteen and fifty pay higher rates than males in that same age range, but by age fifty, the rates are about the same for both genders.

One of the first HMOs in the country, Harvard Community Health Plan, started in Cambridge, Massachusetts, in 1972, and became very, very successful. HMOs were protected by the federal government in terms of price competition with the insurance companies, and given a kind of unnatural competitive market advantage for a long time, and so they prospered.

Today, in almost all HMOs, you must have a

primary care physician: a doctor you see for routine visits, and whose approval you need to get to see a specialist. Many women get aggravated by this policy, quite frankly. Because if you have a child you want to take to a specialist besides the pediatrician, you have to go first to the pediatrician for a visit, and then get a referral. Why do HMOs do this? It is a way of controlling cost for the insurance company.

HMOs were the forerunners in cost control. On the other hand, they also were the forerunners in preventive care. Anybody who has a family, with a couple of kids, loves that $5 office visit. You can take your kid in for any reason. And it is very convenient. No deductibles, no paperwork. Routine physicals are covered and you generally do not have any exclusions in HMOs. Depending on the plan, you can see a psychiatrist, a chiropractor, even get routine dental checkups for kids. And they may offer health education classes, and give you health club discounts and other nice benefits. HMOs have gone a long way in improving the health of the nation by their preventive care philosophy.

A doctor can belong to as many different HMOs as she pleases. That is why you see all the various stickers on some doctors' doors. You may find that the younger the doctor, the more prone she will be to join them, trying to build up her practice. If the doctor is a specialist, say, an eye surgeon at a major teaching hospital, she does not have to join any networks because she's likely to have more business than she can handle. And she does not have to take a discount. Here's how the discount system works:

Your insurance company pays your doctor at, for example, the ninety-fifth percentile of the average cost of a physical exam in your area. So if the physical costs $100, the insurance company probably will pay $95 to the doctor. The doctor, of course, can charge whatever she pleases for the exam. She will not charge you less because you have insurance that will pay her the most. Your neighbor may have a plan with a different company, one that pays the doctor an amount specified by their contract, say, $60 for a physical. No more, no less. There is a contractual agreement for each procedure and HMOs and PPOs have negotiated significant discounts with the doctors who join them in exchange for patients.

Dental plans can work the same way. There is a schedule. If the insurance company pays a dental claim, they are only going to pay so much for a crown or so much for a filling. And dentists know this. That is why the dentist's office is likely to have someone on staff devoted entirely to insurance issues—it takes that much time. And guess who pays for that?

When HMOs were invented, a lot of people thought they would have a much larger share of the marketplace than they do, that employers would substitute them for traditional insurance. That has not been the case.

The HMO is really an extreme form of managed care, which means managing the patient along so that they do not spend too much money or consume too much time or care. When you get right down to it, a lot of women want freedom of choice. You may not mind going to the HMO doctor for your regular checkup and Pap smear, but if you have a life-threatening illness, you may want to be able to search out the best specialist.

Freedom-of-choice issues have kept the traditional plans in business. In a traditional, or indemnity plan, you may be required to pay the first $200 or $300, your deductible. Insurance pays 80 percent of the balance of your bill, then you pay the rest.

> The most famous of all the indemnity programs probably is Blue Cross-Blue Shield. Blue Cross-Blue Shield was invented in Cambridge, Massachusetts, in the 1920s. Were people suddenly sicker? Did they need medical insurance? No. It really was invented because Harvard Medical School was graduating more and more doctors. People did not go to doctors in the twenties. There were few doctors, no one had health insurance. Most women depended on home remedies back then, and on home nursing care if needed. Almost all babies still were born at home. It was almost as if they created the market for doctors by creating Blue Cross. They needed patients.

With the PPO, preferred provider organization, you may wish, for example, to go to the Mayo Clinic in Rochester or to Sloan-Kettering in New York, or to Mass General because you feel these are some of the best medical facilities. Then you would simply pay the deductible. And co-insurance pays an out-of-pocket cost. You have the freedom to choose where and from whom you seek care. That was the insurance industry's invention to compete with the HMOs about a dozen years ago.

Most employers offer some form of health insurance. The PPO is very, very common with employers. Their cost is less than for the HMO. The real cost of health insurance for a family in the most expensive areas of the United States is about $700 to $800 a month. For a single person, it is somewhere around $300.

Insurance is a huge cost for employers. In 1965, private businesses paid $6 billion for health care. In 1980, they paid $64 billion; and by 1991 they paid $205 billion in health care.[1]

What happens if you lose your job? COBRA (Consolidated Omnibus Budget Reconciliation Act of 1986) is an excellent federal consumer protection law that says when you leave your employer, you can continue your medical insurance for eighteen months. If you are a divorced spouse, disabled, or a student in college, COBRA can continue for thirty-six months. Most preexisting conditions also are covered now.

For example, if you are a diabetic and left your employer, the diabetes would not have been covered for twelve months. You couldn't go without insulin for twelve months. The Kennedy-Kassebaum Act, passed in 1997, forbids insurance companies to impose preexisting limitations on a corporate level, except for a couple of very rare reasons. They have got to take the sick people as well as the healthy people. While it is a solution from the social perspective, it certainly is going to continue to increase insurance costs.

If you get a new job, the employer can require a waiting period before you are eligible for insurance. Although it is a hardship for the employee, think how costly and frustrating it would be for the employer to hire someone new, fill out all the paperwork, pay the premiums, and then have that individual quit after a month. So it is not uncommon, especially in smaller companies, to require a waiting period.

MONEY ORDER

I started a new job two years ago last April. And I was not eligible for insurance. Three months later, I was. But as it happened, I found out in June that I was pregnant. So on July 15, when the health insurance coverage began, they wouldn't pay for the pregnancy because they said it was a preexisting condition! I could have avoided telling them I was pregnant, but I didn't want to lie about my baby. That seemed sneaky and wrong. So there I was, the following January, nine months pregnant with no health insurance for the delivery. I went into labor around noontime, and by late evening, it was clear that the baby would be along soon. So we drove to the hospital parking lot and waited there. I was damned if I was going to go in at 11:30 at night, when they bill by the day, starting at midnight, at $995 per day. No way was I going to pay $1,000 for half an hour! So there I was, panting and puffing and trying not to push on a freezing-cold January night until my husband made me go in. Our son was born at ten past midnight.

Situations such as this woman's story were very common until the passage of the Kennedy-Kassebaum Act. Still, many women do not have health insurance at all, because they cannot afford to pay out-of-pocket, or they may work for an employer who does not offer it. They have to pay all health costs themselves, or they don't get health care. This situation can happen even to those who have insurance.

I was skiing this winter and I got an eye irritation and went to see a doctor, and a doctor's assistant saw me. She did not know much about the machine that she was looking through into my eyes. But she was very nice and looked and sort of thought it was not anything too serious. Although I had called my HMO first, I later got a bill for $162. The HMO

refused to pay it because it was not an emergency. They thought I could have waited 'til I got back home to have my eye looked at. I didn't agree. You don't mess around with your vision. I finally paid the bill, but I was furious.

Whichever type of plan you have, be sure to review your coverage annually, or when your family situation changes, to be sure you have the best coverage you can afford.

Medicare

When you turn sixty-five, or when you become eligible for Social Security, you will receive Medicare. Medicare comes in two pieces. The first is called Part A. Everyone who qualifies receives Part A, which covers hospitalization, posthospital care in a very specifically, narrowly defined skilled facility, some home health care for a hundred days maximum, some help with hospice, and that's it!

If you elect to take Medicare B, which as of this writing costs about $50 a month, and is taken out of your Social Security check, you have broader coverage. Medicare B includes: physician services, inpatient and outpatient medical services, some outpatient hospital care, some more diagnostic tests.

Medicare sounds pretty good, until you realize what is missing. Prescriptions, vision care, and dental care are not covered. And so for those, most people buy what is called a "med-gap" policy: a policy that fills in all the gaps. And those can be expensive, but probably are a good idea if you can afford the payments.

Part B covers physician services, and has a low cap (maximum payment to doctor). And so the challenge is then to find physicians who will accept what Medicare will pay.

Just as physicians are not all the same, not all plans are equal. Doing your homework is crucial for any kind of insurance! That's most important.

What to Look for When You Choose a Health Insurance Policy

Lifetime maximum benefits

You may think you would never rack up $1 million worth of bills, but if you need a liver transplant, or have a tumor that needs MRI monitoring, you could exceed that total.

Deductible

How much could you afford to pay "out-of-pocket" per illness or injury before the insurance kicks in? You can make things less expensive for yourself by accepting a high deductible. That's often a very good principle, as you're essentially self-insuring: "I will pay bills up to, say, $500, and anything beyond that would be covered." The result of accepting a high deductible is that you get higher coverage at the upper end.

Renewal

Is the policy automatically renewable? Or can you be dropped for certain illnesses or conditions?

Coverage

What does the policy cover? What does it *not* cover? A good plan generally covers everything except experimental drugs, cosmetic surgery, some limitations on chiropractic—you usually get a certain number of visits per year. Your dental surgery is not covered unless for impacted wisdom teeth, or if you get into an accident and hurt your mouth. There are limitations on any kind of mental or nervous condition or psychiatric visit.

Experimental treatments generally are not covered either. Remember the old days when they were not paying for bone marrow transplants and all the lawsuits around that? Now that they are no longer considered experimental, they are covered.

But even today, with some of the AIDS drugs, you still can have a terrible time trying to get the insurance company to pay for those drugs. Same thing with infertility treatment. It can be very expensive without insurance. Yet they will pay for Viagra!

In general, a good policy should not exclude any of the common illnesses or accidents.

Changing the Health Care System

Medical insurance is an expensive necessity. Health care expenditures in the United States now exceed $3 trillion per year.[2] As of this writing, if you are self-employed, that cost is between $2,500 and $5,000 a year, depending on whether you have single or family coverage. Perhaps there will be a workable sort of nationalized health care one day, if only to relieve the financial burden on individuals, and to ensure some basic level of care for everybody.

Everyone from consumer advocates to former First Lady Hillary Clinton has made efforts—sometimes enormous—to change the health care system. Drug companies, insurance companies, and lobbies such as the one for the American Medical Association tend to protect the interest of the moneyed and powerful, often at the expense of the poor and disenfranchised. We feel that affordable preventive health care and emergency services should be available to every American. Yet, more than 37 million Americans do not have health insurance.

Whether or not we ever get national health

care, we are likely always to have private insurance in this country.

My British clients—corporations that have offices here—tell me that just because they have free health care in England does not mean that they do not have private insurance. They do because they want to be able to go to a special doctor. However, their medical insurance is not "free." They pay for it with a tax. Just like all social democracies, they have higher taxes to pay for everything from pensions to medical insurance.

While socialized medicine covers all who need care, there are many negatives. There may be a long wait time for even critical surgery. Emergency rooms often are overcrowded and patients may have to spend hours waiting for treatment. There are little or no resources available to make improvements to hospitals and other health care facilities.

My dad had his heart surgery at the Mayo Clinic. I spent about three days there in the waiting room. It seemed like 75 percent of the people at the Mayo Clinic waiting for their loved ones were not from the United States. They had all come from Canada and Russia and Pakistan and Saudi Arabia. They came for the best in the world. And the United States likely will always have the best medical care.

As we read in the newspaper almost every single day, the medical insurance picture is changing, it seems, by the minute. Mergers, new regulations—the government tried hard to come up with a good solution, but it is a very complicated and unwieldy problem. Now it is the market that is driving the way health is delivered—very often at the expense of the individual. So protect yourself—shop around!

DISABILITY INSURANCE

Many professionals think disability insurance is the most important kind of insurance you can have. In the United States, we have a system in place to help you pay for your doctors or your hospital bills if you can't: Medicaid. But there is no system in place in this country to send you a monthly paycheck if you cannot work because of an illness or an injury.

Most of us depend on staying healthy enough to earn income to pay our basic living expenses. It may be difficult to imagine yourself or your partner being unable to work, unless you have a friend or a family member who is disabled.

What is disability insurance? It provides a monthly income if you are unable to work due to illness or injury.

People get sick or injured for a whole variety of reasons, and sickness is a much more frequent reason for a disability claim than is an accident. We've seen a thirty-eight-year-old attorney disabled with MS; a dentist with carpal tunnel syndrome; a young mother with a nervous breakdown; a teacher crippled with debilitating depression.

Most of us just don't want to think about being so fragile that we are unable to work. In fact, back problems are the most common form of disability in the United States, often caused not by accident but by strain or injury.

Medical science has greatly increased life expectancy. So as we live longer, the chances of being disabled are greater.

There are three types of disability insurance: group, association, and individual. Group, the type that your employer might make available for you, generally replaces 60 percent of your income. If the employer pays for the benefit, it is provided for you at no cost. And that 60 percent benefit is taxable if you become disabled. So, ultimately, that number is closer to 45 percent after taxes.

Association coverage, offered by an organization or any professional association to which you belong, offers the second-least-expensive coverage. And the most expensive policy is that which you buy yourself, called an individual policy. This policy usually is noncancelable, which means that once you buy the policy, the insurance company cannot change the terms of the contract.

The contractual conditions are very different in these three types of coverage.

Mental and nervous conditions often are excluded from an employer's group coverage. So if somebody is stressed out or is depressed, or has any kind of psychiatric condition, she could get twelve or twenty-four months of treatment, but no disability.

After an enormous number of mental health claims in the seventies and eighties, the insurance companies decided, "We are not paying." Some states enacted laws to force insurance companies to treat mental health problems. In Massachusetts, for example, state health insurance law mandates that insurance companies cover up to $500 of mental health treatment for individuals per year.

In contrast with individual plans, which tend to offer the best coverage, association plans generally pay a lower amount per month, perhaps up to $4,000 or $5,000 a month. For some professionals, that amount does not equal 60 percent of their income, and might be insufficient for their needs. For others, that amount is plenty. Another reason to choose an individual plan over an association plan, if you can afford it, is that the insur-

ance company, and not the association, guarantees those benefits.

For example, one state's dental society called an insurance company and said, "Would you write an insurance disability for five thousand dentists?" But, as it turned out, the dentists had a higher claims experience than CPAs, engineers, or teachers. The insurance company is losing money. They are not required to continue to insure the dentists. So the dental society will have to find another insurance company because it is not guaranteeing the dentists' coverage.

The only way that a consumer can get a contractual guarantee that the insurance company will pay disability benefits if she gets sick twenty years from now is to have a noncancelable, individual policy. The insurance company cannot renege on their promise to pay your benefit. Only you yourself can cancel it.

Even if they go out of business, it still is noncancelable. They have to sell the policies to another insurance company.

If you consider purchasing this type of insurance, be sure you understand the definition of "disability" in the policy. What does it mean to be disabled? You cannot do your own job, or you cannot do any job at all, or you cannot do your job for, say, two years? The group contracts with employers usually say, "the inability to perform your own occupation for twenty-four months and after that time the inability to perform any occupation for which you are suited by education, training, or experience." There is a big difference between the ability to "do your own job," and to "do any job at all," or to be able to "do your job part time." Read carefully before you buy. Make sure the policy you buy would make up the difference if you have a partial disability. Some contracts call it "residual."

My sister just went through breast cancer and she had about a three-month period when she really was not feeling well at all. Some days she couldn't go to work. So she had a partial disability. She lost part of her income, not all of it. She was lucky they did not fire her. The disability policy kicked in after sixty days and paid the difference between a five-day work week and about the two to three days that she could come in while she was going through the radiation therapy.

How much insurance do you need? If you buy it in your early thirties, you may need $2,000 a month to live, but is $2,000 a month going to be okay ten years from now? Probably not, with inflation. So look for a provision that compounds by 3 percent per year to increase with the inflation rate. Most policies have an inflation rider so the income can grow over time. You also want the option to buy more insurance over time, as your income increases, without having to go through the physical exam and the application process again.

Another reason to have your own policy is portability. Many of us work for at least three or four companies in our lifetime. If you change jobs, your next employer may not offer disability insurance, or there may be a long waiting period before you could collect benefits.

The quality of the insurance company from which you purchase your policy is important. Make sure it is rated AA or AAA. Ratings are alphabetical, with AAA the top rating, down to DDD, in which the company might be near bankruptcy.

The insurance industry has been in disarray. Twenty years ago, there were thirty or so good-quality contracts for sale in the marketplace. Now there are only about twelve or fifteen. More and more companies are getting out of the business of disability. It's not profitable for them.

The cost of disability insurance is determined by your age, your occupation, the benefit period, and the waiting period. You always will get asked this question by an insurance agency: "How long could you wait before you needed the money?" Generally speaking, group contracts are for ninety days. Sometimes companies have short-term disability to get you by for those first couple of months. Maternity is a good example of when you might use short-term disability because you will probably be "better" in sixty days. If you have your own policy, you can pick a sixty-day waiting period, a ninety-day waiting period, or a 180-day period. Usually, people pick ninety, which has a lower premium than a sixty-day policy, because they think that they can get by for three months. But that is your decision.

And how long do the benefits last? Generally until age sixty-five, when you become eligible for Social Security.

Since 1987, the cost of disability insurance has more than doubled for women. Some states are now unisex states, which means that men and women pay the same cost-per-dollar benefit if they are the same age. And the cost of disability insurance is based on your age, and on the risk involved in your occupation and your hobbies.

A traveling saleswoman, for example, would pay a higher premium than an accountant. Why? Because she is out and about seeing clients. The accountant generally stays in her office. Coverage for doctors also can be expensive. If you do surgery and thereby risk blood infection, for example, your rates would be much higher than, say, a dermatologist.

For women, disability insurance is 35 percent more expensive than for men. Using those actuarial tables, they determine that the claims submitted and ongoing from women are significantly higher than for men. Why? Possibly because we are more conscious of our health. Women tend to go to the doctor and men do not. Maybe there are more visits because of our reproductive health. Maybe it is because more men seem to need to work as an integral part of their identity, while many women are more comfortable "giving in" to illness or injury. Perhaps we are more conscious of preventive care. Whatever the reason, women's rates have skyrocketed and likely will continue to go up.

As a way to estimate the cost, you might think about the premium as a percentage of your income. It used to be that the annual premium was from 1½ to 2 percent of your income. Now premiums are getting closer to 5 percent.

If you make $30,000 a year, the annual cost of disability insurance would be about $1,500. If you make $50,000 a year, it would be $2,500. The good news is once you buy it, the cost does not ever go up. Let's say you bought a $2,000-a-month policy. Two thousand dollars a month means that the insurance company would send you $2,000 a month if you were disabled. If five years from now, you think you really need $3,000, of course the insurance company will be happy to sell you more, and you will pay more premium at that time. But if you keep your $2,000 policy, they will never raise that premium.

No individual policy will insure you for more than 70 percent of the income you earned while healthy. Unlike automobile insurance, which is regulated by the state, disability insurance rates are not required to remain within certain guidelines. If you do not have disability insurance now, you might want to consider buying it before it is priced even higher.

In some states, you cannot buy disability insurance anymore. Noncancelable insurance is literally unavailable in California. Why? Fraud. The workmen's compensation system there is almost as bad. Florida is the second worst state in the country for disability coverage. You almost cannot get these policies in Florida because the combination of genuine and fraudulent claims have overtaxed the system.

Someone who has an extremely dangerous job—stunt pilots, police officers, firemen—or a dangerous hobby—sky divers, rodeo—usually cannot get disability insurance.

Sometimes, what the insurance company considers uninsurable may seem strange. You cannot get disability insurance if you are a creative writer. What if the writer does not feel like writing that day? You know how creative people are—some days the juices are flowing and other days they are not. So, who is to determine if the writer is disabled? It is a gray area as far as the insurance company is concerned.

What does Social Security do for the disabled? If you have been totally disabled for five months, unable to do anything at all, let alone your regular job, then you may apply to Social Security for what is called SSI. Only about 38 percent of those applications are granted, which means that two-thirds are denied. Social Security would approve a monthly check, and those monthly checks might total about $12,000 a year for a single person, only if you were unable to do any job in the national economy and had a life-threatening illness.

I have a friend who is paraplegic, a single woman, and she collects $525 a month. She had been making $65,000 a year.

Group disability coverage at work is integrated with Social Security, which means that if Social Security paid you, the insurance company would reduce the benefit that *they* paid you. Also, there are limitations on what Social Security will pay.

As with other types of insurance, it is a good idea to review your coverage annually. If, for some reason, you cannot find your insurance policy, you can call the insurance company, and give them your name and your Social Security number. They will tell you your policy number so you then can request a copy of the policy.

LIFE INSURANCE

No one wants to talk about life insurance. Let's face it: who wants to think about, much less plan for, her own death? Although the subject may be unpleasant and complicated, confusing and anxiety-laden, it may help to understand the different insurance products available, and to focus on the benefits of insurance.

What exactly *is* life insurance? It is a binding contract between you and the insurer. You agree to pay a premium, or annual fee, each year, and they agree to pay your survivors a fixed amount of money when you die.

The traditional reasons to have life insurance are "love and money."

The primary purpose of life insurance is to protect dependents from the loss of the "breadwinner's" earnings. How much life insurance do you need? Depends on what you want the life insurance to do. Do you need enough to pay off the mortgage? Do you need enough to provide some income? For how many years?

The first thing to consider is whether or not you even need life insurance.

I have been approached by so many salesmen, I've lost count. The thing is, until someone can convince me otherwise, I really don't need life insurance. No one depends on my income but me. My kids are grown, and if they need financial help, they can get it from their father. My house is nearly paid for, and I don't carry a lot of debt. I don't see the point of insuring my life.

When we got married, my husband took out life insurance, and we review it every year. Because if he died, the income would help pay the mortgage and the child care if I had to go back to work. Recently, we purchased enough to cover college for our three children.

The Presbyterian Minister's Fund was the first company in the United States that offered life insurance, beginning in 1759. Every year, the ministers paid a premium in order to provide financial support for their wives and children upon their death. The way this insurance system was set up, it guaranteed the widow an income until her own death and it also provided the children with incomes for thirteen years after their father's death.[3]

For your survivors, life insurance can help cushion the financial shock of your death. Proceeds from a life insurance policy generally are tax-free—that means your survivors won't have to pay tax on what they inherit from the policy. Also, unlike other parts of your estate, death benefits can avoid probate—that property which has to be approved by the court system before being released to your heirs. Life insurance can be available almost immediately—to help with burial costs, estate taxes, and even current bills.

Some common uses for life insurance are:

- To pay off the deceased's outstanding debt.

- To protect a business from the loss of one of its key people, or to buy out his/her survivors in a business partnership. For example, if you and I own a manufacturing company and we both are married and I die, then you are in business with my husband because I owned the stock and I left it to him. You might prefer to have some money to buy out my husband, so you could own the company outright. You could purchase insurance on my life to cover that situation.

- To create an estate: a way of passing along some assets to your heirs. When one spouse dies, the other spouse can inherit a retirement plan with no taxes involved. But when the second spouse dies, this money is now taxed as income. It is included in the taxable estate. When the second spouse dies and wants to leave it to the kids, 75 percent is going to go for taxes. The insurance indus-

try is pretty creative and actually has come up with a kind of coverage to address just that situation. It's called "second to die" coverage. Or a euphemistic term is "survivorship" life insurance. It kicks in only when the second spouse goes. And it's cheaper than buying two separate policies on two people. And it's also more forgiving in terms of accepting people who might not otherwise be insurable.

- To protect a beloved family home. Grandpa and Grandma have lived on an island in Maine for years—all the family comes in the summer. But when they're gone, if they have not thought ahead, the taxes on something that valuable might be so huge that it would not be feasible to keep the house. A life insurance policy to cover the costs involved can be purchased.

- To pay college expenses for children or grandchildren.

- To create a retirement fund. In this case, the policy's cash value would be tapped before the death of the policyholder. Most often used with variable life insurance, which provides a menu of mutual funds that will grow tax-free, this type of policy can allow the holder to draw money out tax-free as well.

- To replace a charitable gift. Using the proceeds from life insurance can make it possible for you leave money for your heirs while giving to your favorite charity during your lifetime.

- To equalize inheritances. You can arrange for the family business to pass to the child who has been active in the business, while providing an equivalent amount of cash to the siblings.

- Accelerated death benefits. Since 1997, a "terminally ill" policyholder may obtain the death benefits of his or her policy, tax-free. These benefits may be used to pay medical expenses, and help ease the burden on the family.

- To pay estate taxes. To relieve your heirs of the tax burden of inheriting your estate.

Knowing whether or not you need life insurance, and how much to buy if you do, is more of an art than a science. As with other important decisions, it pays to first get all the information you can, and then to trust your adviser, and, perhaps more important, your instinct.

A good insurance agent will sit down with you and ask you to think through what would happen if you died today, next year, in five years. And she can help you figure out how much insurance you ought to have. The whole field has changed in the past generation. It used to be that the family breadwinner would buy enough life insurance to provide for his family for life. But nowadays there are female breadwinners, second and third marriages, prenuptial agreements, and so on. You may want to provide for child care expenses, the children's education, and possibly the mortgage at a minimum.

The Types of Life Insurance

What you want life insurance to do for you and your family helps to determine the type of insurance that is best for you. There are two categories of life insurance: term and permanent.

With term insurance, you pay the insurance company a fixed amount of money, and when you die, money—the face value of your policy—will be paid to your beneficiary. Term insurance is just a simple death benefit. In other words, there is no cash value unless you die. There is no equity in the plan. If you do not die by the end of the specified period of time, or term, the coverage expires and you may choose to renew it, usually at a higher cost. Most people never collect on term insurance, since more than 90 percent of such policies lapse for nonpayment.

Many women in their twenties and thirties and sometimes in their forties will buy term insurance because it is the least expensive type of life insurance. Also, there is a pretty low probability if you are in your thirties that you are going to die soon.

Low probability equals low cost. Interestingly enough, only 1 percent of the insurance death claims are paid from term policies. Why? Premiums for term insurance are based on how old you are. And most people do not keep term insurance when they are in their eighties. It is too expensive.

Actually, the price you pay per year, or the premium, for all life insurance is based on age, but unlike other kinds of insurance, the premium for term insurance goes up every year. Or you might buy a term policy that has a level premium for ten years and then it skyrockets. Companies can be sneaky—the premiums can be something like $300 a year for ten years, then suddenly rise to $2,500 a year. So, what are you going to do then? Drop it? It is so important to read all the fine print before you buy.

Another kind of term insurance is group life. Group life is what your employer would provide.

What percentage of death benefits get paid from group policies? Again, around 1 percent. Why? Because you retire and the insurance goes poof. It is not with you when you are in your retirement years. Again, it is a very profitable business for the insurance companies, because usually not many people use it.

Permanent insurance differs from term in that it does not expire. As long as you keep paying your premiums, you keep the insurance for life. Permanent insurance also has cash value.

You can think of the difference between term and permanent insurance like this: with term, you are renting coverage. You pay a premium every year, and it rises every year, much like renting an apartment. Buying permanent insurance is like owning a home. You are building equity, as with a mortgage. You are issued a premium amount when you buy the policy, and it stays the same. Most planners would argue that for a lifetime plan it's better to own a house. Initially, it is more expensive, but the premium stays the same. Just as when you're paying a fixed-rate mortgage, a chunk of every payment you make goes to build up something that you own.

There are several types of permanent insurance policies.

Until about twenty-five years ago, whole life was the only type of permanent insurance you could buy. This type of policy builds cash value over time, during which the cash value earns tax-deferred interest. You pay a fixed-rate premium each year for your entire lifetime, or for as long as you choose to keep the policy. As long as the premiums are paid, the insurance company promises to pay a fixed amount of cash—the death benefit—to your heirs when you die.

With whole life, part of your premium is actu-ally sitting inside the insurance policy in a cash account. That money builds up slowly over the years, and is not taxed as it grows. That is a nice benefit of life insurance. And, eventually, if there is enough equity in the policy, you no longer have to pay the premium.

Whole life insurance is the most predictable. If you pay $2,000 a year, there is going to be about $20,000 in that policy in about ten years or so, plus the accumulated interest. The insurance company invests your premium dollars in United States Treasury bonds and high-grade corporate bonds.

There is another kind of permanent insurance that is a little more prevalent today: universal life insurance, which effectively is a term policy with a money-market account on the side. But the premiums still go up every year. And every month the company takes the cost of insurance out of the pot. If the premium for whole life is $2,000 and the premium for term is $300, then the premium for universal life is somewhere around $1,000: in the middle.

Variable life insurance allows the cash inside the life insurance policy to be used in a variety of investment options, primarily mutual funds.

If you have money in a certificate of deposit (CD), at the end of the year, you have to report on your income tax the interest that you earned on your CD. So if the CD is paying 6 percent and you earned $100, then you have to pay taxes on that $100. So you did not really earn 6 percent. You earned 6 percent minus the taxes. Life insurance is different. The "inside" cash that stays in the policy grows and earns interest, but doesn't have to be reported each year. The government does not keep track of it. So that the money, if it were earning 6 percent, really is earning 6—minus a few expenses. From a tax perspective, there are advantages: the money in the policy is tax-deferred and the death income benefit is tax-free. Variable life has become more popular than whole life because Americans are optimistic about the economy of the world.

If there is no money in the account, the insurance company does not pay the death benefit. It is not guaranteed. If you're interested in just getting the maximum permanent coverage for the minimum premium, then ordinary universal life probably is wisest for you.

Very often, an old whole life policy can be converted into a modern universal policy that does you a lot more good. For example, you may have held a whole life insurance policy for thirty years, with a death benefit of $20,000. You may be making an annual premium payment of $200 a year. You likely have something like $14,000 of cash value in there. That's your money. When you die, your family's going to get a check for $20,000. How much of that is real insurance? Consider taking the cash value and buying a new universal life policy, for two reasons. First of all because universal life is structured differently—it's structured to provide you with the maximum coverage, whereas whole life is not—and second, because mortality tables are much lower than they were thirty years ago. For the same premium and the money already in the policy, you can now have $120,000 in coverage.

If you decide to change your coverage, be sure to choose a reputable agent. There are insurance scams in which an unscrupulous agent tries to get you to sell all your whole life insurance policies and buy one new one, so she could get a big commission. This practice is called "churning" if done by a stockbroker. Very rarely does it make sense to give up a permanent insurance policy,

because you pay the cost in the early years. The commissions come out of the early years.

Most insurance agents are paid a proportion—usually more than 50 percent—of the first year's premium. Some less ethical agents, therefore, push the most expensive kind of coverage to boost their commissions.

When you do review your life insurance coverage, reexamine the purposes for which you need coverage. While everyone's needs are different, of course, if you plan to use life insurance to cover loss of income, as a rule of thumb, the wage earner should be insured for approximately eight times his or her earnings.

LONG-TERM-CARE INSURANCE

Many of us have insured our cars, our homes, our health and lives, but we face the future unprotected from one cost that easily could consume our life savings in a matter of months—long-term care.

"Long-term care" refers to a wide variety of health, personal care, and social services for those who are chronically ill or unable to care for themselves.

Some studies show that two or more out of every five people (43 percent) turning sixty-five will need extended home care or nursing home care at some point in their lives. The *New England Journal of Medicine* reports this number increases to more than 50 percent once an individual reaches seventy-five years of age. At an average cost of $47,000 per year in the United States, up to $75,000 per year in major Northeast and West Coast cities, and projected to triple in the next two decades, it is clear that a family's assets quickly can be depleted.

You may not yet be aware of long-term-care (LTC) coverage because it is relatively new, but it is becoming more and more common as the baby boomers hit the demographic curve. Long-term care is the fastest growing segment of the insurance industry. A long-term health care policy is coverage that will kick in with a stream of cash to help you pay bills, if you are ill for some time or need care for an extended period. Long-term care is not something that is covered under your normal health insurance. It is a separate kind of insurance and must be purchased separately.

To most people's surprise, Medicare does not cover extended care. A recent study showed that 81 percent of older people thought that Medicare covered everything. That is a potentially disastrous misconception because long-term care costs can be the biggest financial drain for older women.

Medicare does not cover long-term care beyond a maximum of twenty days, plus eighty days' secondary care, and it only covers *skilled* care following a three-day hospitalization. That means that home health care also is not covered by Medicare if you do not need a skilled nurse. As of this writing, twenty-four-hour-a-day home health care costs more than $100,000 per year. Most long-term care is of a custodial nature and except for private pay or welfare's Medicaid program, only LTC insurance will cover these expenses. Medicare pays for only a small fraction of nursing home costs and Medicaid pays for almost half.

To qualify for long-term-care Medicaid, an individual must spend down her assets to a near-bankruptcy level of $2,000. These countable or nonexempt assets include such items as cash, savings and checking accounts, stock, bonds, IRAs, Keoghs, 401(k)s, CDs, investment rental property, vacation home, second vehicles, whole life insurance with cash surrender value, above a certain amount, and deferred annuities under certain conditions.

Medicaid also may place a lien on your primary residence, making it doubtful that your home can be passed on to your heirs.

> *My grandma, who is in her nineties, fell and broke her hip while pruning the bushes in her yard in Ohio. She was not expected to return home from the nursing home, to which she was admitted after her hospital stay. Her home of sixty-five years and its contents were put on the auction block to pay back the lien Medicaid had placed on her property. The family went to the auction to bid on and try to buy back some of those irreplaceable family heirlooms, mostly of value only to the family.*

Instead of spending their life savings, an increasing number of people are choosing to purchase an LTC insurance policy that provides benefits for all levels of care, namely nursing home, extended home health care, assisted living, and adult day care. Some plans will even pay benefits to make necessary structural changes to your home—for example, widening doors, putting in ramps—and for making it possible for you to stay at home as long as possible—for instance, with a "lifeline" telephone device or caregiver training.

Levels of Long-Term Care

- *Skilled care.* Around-the-clock care provided by a licensed professional under a doctor's supervision.

- *Intermediate care.* Care provided by skilled medical staff, but not on a daily basis.

- *Custodial care* (also known as "non-skilled" care). Assistance with daily needs like eating, dressing, bathing, etc., which does not require skilled medical staff.

People of all ages up to age eighty-nine generally are eligible for LTC insurance. Because the policies are health underwritten and the premiums are age-related, it is advisable to consider coverage at an early age, prior to any serious health diagnosis.

In terms of lowest cost, most professionals suggest that the best time to buy LTC insurance is in your early fifties. As with life and disability insurance, most people do not want to address the issue of needing LTC insurance. So many put off thinking about it until they are in their mid-sixties or early seventies. LTC insurance is much more liberal than disability insurance in terms of how you qualify. A mobility problem, Alzheimer's or other cognitive impairment, and certain other medical conditions would make you ineligible, but most other stable health conditions would be covered. If you are diagnosed with one of these illnesses once you have a policy, you would be covered.

How much does it cost? Well, of course it depends on your age, your health, where you live, and the variables that you choose: how long you wish to wait—between zero and a hundred days—and lean on your savings before it kicks in, whether you want $50, $75, $125, or up to $300 a day, whether you want the benefits to pay for three years or five years or for your lifetime, whether you want inflation protection. As of this writing, the annual LTC premium for a woman in her seventies might be $3,000.

My mother, who is seventy-one years old and living in San Antonio, pays $2,800 a year for a policy that will give her a benefit of $125 a day if she had to go into a nursing home or $75 a day for a visiting nurse. In the Northeast and in larger cities, the cost could be a lot more, and her estate would be more at risk.

It's a very good idea to coordinate your long-term health care insurance with estate planning (see chapter 8).

Some states have strict regulations about LTC insurance, regarding preexisting conditions, refunds for changes of mind, underwriting, and replacing one policy with another, to name a few. So the days of the fly-by-night policy are gone. Many planners feel that LTC is an important type of coverage you should at least consider, for your parents and for yourself, especially since statistics show that the average distance between caregivers and parents is 100 miles.

Others have quite a different idea about long-term-care insurance, pointing to some of the drawbacks.

For example, there is no guarantee that insurance companies cannot raise the premium in the future. For some women, the major consideration is one of lifestyle: if the premiums are just too high for their budget, and they would have to sacrifice food or other necessities to meet the payments, then long-term care insurance may not make sense. Others know that nursing home care is not an option for them:

I have a big house—too much room for just me. I'm thinking of organizing a collective house, you know, back to the commune, mixed ages. I'm not going to live in a nursing home, no matter what. I plan to stay right here 'til I die.

My uncle had been reclusive all his life—really liked his privacy. He was profoundly deaf, and did okay on his own until his heart attack. He was put into a nursing home and at first had a private room, which suited him just fine. Then he ran out of money and the government of course wouldn't pay for a private room. I know it was having to share that small room that finally did him in. I'm the same way. A nursing home is just not for me.

Some companies offer stand-alone home health policies at a much lower cost. These do not cover nursing home costs, but will cover someone to come in and help care for you at home. Seventy-five percent of all nursing home residents are women. And of the 7 million caregivers in this country, more than two-thirds are not professional caregivers, but rather women who are juggling careers, obtain a leave of absence, or take early retirement in order to provide care for an elderly relative.

At what point should you consider LTC insurance for yourself or for your parents?

I would say sixty is a magic age. My husband just turned sixty and right before his birthday I thought, "Oh my gosh! We better look at this for you because

the premiums start to go up significantly when you hit sixty." So we found a great policy for him at age fifty-nine and we signed it the day before his birthday. And then because I'm such a young thing— I'm only fifty-three—I could sign on too at a much lower rate. I got a 10 percent discount for being his spouse!

When thinking about purchasing an LTC policy, definitely shop around, and definitely talk to a professional. And be careful! Typically, group policies are not as strictly regulated as individual policies.

For example, a large and reputable association offers a policy to its members. Many women innocently assume that this must be the best policy precisely because the organization is large and reputable. But the policy is not clear as to whether or not it covers Alzheimer's disease. Well, half the people in long-term-care facilities have Alzheimer's. So, do you want to buy a policy that isn't clear about something so important?

"Preferred health" discounts also are available for those in exceedingly good health.

MOST COMMON REASONS GIVEN BY THOSE BUYING LTC INSURANCE

"So I can preserve my financial independence and avoid having to rely on others." (69 percent)

"To protect my assets." (67 percent)

"To be able to afford the health care I need." (66 percent)

"To ensure adequate income if my spouse dies first." (59 percent)

"Because the government will not take care of me." (54 percent)

"Freedom to choose from where and when I get my health care." (50 percent)

"So I don't have to depend on Medicaid." (50 percent)[4]

What to Look for in a Good Long-Term-Care Plan

The trauma of long-term care is hard enough. A good plan will not require prior hospitalization and should cover preexisting conditions such as Alzheimer's and Parkinson's disease.

Make sure the plan is "qualified," allowing for federal tax benefits and other recent government incentives. The plans should pay for home health care and assisted living, not just care in a nursing home. Inflation riders should be offered and carefully considered prior to age seventy. Many people are living well into their nineties and even longer. Who knows what medical science has in store?

Check to see what services are covered: skilled care (daily nursing and rehabilitation under supervision of skilled medical providers, i.e., registered nurses and doctors), intermediate care (the same, except that you require only occasional nursing care), custodial care (help with daily activities), home health care? How much does the policy pay each day/week/month for each type of care you select? For how long will the benefits last, and what is the maximum lifetime benefit?

Do you want stand-by care—someone who comes in and helps you only when you need help—or hands-on care—someone who helps you all the time?

Must you wait before preexisting conditions are covered? Does the policy require a doctor's certification of need? Is the policy guaranteed to be renewable? What is the age range for coverage? How much does it cost? Will the company waive the premium if you have been in a nursing home for a certain number of days?

Long-term-care insurance may or may not be right for you. If you do need long-term care, but

could be at home, who will provide that care? Do you and your children or spouse have different expectations for your old age? We suggest that you talk about these issues with your family and loved ones. Planning for the future—even for a less-than-optimal future—gives you a measure of control over your life, and helps you to grow older with dignity and confidence.

AUTOMOBILE INSURANCE

The same night I was at the Financial Literacy Project class learning about auto insurance, my husband and daughter were in a car accident which left our vehicle wrecked. I immediately took charge. Even though my husband and daughter looked okay, I got them appointments for X rays and doctors' visits right away. We had to rent a car to get to the appointments. Without the class, I would have been unaware that we were even entitled to a rental free of charge. I suppose we would have found out all eventually, but I was newly informed and able to get the job done efficiently. We had a rental for more than a month, until we settled the claim with the insurance company—and paid not a penny!

I was rear-ended by a drunk driver. He was going sixty-five, so my car really flew through the air, which is why I have this back condition. He was a deadbeat. He had only the minimum coverage required by law. This time I was smart—I had bought the rider on my insurance policy which says that if you're hit by an underinsured driver, then you turn to your own company and they will make up the difference up to $100,000. And I had to fight for that too and produce stacks and stacks of records.

If you own or drive a car, you need some form of auto insurance. What kind of insurance and how much you need may be mandated by state law. Like other forms of insurance, auto insurance can protect you against catastrophe or even minor damage. Car owners must carry a minimum level of liability insurance, which varies depending on where you live. In states without mandatory auto insurance requirements, uninsured drivers must prove that they can pay the minimum required by their state.

Your auto insurance policy covers you, the particular car, and other "insureds," who include your spouse and other family members living in your household. An "insured" also may be anyone to whom you, the owner, gives permission to use the car, as limited by coverages.

Auto insurance can be expensive, and premiums are continually rising. More expensive cars (making them more expensive to repair), an increase in accident-related medical bills, a greater prevalence of auto theft, and a greater number of claims with a greater number of cars being declared a total loss—all these factors contribute to ever-higher costs.

In addition, many individuals and consumer advocate groups such as the Consumers Union, as well as insurance companies, believe that a major factor contributing to high auto insurance premiums is the system that assigns blame to one or more parties to an accident. Used in most states, the "fault" system means that an individual can be held responsible in a court of law for damages. In contrast, a "no-fault" system limits the liability of the person who caused the accident. The no-fault system tends to reduce the number of smaller lawsuits and speeds up the investigation process, both of which cost insurance companies time and money. But the jury is still out: in states that have or that have tried no-fault, there is no clear evidence as to whether or not premiums have been lowered.

Today, there are approximately six thousand insurance companies in the United States. The insurance business is one of our most powerful industries, generating premiums well in excess of $406 billion per year.

All insurance companies have both good points and bad. It is very important that you choose an independent insurance agent who is familiar with both you and the many different companies, so that she can help you select the company that offers the best coverage for you. A good agent also will help you to better understand and influence the "gray areas" of interpreting your policy.

Understand that your auto insurance should change over the years. You need a policy tailored to what you need *right now,* so don't just keep renewing the same policy without reviewing it yearly.

Auto insurance costs vary widely. How much you pay for coverage depends on many variables, the most important of which are where you live, the number of years you have been driving, and the model of car you drive:

- *Territory.* The neighborhood or area in which you live. Since most accidents happen close to home, rates for a particular territory are based on the number of claims within that territory, as well as on the town's theft rates.

- *Your age and gender.* Those who have been driving fewer than six years or who are older than sixty-five tend to be involved in more accidents, and so can expect to pay a higher premium.

Younger unmarried men are involved in a greater number of accidents, so in some states, premiums are higher for those in this group.

- *Use of automobile.* The fewer the miles driven annually, the lower the premium. If you use your car primarily for personal, rather than business, use, your premium probably will be lower.

- *Make and model of car.* The safer the car, the lower the premium. Cars that are more expensive to purchase and to repair tend to be subject to a higher premium. The same is true of new cars as opposed to used cars.

- *Your driving record.* If you are a careful driver with an accident-free record, you will pay a lower premium. Drivers with violations, such as speeding, drunk driving, driving to endanger, running red lights, or even driving with an expired state inspection sticker, can expect to pay a higher premium.

- *Type of coverage.* If you choose a higher deductible, you will pay a lower premium. The more liability coverage you buy, the greater your overall cost. You also may select certain optional coverages that will increase your premium.

Costs vary widely by location and by company. It is so important to shop around and to find the best deal. A good insurance agent can help you find the coverage that is right for your driving style and your budget. You may qualify for a number of different types of discounts offered by insurance companies. Among the common discounts given are for completing a driver's education training program, insuring more than one car with the same company, buying both auto and homeowner's insurance from the same company, installing antitheft devices, honor roll or dean's list discounts for good students, and mature driver discounts for drivers older than fifty, fifty-five, or sixty-five, depending on your state.

There are different coverages available. Some are mandatory and others are optional, depending on the state in which you live. Again, a good agent can guide you to finding the coverage best for you. The type of coverages include:

- *Bodily injury liability.* Pays claims against you and the cost of your legal defense if your car injures someone.

- *Property damage liability.* Pays claims and legal costs for damage to the property of others caused by your car.

- *Medical payments.* Pays medical expenses resulting from accidental injuries for you and the passengers in your car. This is good coverage to have if you often

Each year, there are approximately 30 million auto accidents in the United States—one for every five licensed drivers—resulting in a cost of nearly $100 billion in medical expenses, emergency services, property damage, legal and court costs, lost productivity, public assistance programs, and insurance administration expenses.

have people in and out of your car—if you drive a carpool, are a Scout leader, etc.

- *Personal injury protection (PIP).* In states that have a "no-fault" system, PIP covers your medical expenses up to a fixed limit.

- *Uninsured or underinsured motorists.* Pays for damages caused by drivers who have insufficient or no coverage, or by hit-and-run drivers.

- *Towing/labor.* If you get a flat tire or run out of gas. If you have purchased collision coverage, the tow resulting from a collision is reimbursed under collision. The same is true for a tow resulting from comprehensive damage.

- *Substitute transportation.* Covers cost of rental car, if your car has a covered loss. Common choices are $15/day, $30/day, or $100/day. Insurance from the other party to the accident will pay for rentals only if they are legally liable for the damage.

- *Collision.* Pays for damage to your car resulting from a collision, up to the actual cash value of your car, subject to the deductible clause.

- *Comprehensive.* Pays for damages to your car if it is damaged by fire, flood, vandals, animal collision, or if it is stolen. Glass loss is included under this coverage.

You may purchase collision and comprehensive coverage with a deductible. That means you

agree to pay a certain dollar amount—$300 or $500, for example—of any claim before the insurance company pays the balance. By avoiding most very small claims, the company saves money and premiums are lower. In addition, you should buy a policy with a waiver. A waiver is an inexpensive addition to your coverage that enables you to avoid waiting for reimbursement, when you are not at fault, and you know who is at fault.

It's so important to be covered at the upper levels. But there's a chance to stretch your insurance dollars by saying, "I'll fix dents myself." In other words, can you live with a $500 deductible in exchange for a much lower premium?

I have a daughter who's a sophomore in college, and she likes to drive the car when she's home. Extraordinarily expensive! Well, I found out that there are a few companies that allow you to put your student on and off as he or she comes home from college, and then goes back to college, rather than have them listed as a year-round driver. That has saved us hundreds of dollars each year.

There are many other ways to save money on your insurance premiums. As with other types of coverage, it pays to shop around. Some insurance companies will do direct writing. They offer big discounts to consumers because they aren't paying agents a commission. However, the drawbacks of not having an agent, who will advocate and explain and help you through all insurance procedures, may not outweigh the benefits of saving money.

HOMEOWNER'S INSURANCE

Homeowner's—or renter's—insurance covers your home and the property in your home in case of fire, theft, damage, lightning, falling trees, and other disasters, and helps to pay for injuries to those on your property or to those caused by members of your household. Unless you easily can afford to replace your home and its contents, it is a good idea to have some protection against loss. If you rent, you still may want to have insurance on your personal property. If you hold a mortgage on your home, the lender will require that you purchase insurance.

Compared to auto insurance, premiums for homeowner's insurance remain quite stable over time. This is due to a number of factors, most obviously that there are far more auto accidents and so chances are greater that a claim will be made against an auto insurance policy than against a homeowner's. Also, liability claims are much more common for cars. Like auto insurance, homeowner's insurance is based on where your home is located. If you live in an area where there is high crime, or in a tornado zone, your premiums will be higher. The distance from your local fire department, and even from the nearest fire hydrant, also may be factors.

For the insurance companies, homeowner's insurance is very profitable, so it pays to shop around. You may wish to buy from the same company as your auto insurance, as you might qualify for a discount on both types of coverage. Other ways to save on homeowner's insurance are to install smoke detectors or burglar alarms, to build the house with fire-resistant materials, and to ensure that all occupants are nonsmokers.

Several years ago, my husband and I bought a wonderful old farmhouse in the country. And four years ago we loaned it to some people who were down on their luck. Just a couple of days before we gave them the keys, my husband said, "You know, I wonder if we ought to look at our insurance some more, update it?" So sure enough we looked at it and it was way out-of-date. So we bought an up-to-the-minute policy. Now, we didn't realize quite how poor these people were, and they made the decision not to use the furnace in the winter but to stuff the fireplace nonstop with pine logs. Well, they are all right—they just barely made it out with their lives—but our house went up in flames. And we had to go to the company and say, "Okay, folks, pay up." Needless to say, we were not their favorite customers. It took a little while, and really took some knowledge about how insurance companies work, to make them do their duty, but they did and we now have a gorgeous new house in New Hampshire. My point is: Make sure you have the replacement cost, because otherwise the insurance company is going to pay you for what a second-hand depreciated house would be worth. And replacement cost means, "If I had to build again from scratch, what would it cost today?"

A homeowner's policy consists of two parts: property protection and liability coverage. Protection of property includes: the dwelling, other structures on the property, personal property, loss of use, and miscellaneous coverages. Liability coverage includes bodily injury or property damage, such as a neighbor's tree smashing your garage roof. Homeowner's insurance generally covers any loss or disaster, with the exception of flood or earthquake. Mud slides and riots may not be included. Perils commonly included are fire, lightning, windstorm, hail, ice and snow, explosion, falling objects, window breakage, smoke damage, a car or aircraft crashing onto or into your property (home, pool, lawn), accidental damage to household systems, such as electrical and plumbing systems, and vandalism and theft.

Lloyd's of London, dating back to the seventeenth century, is thought to be at the root of our modern-day insurance system. But rather than an insurance company, it was actually a coffeehouse at the dock where investors (known as underwriters) and merchants met to negotiate insurance protection for shipping cargo across the seas. Around the same time, in 1667, fire insurance was established in London after a major fire the year before left hundreds of thousands of people homeless and destroyed almost fifteen hundred buildings.

The first fire insurance company in the United States was the Friendly Society for the Mutual Insurance of Houses Against Fire, created in 1734. They based insurance rates on the construction of the building and developed a risk classification system. Early fire insurance policies varied from state to state and company to company. These discrepancies led to numerous consumer complaints and court cases that ultimately resulted in a uniform fire insurance policy: the 165-line New York fire policy of 1943. It was the only insurance policy to become standardized by law and was the foundation for all future property insurance coverage.[5]

The most common kinds of coverage are:

Dwelling coverage. To determine a sufficient amount of coverage, ask yourself, "How much would it cost to replace the home today?"

Liability insurance protects you against lawsuits arising from things that happen to others on your property. You likely will want enough insurance to cover your assets—two times your assets is better.

Personal property coverage. This amount is calculated from the amount of dwelling coverage. Usually, this figure is 50 to 75 percent of the dwelling coverage. In order to be able to document your property, you will need to list every item you own, the original purchase price, its condition, and the date of purchase. For special valuables, you can add a floater to your policy.

For personal property coverage, you can get jewelry appraised. Most reputable jewelers will do that for you. Sometimes they charge you 10 per-

cent of the value of the item. So if you have a really expensive item, it would cost you a lot of money just to have the appraisal done. In that case, you might be better off keeping the item in your safe deposit box. Some jewelers will give you a discount if you bring in a number of items at once. But if you bring in just one ring, and the value of the ring is $2,000, they may charge you $200.

Another thing you can do yourself for much less cost is to rent or borrow a video camera and go around the house taking pictures of all your valuables. You can describe them as you go, state if they are family pieces, and when and where you got them.

I wish I'd had a floater on my personal property coverage. I lost all my grandmother's jewelry when our house was robbed. Since I had never taken the time to itemize it, all the insurance company gave me was a check for twenty-five hundred dollars. I'm sure it was worth more than ten times that amount. But how do you get a floater if you don't have receipts for things, like old jewelry?

You also can keep records on your computer. But be sure to make a backup copy and take it to a trusted neighbor, to a family member or friend, or to your safe deposit box. If the backup is sitting right next to the computer that burns, you'll lose the backup.

The best advice about homeowner's insurance is to update it regularly. Review it every year, when you review your investments and your goals.

Excess liability insurance. Even if you have good homeowner's and good auto insurance coverage, you still should consider buying excess liability coverage. In other words, if you hurt someone else or someone thinks you've hurt him, he is likely to sue, so regular policies do include some coverage. But it's well worth supplementing that coverage with what is called an "umbrella" policy. It costs only about $150 a year, and basically protects you against being sued if, for example, your mailman steps on a roller skate. It wouldn't cost you much to be insured for $1 million. So in today's legal climate, it makes sense to consider this relatively low-cost coverage.

Other kinds of insurance. There seems to be insurance for every conceivable type of loss. If you're worried about it, chances are some insurance company is willing to cover your risk—for a price! Some of the other common—and less common—kinds of insurance include: pet health insurance, cancer insurance, life insurance for children, child support insurance to cover loss of income of the one who is making the payments, adoption insurance against the birth mother changing her mind, travel insurance, car rental insurance, credit card insurance, mortgage life insurance, safe deposit box insurance, wedding insurance (to cover nonrefundable deposits on hotel, caterer, and band, for example), and even theater ticket insurance!

It may help to think of insurance—to cover your income, property, and potential expenses or losses—as similar to the foundation of a building. Good insurance, properly chosen and reviewed on a regular basis, can keep your whole financial plan from crumbling.

7: Making Money Work for You

Contributing Author:

Karin Hedberg

"When's the best time to start investing? Yesterday. When's the second best time? Today."
—CLAIRE JOSEPHS HOUSTON, DIRECTOR,
WOMEN SUPPORTING WOMEN CENTER, EXETER, NEW HAMPSHIRE

IN THIS CHAPTER, YOU WILL LEARN:

- Why you should invest

- How compounding can increase your money

- How to determine your investment style

- The types of investments

- Managing risk

- How to choose and use a financial professional

So far, you are tracking your spending and expenses and have begun to save some money every month. You have protected yourself against loss or disaster by choosing the proper insurance. You have set your goals. You have made a plan to achieve those goals.

As you read in chapter 2, each of your important goals has a cost in terms of time, resources, and money. Perhaps you can save enough cash for your shorter-term goals, like a new coat or a vacation next winter. But how can you plan to reach your long-term goals? Saving money in a bank is one option, but banks generally pay a fairly low interest rate, that is, the money the bank pays you for the use of your money over time.

By investing in stocks, bonds, mutual funds, or other investment vehicles, you often can earn a much greater return, or yield, on your money.

Many people—men and women—feel intimidated by the idea of investing. Investing has a whole language of its own; terms we hear daily, but may not understand: "Dow Jones Industrial Average," " 'bull' or 'bear' market," "Wall Street," "NASDAQ."

It may be helpful to understand that investing is simply putting out energy—in this case, "green energy" or money—with the hope of getting more or something better in return.

We all make investments all the time. Women, especially, tend to put a lot into relationships. We may spend a huge amount of effort making our home warm and wonderful. We may delight in the time we set aside to work in the garden, for example, or on a favorite hobby or other creative pursuit. We invest energy in our children, our pets, our jobs, and in taking care of our health. We choose carefully, so that we are putting our limited resources into things that will bring us pleasure—in other words, into things that will pay off, not necessarily in dollars and cents! Whether we are putting in time, energy, effort, or love, both risk and reward are involved. Investing our money is not very different—it's just moving the same know-how into a different arena.

When should you begin to invest? Many financial advisers recommend that you first should have enough money to cover three to six months' living expenses, set aside in an interest-earning savings account or other safe but accessible place, in case of emergency or temporary disability.

Many women find it hard to accumulate that much cash. As with other projects, this may be easier to accomplish if you break it down into small steps. A good initial goal might be to save one month's expenses, then to increase your savings until you have two months' expenses set aside, and so on. When you have three months' expenses saved, you may feel that you can afford to begin to take some investment risks with your money. Even when you start investing, you should continue to add to your savings. Investing and saving are just ways to build wealth by different means.

The easiest and safest way to earn high interest on your money is to pay off all your credit card debt.

My financial planner told me it was not a good idea to put money into a savings account until I had paid off my high-interest credit cards. Emotionally, I found that very hard to accept. I didn't want to be without any savings. But she helped me to understand that by owing 18 percent interest on the outstanding debt, and earning only 3 percent interest on the savings, I was actually losing money!

WHY INVEST?

Why should you invest? Why do you need anything more than a checking and savings account at the bank?

The three most common investment objectives are to keep what you already have, to earn income, and to increase your wealth. As you read on, you will learn that certain investments can offer protection against inflation, while some are beneficial in reducing your income tax burden.

There also are reasons to invest that are not strictly financial. As you have read, and will read further in chapter 10, how you spend, donate, or invest your money can reflect your core values. Perhaps you work for a company, and want to invest in that company. Or you may feel strongly positive about your nation and/or about the capitalist system. You may want to own shares in a particular company whose products or services you like, or you may wish to help your city or town pay for a new school or for new road construction. Investment vehicles are available to address these kinds of goals.

But perhaps the most compelling reason to invest is compounding.

And the sooner you can start investing, the more money you are likely to make.

COMPOUNDING

Compounding is a seemingly miraculous way to build your money. With any interest-bearing account, your money earns some interest. With the right investment vehicle, both interest and appreciation is added to your original investment, the principal, so you also are earning interest on your interest. This total becomes your new principal, or basis, upon which you earn interest during the next term. This process is repeated each period your money remains invested. This mathematical wonder is called compounding. And the total can build fast!

For example, if you were to start at age eigh-teen and save $2,000 a year for just five or six years in a tax-deferred account, the yield will be many times more than starting thereafter and saving $2,000 every year until age sixty-five (see chart).

TIME IS ON YOUR SIDE: THE AMAZING POWER OF COMPOUNDING INTEREST AND TAX DEFERRAL

	Investor A		Investor B			Investor A		Investor B	
Age	Year-end Contribution	Year-end Value	Year-end Contribution	Year-end Value	Age	Year-end Contribution	Year-end Value	Year-end Contribution	Year-end Value
18	$2,000	$2,200	$0	$0	44	$0	$153,870	$2,000	$126,005
19	2,000	4,620	0	0	45	0	169,257	2,000	140,805
20	2,000	7,282	0	0	46	0	186,183	2,000	157,086
21	2,000	10,210	0	0	47	0	204,801	2,000	174,995
22	2,000	13,431	0	0	48	0	225,281	2,000	194,694
23	2,000	16,974	0	0	49	0	247,809	2,000	216,364
24	2,000	20,872	0	0	50	0	272,590	2,000	240,200
25	2,000	25,159	2,000	2,200	51	0	299,849	2,000	266,420
26	0	27,675	2,000	4,620	52	0	329,834	2,000	295,262
27	0	30,442	2,000	7,282	53	0	362,817	2,000	326,988
28	0	33,487	2,000	10,210	54	0	399,099	2,000	361,887
29	0	36,835	2,000	13,431	55	0	439,009	2,000	400,276
30	0	40,519	2,000	16,974	56	0	482,910	2,000	442,503
31	0	44,571	2,000	20,872	57	0	531,201	2,000	488,953
32	0	49,028	2,000	25,159	58	0	584,321	2,000	540,049
33	0	53,930	2,000	29,875	59	0	642,753	2,000	596,254
34	0	59,323	2,000	35,062	60	0	707,028	2,000	658,079
35	0	65,256	2,000	40,769	61	0	777,731	2,000	726,087
36	0	71,781	2,000	47,045	62	0	855,504	2,000	800,896
37	0	78,960	2,000	53,950	63	0	941,054	2,000	883,185
38	0	86,856	2,000	61,545	64	0	1,035,160	2,000	973,704
39	0	95,541	2,000	69,899	Less total invested:		(16,000)		(80,000)
40	0	105,095	2,000	79,089	Equals net earnings:		$1,019,160		$893,704
41	0	115,605	2,000	89,198	Money grew:		64-fold*		11-fold*
42	0	127,165	2,000	100,318	*Assuming a 10% rate of return, and that no tax is paid on				
43	0	139,882	2,000	112,550	accumulated interest.				

THE RULE OF 72

At what point will your money double? To find out, you can use what's known as the "Rule of 72." The Rule of 72 works like this: 72 divided by the rate of return equals the time in years for your money to double. For instance, 72 divided by a 10 percent rate of return means your money will double in 7.2 years. The Rule of 72 shows the importance of your rate of return. The higher the rate of return, the quicker your money will double. If you were earning only 3 percent, then it would take twenty-four years to double your money. And if you are lucky enough to find an investment with a twenty-four percent rate of return, you would double your money in just three years.

FINDING YOUR PERSONAL INVESTING STYLE

As with the way you dress, decorate your home, or choose a new car, investing can be a reflection of your personal style. Are you a risk taker or are you more cautious? Do you want to spend a lot of time managing your investments, or would you rather have someone else do it for you? How much time do you have? That is, can you afford to invest your money and leave it alone for ten years? For twenty years? Or will you need the money sooner to pay for college, or to start a new business? How can your investments reflect your important values?

It is important to think about these questions *before* you begin investing, so you can pick the investments best suited to your needs and financial goals. Keep in mind, however, that your investment style can and likely will change as your goals and your needs change. But just as you have determined your net worth as a starting point for financial planning, gaining an understanding of

your investment style, or comfort level, is a good place to begin.

Investments can be sorted in a number of ways, which reflect the questions above. They can be described by type, by amount of risk involved, or by whether "active" or "passive"—that is, whether the investor herself or a mutual fund manager investigates and purchases securities, or whether investments are purchased according to a predetermined "index." As you read, think about which investments may be right for you.

TYPES OF INVESTMENTS

We asked our students, "What do you think makes a perfect investment?" They answered:

It would have to be safe.

Has a high return—it earns a lot of money for you.

Predictable return with guaranteed growth.

Tax-free and no penalty for withdrawal.

You can get at it when you want to, meaning it's liquid.

No special education required—anyone can do it.

So the "perfect investment" would be low risk, high yield, tax-free, liquid, and you wouldn't need any skill or knowledge to make the investment. Of course, such an investment does not exist. But you can explore ways to make your investments suitable for your goals.

"Liquid" means the ability to convert the asset to cash. You can gain access to the money in your savings or checking account by making a bank or ATM withdrawal or by writing a check. A U.S. savings bond can be redeemed in a few minutes. Real estate and collectibles are much less liquid, as each could take some time to sell.

The most common investments are described below, roughly in order of safest to most risky. The general rule of thumb is: the safer the investment, the less you are likely to earn from it.

Cookie jar/piggy bank

Your cash is exactly where you put it, and when you open the bank, you will have the exact amount you put in. However, the actual value of cash not invested elsewhere decreases over time due to inflation.

Bank

Savings account, certificate of deposit (CD), money market.

Savings and checking accounts

Money is safe and insured by the federal government, up to certain limits. Some accounts may have a small interest rate, usually not enough to keep pace with inflation. Highly liquid, however, these are good vehicles for monthly living expenses and short-term savings.

Certificates of deposit (CDs)

Cash you loan to the bank for a specified period of time: often six months, twelve months, eighteen months, twenty-four months, up to five years. Usually, the longer the term of the CD, the higher the interest rate, with shorter-term CDs just earning the rate of inflation. To encourage you to keep your money in the certificate for the full term, banks may impose a penalty for early withdrawal. This penalty often is one month's interest, sometimes more. With a few exceptions,

---

"Inflation" means a movement toward higher prices. Correspondingly, the value of your money decreases. For example, in a year in which the inflation rate is 3.5 percent, you may spend $10.35 to buy what cost just $10 last year. If you keep your money in a cookie jar, it will lose buying power, or value, over periods of inflation. With just a bit more arithmetic, you see that a 5 percent rate of return on, for example, a bank CD is really yielding only 1.5 percent return of value (5 percent paid minus the 3.5 percent rate of inflation). This rate, minus the income tax you would have to pay on the interest earned, is the "real rate of return" and is what you actually earn on your money.

---

the penalty will not decrease your original investment.

Money market fund

Offered by a bank or brokerage, a money market is a type of mutual fund. Generally, money market funds are invested in safe, short-term securities. They are highly liquid, and usually are very stable—that is, the share price will not fluctuate. Money markets or CDs may be a good choice for your emergency savings, perhaps three of your six months' set-aside living expenses.

U.S. savings bonds, U.S. Treasury securities

U.S. savings bonds are available from banks and from the U.S. Treasury. The minimum investment is $25. U.S. Treasury securities ("T-bonds," "T-notes," and "T-bills"), available through banks, brokerages, and financial institutions, are issued by the United States and offer moderate income with the lowest risk.

Your home and other real estate

Your home has value on so many levels: shelter, of course, plus property rights. As a financial asset, your home offers significant tax advantages and potential for appreciation. Your home is also considered a safe, low-risk investment. Real estate investments other than your home are considered very risky. Second homes, rental property, commercial buildings, and raw land all are considered speculative, with potential for high profits and some tax advantages. In addition to the issue of investment safety, these properties require specialized knowledge and management skills.

IRAs, 401(k)s, and pension plans

IRA stands for individual retirement account and is offered by banks, brokerages, and financial institutions. There usually is an annual fee, ranging from $25 to $50, to service your account. There are several kinds of IRAs: the traditional IRA, the Roth IRA, and the education IRA. IRAs, 401(k) plans, and pension plans offer planned saving and investment programs for retirement. Earnings on qualified plans may be tax-deferred until withdrawal. Each of these programs has its specific rules and requirements with penalties imposed for withdrawal before the age requirements. These retirement plans, described further in the next chapter, offer the flexibility to invest in stocks and mutual funds. The safety and growth potential are based on your investment choices.

Life insurance

As you read in the last chapter, some types of life insurance, notably whole life and universal life, have an investment value. The company will pay you a calculated interest rate based on the underlying investments of the company, and, if you get what is called a "variable rate," you literally can take the cash value of your life insurance policy and invest it in mutual funds. With a cash value, you may borrow or take withdrawals, which, unless replaced, will reduce your death benefit. And you also may make loans to

---

"Securities" are any type of investment that is secured by assets. Examples of securities are stocks, bonds, CDs, and mutual funds.

yourself against the cash value of your life insurance.

Annuities

Available through banks, brokerages, and insurance companies, an annuity is a popular retirement savings plan with a defined payout schedule that begins at a predetermined date, usually at retirement. Like an IRA, interest and earnings accumulate tax-deferred. As with life insurance, proceeds avoid probate upon the owner's death and partial withdrawals of cash value are allowable. Unlike IRAs, annuities have no age requirement to begin taking withdrawals and usually offer several retirement payout options.

Bonds

When you buy a bond, you are loaning money to the government or to a corporation, which pays you interest on your money. Two rating services, Standard & Poor's and Moody's, rate the potential safety of bonds by designating each a letter grade, from triple A (safest) down to C (riskiest). There are several different kinds of bonds, with three main types.

Municipal bonds

Your city or state puts together a project, for example, a new high school or a new highway. It will "put up" a bond to attract investors, or, for example, may construct a toll booth with the money collected going to the new road. If you are a resident of the municipality offering the bonds, you will get a tax break for investing in those bonds. If your town of residence "floats" (offers for sale) a bond because it wants to build a new school, and you invest, then your investment will be tax-exempt from federal, state, and local taxes. Municipal bonds are a good way to get tax-free earnings, important to those individuals in a very high tax bracket.

Government bonds

Federal government bonds are the most stable, as they have the backing of the federal government. Although subject to federal tax, they are exempt from state and local taxes.

Corporate bonds

With corporate bonds, you are loaning money to a company, which will pay you a specified amount of interest on that investment. If something negative happens to the company, bondholders would get paid before common stockholders. Corporate bonds are taxed at the federal, state, and local levels.

Stock

Whereas a bond represents "loanership," common stock represents "ownership" in a company. When you buy stock in a company, you actually own a piece of the company and share in its growth and profitability, as well as in its loss and hardships. Some common stocks pay a dividend to the shareholders, which is a portion of the corporate profits. Some stocks do not pay a dividend and your investment grows as the stock price appreciates. Over the long term, stocks probably are the best investment you can make. Stocks generally increase in value. And, as far back as records have been kept, on average, stocks have outperformed all other types of investments. But you will need to have the patience to leave your money invested in stocks for a number of years—maybe twenty years or longer. When considering purchase of stock, you may wish to look at whether the company makes products or delivers

> **The rate of return equals today's value of your investment less the dollar amount you invested at the beginning, divided by the total dollars you invested. So if today's value is $2,000 and you had invested $1,500, that would be $500/$1,500, or a 33⅓ percent rate of return. Say you invested a certain amount of money initially, and now are adding to it regularly. How do you figure out the rate of return?**
>
> **Take the value today minus the total amount invested, then divide it by the total amount invested, giving you the rate of return over time. Divide that by the number of years you've invested, and you will find the average annual rate of return.**

services that you and your family enjoy and use regularly, as well as just at the stock's rate of return.

The rate of return for your stocks is listed in some newspapers, such as *The Wall Street Journal.* Or if you get a *Standard & Poor's Report,* available at any public library, you will get much information about the stock itself, as well as the "earnings" or rate of return. *ValueLine,* also available at the library, is another recognized source of stock information.

Mutual funds

Mutual funds are useful for people who want to own stocks, but want someone else to do their stock picking for them. Investing in a mutual fund is buying a share of a group of investments. You are not directly investing in one company, but you are reaping the larger benefits of sharing the investment in many companies. Usually, there is less risk involved than with buying only one stock. More about mutual funds later in this chapter.

Higher-risk investments

Precious metals, fuels, commodities, collectibles, futures, options. Values of silver, gold, commodities, and collectibles can rise and fall sharply due to inflation and economic instability. Futures and options are investment strategies that require specialized training and are considered the riskiest investment types.

TYPES OF INVESTMENT RISKS

Each type of investment described above is subject to one or more common risks. They are:

Inflation risk

You want to make sure that your investments earn more than the rate of inflation. If your investments can't keep up with inflation, your investment will lose its future value and its spending power.

Interest rate risk

Some investments are interest-rate sensitive. Bonds are particularly sensitive to interest risk. When the interest rates go up, the bond prices go down. When the interest rate lowers, the bond prices will go up.

Economic risk

Some companies and industries will be more sensitive to changes in the economy. For example, in a healthy economy, people will buy more cars and builders will build more houses, but when the economy slows down, so do the sales, which affects a company's bottom line and the value of its stock.

Market risk

When investing in the stock market, you want to look for a company that is healthy, and hope for a good return on your investment. But general downward movements in the market will pull down stocks of many companies, whether or not each is a fundamentally strong company. So how other stocks in the market are doing will affect your stock.

Specific risk

When a company goes bankrupt, or there is a disaster—for example, a company's product or actions cause loss of life—the price of its stock is very likely to go down.

Legislative risk

When the government changes the rules regarding taxation or regulation of investment strategies that adversely affect the outcome of the investment. For example, in the 1980s and 1990s, many investors lost money in limited partnerships that were negatively affected by the tax law changes in 1986 and beyond.

MANAGING RISK

Just as each type of investment comes with its own set of risks, there are several different ways to protect yourself from risk in the market. First, consider the amount of time you can invest in the market. If you can invest over a longer period of time, the fluctuations will average themselves out. This factor is important when you are working on achieving your long-term goals, such as saving for a college education or for retirement.

Generally, the best time to invest is *now*. And as you just read, the earlier you invest, the longer that money will be compounded.

There is a saying in the industry: "It isn't timing the market, it's time in the market." In other words, it's impossible to time the market for yourself: to make sure you are buying at the right time and selling at the right time, because nobody can predict the future. Dollar cost averaging, asset allocation, and diversification are three common ways to manage your risk. Investing in mutual funds is another common strategy for managing risk.

Dollar cost averaging

Investing the same amount of money at the same time intervals: once a month, once a year, once a paycheck, is known as "dollar cost averaging." Here's how it works. If you invest $100 once a month in a mutual fund, you are buying shares of that fund, and the share price may, of course, fluctuate each month on the day you buy. When the price is high, say $10 a share, you will be buying ten shares for $100. With the same $100 investment, when the price of the stock is low, say, $2.50, you will be buying forty shares.

So you buy a greater number of shares when the price is low and less when the price is high. After six months, you will have invested $600. And if, for example, your shares cost $2.50 each for two of those months, and $5 each for two months, and $10 each for two months, you now would own a total of 140 shares, at an average price of $4.28 per share. If you had bought $600 worth of shares when they cost $10 each, you would own only sixty shares. Or if you wanted 140 shares, and bought them when the price was highest, you would have paid $1,400. Over time, you tend to do well with dollar cost averaging.

Asset allocation

Probably one of the most important things you can do to protect your money is to allocate your assets to different asset classes. For example, you have some cash, which is nice and liquid, then you buy some bonds, which are really safe, and then some other more risky investments, like mutual funds and stocks, which you are going to hold over a longer period of time. By dividing your money into different types of investments, you reduce your risk.

A private company was going public and offered its stock to customers first. I bought the minimum number of shares (50) at the customer price of $5 per share. Then the company went public. My $250 investment shot up to $700! It was the first time in my life I ever bought stock. Using the confidence that the Financial Literacy course instilled in me (as well as my newfound ability to read the prospectus), I followed my hunch, and won!

Diversification

A third way to reduce your risk is to diversify your assets within each allocated segment by going across different sectors of the market, for example: pharmaceutical companies, utilities, or high-technology companies. If there is a downturn in one sector, the other sectors may remain strong.

Mutual funds

If you only have a little bit of money to invest, it is more difficult to allocate or diversify. If you invest in a mutual fund, you have found a way to diversify without spending a lot of money. When you buy into a mutual fund, your money is pooled with the money of many investors to buy and sell stocks and/or bonds. Because many investors contribute to a mutual fund, there is a larger pool of money to diversify, to get lower prices by buying in larger quantities, and to hire an experienced professional to manage the fund.

There are different types of mutual funds, notably: income, value, growth, international, global, and sector funds. The kind with which most people are familiar is professionally managed, either by a team or a manager. These funds are liquid, meaning you buy and sell, depending on the type of shares you have, and you get regular reporting. All mutual funds have fees attached. They are paid either when you open the account, when you close the account, or are spread out over the life of the account. There are no "no-fee" mutual funds.

Before you invest in a mutual fund, you first must be clear about your financial and personal goals, and your investment style. Are you looking for maximum safety, for maximum earnings, or for a combination of both? Are you concerned with the politics or practices of the companies included in the fund? A little research will help ensure you select the funds that meet these goals.

ALIGNING YOUR INVESTMENTS WITH YOUR VALUES

As we already have said, you likely will want your investments to reflect your values. Is the rate of return the most important factor in a mutual fund you are considering? Or maybe you are willing to give up a little bit on the rate of return to make sure that your investments are socially responsible. Several mutual funds are built and marketed on the strength of being sensitive to certain causes.

You may not want to buy stock in companies that produce tobacco or weapons, for example. Or you may be looking to invest in companies that are known for family-friendly policies, or which have a higher rate of women in executive positions. It may be important for you to invest in a company that does not pollute, or in a firm that "gives back" to its community.

There is a perception that these companies usually offer a lower rate of return. You need to look closely at how they are managed. Companies such as Dell, Xerox, and IBM also offer good rates of return, and tend to be woman-friendly, environmentally conscious, and offer on-premises day care, for example. Ben and Jerry's and Newman's Own, among others, are companies known for their generosity to the community.

No matter which mutual fund you are considering, you must get a prospectus. This document shows you exactly what companies are in your mutual fund. It will tell you who manages your mutual fund, whether a management team or an individual, and the tenure and history of that person or team. It gives you the different management fees charged and explains the different types of shares, the different types of withdrawal, the different ways that you can invest, the procedures for automatic deposit and withdrawals.

A prospectus also will give you portfolio histories—how well the fund has performed in the past. And it should give you all the information that you need to know about how to buy it and how to sell it and about the company behind it.

Reading a prospectus can be really difficult—especially the first time—but it is crucial if you are going to make an intelligent investment. Use the table of contents. Don't be afraid to ask questions, and keep asking until you understand the answers. If you have trouble with the prospectus, you can ask someone who is licensed to sell mutual funds.

By law, a registered representative only can read from the prospectus. When she gives you a prospectus, she can't have anything paper-clipped, the pages can't be turned down, nothing's going to be highlighted, and she cannot tamper with or change the prospectus in any way. She is not allowed to highlight because people tend to read only what's highlighted and that's a misrepresentation. You need to know all the information.

INVESTMENT CLUBS

An investment club is a group of people interested in joining together to invest in the stock market. They meet regularly, share investment goals and principles of investing. Each contributes a fixed amount of money on a regular basis, depending on the needs and wishes of the members. Members share responsibility for researching and reporting on prospective companies the group wishes to purchase. Earnings may be reinvested, or stocks may be sold, at the group's discretion.

In the early months of the club, members may spend much of their time doing research and building up an investment fund. Initial forays into the market may come as late as one year or more into the life of the club. As members help to educate themselves and each other, they re-

The most recent numbers show that all-women investment clubs earned an average return of 21.3 percent, whereas all-men investment clubs earned an average return of 15 percent.[1]

port a general rise in confidence. You can leverage the research and knowledge that's shared in the club into your own investment strategy.

For me, investing in individual stocks was a scary prospect. There was so much to know! Which companies? What did all those terms mean? How could I ever gain the skills and knowledge I needed to become an intelligent investor? How could I choose stocks that would meet my goals? Being a part of Womankind's first investment club was a very powerful way for me to understand the multiple facets of the market. Learning with other women gave me the confidence to get over that fear and just jump in. What a thrill it was when we bought our first stock!

Joining an existing investment club, or forming one of your own, is an excellent way to teach yourself about investing, and begin to grow your money to help you reach your important goals. You also will want to think about building your own investment portfolio.

CHOOSING AN INVESTMENT/FINANCIAL PROFESSIONAL

A broker or financial adviser offers the benefits of expertise, an objective perspective, and dedication as a full-time professional. Choose your financial adviser as carefully as you would your

doctor. She or he should be someone you trust, who is specially trained, has affordable fees, and is someone with whom you feel comfortable sharing private information and concerns. Talk to friends and coworkers for a personal referral, go to the Yellow Pages to find companies you feel have a good reputation, or attend seminars and workshops to meet experts in their field.

Financial advisers come with many titles, such as financial planner, investment consultant, stockbroker, or registered representative. The designation a professional uses is determined by federal or state licensing requirements or the companies that hire them. It is best to find the one professional who can serve and help you meet your financial goals.

Find out about their areas of expertise, like retirement planning, insurance planning, or cash management, and choose one who meets your needs. Ask for a personalized financial plan, considering your individual goals. Learn how they will work with you, how often you will meet or review your plan. Understand how they are compensated, how fees are calculated, and the services you may expect from them.

Before I started investing, I was frightened, because I didn't understand the stock market or how it worked. A dear friend explained it like this: "Choose a broker whom you can trust and tell him or her to send you three choices of stock. It's no harder than picking out fabric for a sofa. Sometimes your choice turns out to be great, sometimes you just have to live with it."

You may want to check their license registrations by calling the National Association of Securities Dealers (NASD) at 800-289-9999, or the Securities and Exchange Commission (SEC) at 202-942-8088. It is important to feel comfortable with your qualified adviser. If for any reason you feel that you can no longer work with her, ask her manager to reassign you. The offices are required to take in, record, and attempt to resolve any disputes.

Now I am able to make more informed investment decisions with my financial adviser, not just on his advice.

Financial professionals charge in a variety of ways. Be sure to ask before you hire them, so you are not surprised! Some investment professionals charge an hourly fee—$200 to $500 an hour is not uncommon. And you can invest in whatever you want. They may even place trades for you. You do not pay any commission, you do not have to pay any sales tax. You might have to pay a small ticket charge, but that is charged by the company with which they are placing the trade.

So what's the minimum investment amount you have to put out there before it pays? If you have to pay $300 an hour, you have to be dealing with a fair amount of money to make it worth it.

I disagree. I pay $300 an hour, but I consult with my adviser only for a couple of hours each year, and I know he's saved me or helped me make much more money than that with his good advice. To me, it's worth it!

Another way financial professionals get paid is by commissions based on the transaction. They give their advice for free. They set up a financial plan for you and hope you will invest with them, or buy insurance from them. In those cases, they do charge a commission.

My bias is toward financial planners who charge on a flat-fee basis or by the hour. What's most important is to understand what you are paying for and how you are paying. There is nothing wrong with commissions as long as they are disclosed up front. But a lot of women do not know to ask, "What are the commissions?" You do not always see them coming out of your account on paper. If you buy someone's time, you know pretty much what you are getting. And if you want to get out, there is no penalty. Sometimes with commission products it is hard to get out.

A discount broker differs from a full-service broker, in that you do all your own research, and you just direct the discount broker how you want her to trade. You call up a discount broker and you say, "I want to invest in this, this, and this." And that's why you are paying a discounted fee, because you are not getting the benefit of her knowledge, or her license. A discount broker cannot tell you what you should invest in or not invest in. She cannot even tell you that the company that you want to invest in right now just announced bankruptcy. She is not allowed to give you any information about the company; she simply can "take a ticket," or place the order. If you are a skilled and knowledgeable investor, then a discount broker may be a good choice for you, because you are not paying for expertise. But you also are not getting professional advice.

Also, discount brokers do not know you, or your particular situation, or what investments may be right for you. A full-service broker not only will do a financial plan for you, but also is bound by the rules of suitability. In other words, she cannot make an investment for you that isn't suitable to your financial background and risk tolerance.

Say you are retired and are living on the income of your investments, and all of a sudden, your broker tells you about a great opportunity for a limited partnership that ties up your money for ten years—in other words, you could not get to your money without a huge penalty if you take it out. That is not a suitable investment for you, and it is unethical for a broker to recommend it.

A full-service broker will take a look at your entire situation, and give you an assessment of your investments. That's the basic difference between the two: just how much you want to be advised. Nothing more. You are getting the same stock, the same stock price; with fewer fees with a discount broker and advice on what and how to buy with the full-service broker.

We were cleaning out the attic in my grandmother's house, and we found a certificate for stock in the telephone company—we found it had a lot of value.

Now most trading is done electronically. You can request a certificate, say, if you want to give stock to a child as a gift, but certificates can get burned, or lost, or stolen.

When you buy these investments, you can do it yourself, you don't always have to go through a broker to do it. This is often the case when the company for which you work pays you in stock.

Another way to "do-it-yourself" is by on-line trading. On-line trading has attracted many individuals who wish to buy and sell securities on their own, in their own account. By taking on the task and responsibility of managing their own accounts, individual investors may trade anytime

for a lower cost. The Internet is a great source of information, research, and how-to references. Keep in mind that this powerful resource is anonymous and mistakes—even misrepresentations—can happen. Be cautious of any information you may come across on a particular investment; know the trading process and the real costs associated with trading on-line *before* you invest.

REVIEWING YOUR INVESTMENTS

One important question to ask your financial adviser is: "How often will we review my investments?"

You should review your investments at least once every year. Some women pick their birthday. Just see how you did that year and where you want to go for the next year. There are some years you may take a hit, so focus on "What is my time horizon?" "Was the market bad this year?" "Are my investments still doing well?"

Has your situation changed? Are you no longer saving for education? Did your children graduate, or do they now have other means of paying, such as a scholarship? Are you now planning to retire early? A divorce can make a huge financial difference—what happens to your financial investments? Will you need this money right away? You might want to move it to something more liquid.

Then, too, large purchases are going to affect how you invest your money. You may move to a smaller home: you'll have more money to invest. Or you may get a bonus at the end of the year. That's some money to invest. Or you just found out that your child needs braces or you need a new roof: you will have to free up some of your money.

After taking the course, I realized that I could save more than 15 percent of my annual income in high-yielding CDs so that in ten years I'll have a chunk of money, insured and not at risk, I otherwise would have frittered away. Even if you only can save $50 a month, you will have saved *$6,000 in ten years, not including compound interest.*

Thoughtful investing can be the most important tool in helping you reach your goals, and can help you to feel more confident about your financial future. Investing also is an important component of retirement and estate planning, discussed in the next chapter.

8: Planning for Long-Living Women

Contributing Authors:

Rachel Barenblat, Katharine M. Berlin, Jennifer Lane, and Leslie Sleeper Madge

"We need to think about money as we do about our children: You patiently plan and work hard to get it, you wisely nurture and grow it, and when the time comes to let it go, you experience great joy and independence (and it may also take care of you in your older days!)."
—SUZY SAYLE JIMERSON, CLINICAL NURSE SPECIALIST

IN THIS CHAPTER, YOU WILL LEARN ABOUT:

- Retiring the idea of retirement: new ways of looking at your later years

- Planning for retirement: a traditional view

- Thinking about creating your legacy

- Estate planning for maximum benefit

PART I: RETIREMENT

"Retire" comes from an old French word meaning "to withdraw" and the word originally was used in a military context. Only in the mid-seventeenth century did "retire" come to mean "to withdraw from a [work] position for more leisure."

Retirement, in the sense of a deserved vacation from work that comes when one reaches age sixty-five or so, is a new concept. In the early part of the twentieth century, people didn't retire at all. Generally, people worked until they died, which usually was around age fifty, points out Carol Vinzant in a recent issue of *Fortune*. "Nowa-days, of course, people live longer and expect a smoother ride at the end of life," she writes. "Thanks to Social Security, two generations have had one."

Created in 1935, Social Security was instituted to protect the American worker from impoverishment in the years between retirement and death—an average of about five years at the time. The theory was simple: pay a portion of your paycheck each month in Social Security tax, and receive a pension to live on when you finish working. But changes in generation size and makeup, and increasing life expectancy, mean that Social Security is unlikely to be able to continue providing retirement security, at least not the way it has done so in the past.

Add to this the awareness that most women live longer than men, drop in and out of the workforce to raise families or care for aging parents, tend to have lower-paying jobs than men, and often are not adequately protected by traditional pension plans, and it becomes clear that Social Security may not be a safety net on which women can depend.

Since the 1950s, people have been retiring at

The median income for U.S. women older than sixty-five is $8,200, including Social Security. (Source: U.S. Department of Labor)

Women tend to spend between 11 and 14.5 years out of the workforce as compared to slightly more than 1 year for men. (Source: U.S. Department of Labor, Women's Bureau)

More than 50 percent of women between twenty-five and sixty-four years of age do not participate in a pension plan, and only approximately 20 percent of women older than age sixty-five receive a pension. (Source: U.S. Internal Revenue Service)

an increasingly young age, but the trend slowed by 1985, and now may be reversing. It is no longer clear whether women, in years to come, will be able to retire earlier. Despite Social Security's good intentions, retirement still is a luxury for many women.

I got a late start. During long years at low-paying jobs as a single parent, I was accumulating debts, not savings. I'm on track now, but it's a big deficit to overcome. I will have to work much longer than is traditional just to get by.

I give thanks that I'm a nurse, because if I need to supplement Social Security, I can work one or two days a month.

I've farmed my own land for fifty-eight years. If I don't work, I don't live.

It's one thing to retire from a job with a pension, but what happens to the working woman with no retirement package, or a working woman whose family depends on her salary? Factory workers, waitresses, cafeteria cooks, housecleaners: some women would love to stop their daily grind, but can't afford to stop working.

Whether we love our jobs or hate them, Americans believe in work. The nation's Puritan roots include a strong belief in the Protestant work ethic and the power of work. Our national mythology, which says that anyone who works hard enough can pull herself up by her bootstraps and become wealthy—not to mention president—places work at the center of our self-definition as a nation. Although most women tend not to be defined by work nearly as much as most men, this attitude affects the way we approach retirement. For in addition to issues of financial security, retiring from work requires redefining one's sense of self, community, and daily structure.

In three months, I will be without a profession. Where does that leave me? Without an identity? Without an intellectual community? Without a focus? Without a job to do?

I will be an active part of any community, defined by location or common interests. My self-definition doesn't come from my job. It's a big part of who I am, but not all. I hope my sense of self will evolve as my circumstances evolve.

154

You may begin to think about moving to a different city, learning a new language, taking up a new hobby or expanding a hobby into a thriving business, or simply taking all the time you want to be with family and friends, or to catch up on reading.

My plan is to begin work on a doctorate when I'm seventy. Let's face it—there are only two good reasons for getting an advanced degree. One is to improve career and earning opportunity. Too late for me there. The other is for the deep pleasure of learning for learning's sake. I want to be free of all other responsibilities when I finally go back to college.

Many universities and local colleges offer free or reduced tuition for long-living women and men. Elderhostel, a Boston-based program, offers low-cost, short-term study programs at locations around the world.

My husband and I have been doing an Elderhostel week each year for the last seven years. We've been in five states so far, studying everything from geology in Palm Springs to Appalachian music in the Daniel Boone Forest in Kentucky to T'ai Chi in Vermont. What fun!

Retirement also can affect women on an emotional and psychological level. The job of housewife and mother—a fundamental role for many women—isn't something from which one can retire. For many women, their longest-running job never ends and the idea of retirement seems like a mockery.

I had four kids—the last when I was twenty-two. I'm forty and a grandmother. My oldest girl had some problems with drugs, and I'm raising her two boys, who now are six and eight. I told them,

"When you are old enough to have babies, you'd best be able to take care of them. I'm not going to be Mama all my life." But they know I'd help them the same way if they needed me.

Little kids, little problems; big kids, big problems. My son just got divorced, and moved back home. It's only temporary, but I find myself baking his old favorite meat loaf and doing his wash!

My husband retired last June. We had always looked forward to his retirement, but now I just keep thinking of that old saw, "I married him for better or for worse—but not for lunch!" When I go out shopping, he pouts. When I talk on the phone to my friends, he hovers. When I go out to my bridge club on Wednesdays, he tries to think of some errand nearby so he can drive with me. It's getting so that the only peace I get is in the bathroom!

Many women shun the traditional view of retirement:

Why would I want to retire? It took me nearly forty-five years to find work that I love. I plan to keep at it until I drop.

Retire? What am I supposed to do? Move to Florida and sit around on the beach?

I loved being a teacher, and now that I'm sixty-five I can take the skills I've learned and use them in a new way. I don't quite know yet what I will do next, but I definitely will not spend the next thirty years on the golf course all day.

I watched my father, and then my uncle, drop dead shortly after each retired. I think they simply didn't know how to go on without working. I plan to start a new business when I leave my job in three years.

Retirement depends on so many factors: work, savings, Social Security, family, partner or spouse's work and savings, physical and emotional health. It is impossible to predict what any one woman's retirement will be like. Some factors, like savings, can be controlled. Others, like health, cannot. Like a game, retirement requires a combination of skill and luck.

The ingredients for a happy retirement? Good health, friends and family, thoughtful transitions, and financial order.

Portions of the previous section originally appeared in *The Women's Times*, Pioneer Valley (MA) edition, November 1999, in "Life After Work: What Retirement Means to Women," by Rachel Barenblat. Reprinted with kind permission.

Planning for Retirement: A Traditional View

You are never too young or too old to start planning for your retirement years. Whether you live alone, with your parents, with children, and/ or with a partner, it is important to remember that you are solely responsible for taking care of yourself. You may expect help from your spouse or children, but it is not a good idea to depend on them. In fact, after investment planning, retirement planning is the number one reason why people seek the advice of a financial professional.

My husband and I are getting divorced. Since our marriage twenty-eight years ago he's always handled our finances. I paid the bills and balanced the checkbook, but every time I asked about retirement, he said he was handling it. He's very smart, an electrical engineer, so I was happy to let him deal with making investments. Well, now I'm finding that he wasn't handling it. I'm fifty-one and haven't worked since I was married. What am I going to do?

Many women sorely underestimate the amount of money they will need for retirement. One traditional rule says that one needs 70 to 80 percent of one's pretax income for a comfortable retirement. We offer three different profiles, and invite you to choose the one that best matches your life now, and your plans for retirement: women who will need either 65 percent, 75 percent, or 85 percent of their current income. The "65 percent" woman now saves a lot—15 percent or more of her salary. She tends to have a high income, owns her own home, either alone or with a spouse/partner, and plans to cut back on her lifestyle. The "75 percent" woman saves less—5 to 10 percent of her salary—has a modest mortgage payment or pays rent, and plans to maintain the same standard of living. The woman who will need 85 percent of her current income doesn't save, holds a significant mortgage or pays high market rent, and plans to maintain her lifestyle.

Trying to calculate your retirement needs can be very difficult, and many people take it too lightly. What often happens is that they get such a huge number that they never start saving, or they get such a low number that they wrongly decide that no action is necessary.

Decide which profile best fits you, and use the appropriate figures in the worksheet that follows. Please remember that this worksheet should not be considered as a replacement for a retirement review with a professional adviser.

RETIREMENT PLANNING WORKSHEET

To complete this worksheet, you will need a calculator, current investment and other financial records, and a copy of your Social Security earnings to date. (If you don't have one, you can call the Social Security Administration at 800-772-1213 to order one, or visit the SSA Web site: www.ssa.gov.)

Step 1

Write a short paragraph describing your retirement or future lifestyle expectations.

_____

_____

_____

_____

_____

_____

_____

Step 2

List your assumptions.

1. In how many years do you want to retire or change your lifestyle? _____ years

2. If you were living that lifestyle now, how much would you be spending each year?
   $ _____

   This amount should be in today's dollars. We'll help you make adjustments for inflation in the remainder of this worksheet. Remember that many people find they'll need 70 percent to 80 percent or even more of their current income to support their ideal after-work lifestyle. Estimating this amount is harder the number of years you are away from making this change, but

it's important to take a rough guess now so that you can develop an accurate savings budget.

It's possible that once you've completed this worksheet you'll need to make adjustments to any number of these assumptions. This is okay and is expected. In fact, it's important that you revisit this worksheet frequently and make adjustments to it as you move toward your goal.

3. What do you think inflation will average between now and then? _____ %

   This is a difficult assumption to make and is the reason that you should frequently revisit this calculation to make adjustments. Inflation as measured by the change in the consumer price index (CPI) has ranged from 5.63 percent per year in the 1940s to 1.98 percent in the 1950s to an average of around 5 percent through the 1960s, 1970s, and 1980s. In 1979, 1980, and 1981, inflation averaged more than 10 percent per year. In the 1990s it started around 5.4 percent and has decreased to 3 percent through the first four months of 2000.

   Since no one has a crystal ball—and in an attempt to err on the conservative side—it's suggested to use an inflation assumption equal to current inflation plus 1 percent. For example, for the twelve months preceding September 2000 CPI increased 3.8 percent. In this case, you should use 4.8 percent as your assumption.

4. How long will you be retired? _____ years

   This is another tough assumption to develop and will need to be revisited frequently. Many financial planners are now planning for their clients' retirement to last well into their nineties or even older.

5. How much return can you expect on your savings? _____ %

It's very important that you don't overestimate the amount you will earn on your investments. Use the amount that you are making on any current investments or 8 percent—whichever is less. If you are a conservative investor, you might consider using a lower number like 5 percent or 6 percent. This worksheet assumes that you are planning the same return on your portfolio after retirement as you have before retirement. (This is done to shorten the calculation—please speak with a financial adviser about a more precise estimate.)

Step 3

Estimate that portion of your retirement income that will come from savings.

The numbers generated here are only an estimate. Accurate retirement planning considers many factors that are not dealt with in this worksheet. One of these factors is the effect of taxes on your retirement plan funds when they are withdrawn from your account. Please review the results on this worksheet with your financial adviser.

1. What income will you need in retirement? (From the assumptions in Step 2.)
$ _____

2. How much of this will be provided by Social Security? $ _____
Multiply the monthly amount shown on page 2 of your Social Security statement by twelve.

3. How much of your target annual income will be covered by pension benefits? (Multiply this number by 60 percent if it will stay the same—as opposed to a benefit that has a cost-of-living adjustment.) $ _____
Speak to your spouse or your spouse's human resource department for information on your pension benefits.

4. How much annual income will you earn in your new position (part-time employment, new business etc.)? $ _____

5. Target annual income from savings.
Subtract your Social Security benefit, pension, and other income from your target income to see how much income from savings and investments will be needed to make up the difference
(Question 1 minus 2, 3, and 4). $ _____

Step 4

Estimate your target nest egg:

1. What will your target savings income be in future dollars? $ _____
Multiply your target income from Question 5 above by factor given in Chart A.
Use Chart A with the number of years until retirement on the left and the inflation rate at the top.

2. Calculate the "real return" on your investments after inflation. _____ %
- Add 1 to the return percentage you used in your assumptions in Step 2 (Part 5). For example: if your return assumption was 6 percent or .06, the result here would be 1.06.
- Add 1 to the inflation percentage you used in your assumptions in Step 2 (Part 3).
Once again, if your inflation assumption was 4 percent or .04, the result here would be 1.04.

- Divide your new return percentage by your new inflation percentage.
  In our example, this would equal:
  $1.06/1.04 = 1.0192$
- Subtract 1.
  $1.0192 — 1 = .0192$
- Multiply by 100.
  $.0192 \times 100 = 1.92$ percent
  This means that after inflation of 4 percent your investment return of 6 percent is really 1.92 percent. This is the most important (and difficult) part of the retirement calculation.

3. Calculate your target nest egg. $ _____

Multiply your savings income target from Number 1 above by Factor B from the chart.

Use Chart B with the number of years in retirement on the left and the real return percentage at the top.

Step 5

Decide how much you should be saving on an annual basis.

1. Project the growth of your current investments. $ _____

Multiply the value of your current investments by Factor A from the chart.

Use Chart A with the number of years to retirement on the left and the estimated investment return from Part 5 of your assumptions at the top.

2. Subtract this amount from your target to get the additional amount that you need to save. $ _____

3. Calculate your level annual savings target by dividing this number by Factor C from the chart. $ _____

Some things to keep in mind:

a. This worksheet should be used to estimate what you should be saving toward your retirement or lifestyle-change goal.

b. Once you have made this rough calculation, you should consult with your retirement adviser to adjust your numbers as necessary.

c. Complexity does not allow us to present the calculations for an increasing retirement savings target. With this type of plan, the saver starts with a lower savings amount and increases it on a regular basis. If you think that might be easier for you to budget, contact a financial professional for help.

FUTURE VALUE FACTORS
CHART A

Periods	1%	2%	3%	4%	5%	6%	7%
1	1.0100	1.0200	1.0300	1.0400	1.0500	1.0600	1.0700
2	1.0201	1.0404	1.0609	1.0816	1.1025	1.1236	1.1449
3	1.0303	1.0612	1.0927	1.1249	1.1576	1.1910	1.2250
4	1.0406	1.0824	1.1255	1.1699	1.2155	1.2625	1.3108
5	1.0510	1.1041	1.1593	1.2167	1.2763	1.3382	1.4026
6	1.0615	1.1262	1.1941	1.2653	1.3401	1.4185	1.5007
7	1.0721	1.1487	1.2299	1.3159	1.4071	1.5036	1.6058
8	1.0829	1.1717	1.2668	1.3686	1.4775	1.5938	1.7182
9	1.0937	1.1951	1.3048	1.4233	1.5513	1.6895	1.8385
10	1.1046	1.2190	1.3439	1.4802	1.6289	1.7908	1.9672
11	1.1157	1.2434	1.3842	1.5395	1.7103	1.8983	2.1049
12	1.1268	1.2682	1.4258	1.6010	1.7959	2.0122	2.2522
13	1.1381	1.2936	1.4685	1.6651	1.8856	2.1329	2.4098
14	1.1495	1.3195	1.5126	1.7317	1.9799	2.2609	2.5785
15	1.1610	1.3459	1.5580	1.8009	2.0789	2.3966	2.7590
16	1.1726	1.3728	1.6047	1.8730	2.1829	2.5404	2.9522
17	1.1843	1.4002	1.6528	1.9479	2.2920	2.6928	3.1588
18	1.1961	1.4282	1.7024	2.0258	2.4066	2.8543	3.3799
19	1.2081	1.4568	1.7535	2.1068	2.5270	3.0256	3.6165
20	1.2202	1.4859	1.8061	2.1911	2.6533	3.2071	3.8697
21	1.2324	1.5157	1.8603	2.2788	2.7860	3.3996	4.1406
22	1.2447	1.5460	1.9161	2.3699	2.9253	3.6035	4.4304
23	1.2572	1.5769	1.9736	2.4647	3.0715	3.8197	4.7405
24	1.2697	1.6084	2.0328	2.5633	3.2251	4.0489	5.0724
25	1.2824	1.6406	2.0938	2.6658	3.3864	4.2919	5.4274
26	1.2953	1.6734	2.1566	2.7725	3.5557	4.5494	5.8074
27	1.3082	1.7069	2.2213	2.8834	3.7335	4.8223	6.2139
28	1.3213	1.7410	2.2879	2.9987	3.9201	5.1117	6.6488
29	1.3345	1.7758	2.3566	3.1187	4.1161	5.4184	7.1143
30	1.3478	1.8114	2.4273	3.2434	4.3219	5.7435	7.6123
31	1.3613	1.8476	2.5001	3.3731	4.5380	6.0881	8.1451
32	1.3749	1.8845	2.5751	3.5081	4.7649	6.4534	8.7153
33	1.3887	1.9222	2.6523	3.6484	5.0032	6.8406	9.3253
34	1.4026	1.9607	2.7319	3.7943	5.2533	7.2510	9.9781
35	1.4166	1.9999	2.8139	3.9461	5.5160	7.6861	10.6766
36	1.4308	2.0399	2.8983	4.1039	5.7918	8.1473	11.4239
37	1.4451	2.0807	2.9852	4.2681	6.0814	8.6361	12.2236
38	1.4595	2.1223	3.0748	4.4388	6.3855	9.1543	13.0793
39	1.4741	2.1647	3.1670	4.6164	6.7048	9.7035	13.9948
40	1.4889	2.2080	3.2620	4.8010	7.0400	10.2857	14.9745
41	1.5038	2.2522	3.3599	4.9931	7.3920	10.9029	16.0227
42	1.5188	2.2972	3.4607	5.1928	7.7616	11.5570	17.1443
43	1.5340	2.3432	3.5645	5.4005	8.1497	12.2505	18.3444
44	1.5493	2.3901	3.6715	5.6165	8.5572	12.9855	19.6285
45	1.5648	2.4379	3.7816	5.8412	8.9850	13.7646	21.0025
46	1.5805	2.4866	3.8950	6.0748	9.4343	14.5905	22.4726
47	1.5963	2.5363	4.0119	6.3178	9.9060	15.4659	24.0457
48	1.6122	2.5871	4.1323	6.5705	10.4013	16.3939	25.7289
49	1.6283	2.6388	4.2562	6.8333	10.9213	17.3775	27.5299
50	1.6446	2.6916	4.3839	7.1067	11.4674	18.4202	29.4570

FUTURE VALUE FACTORS
CHART A

Periods	8%	9%	10%	11%	12%	13%	14%
1	1.0800	1.0900	1.1000	1.1100	1.1200	1.1300	1.1400
2	1.1664	1.1881	1.2100	1.2321	1.2544	1.2769	1.2996
3	1.2597	1.2950	1.3310	1.3676	1.4049	1.4429	1.4815
4	1.3605	1.4116	1.4641	1.5181	1.5735	1.6305	1.6890
5	1.4693	1.5386	1.6105	1.6851	1.7623	1.8424	1.9254
6	1.5869	1.6771	1.7716	1.8704	1.9738	2.0820	2.1950
7	1.7138	1.8280	1.9487	2.0762	2.2107	2.3526	2.5023
8	1.8509	1.9926	2.1436	2.3045	2.4760	2.6584	2.8526
9	1.9990	2.1719	2.3579	2.5580	2.7731	3.0040	3.2519
10	2.1589	2.3674	2.5937	2.8394	3.1058	3.3946	3.7072
11	2.3316	2.5804	2.8531	3.1518	3.4785	3.8359	4.2262
12	2.5182	2.8127	3.1384	3.4985	3.8960	4.3345	4.8179
13	2.7196	3.0658	3.4523	3.8833	4.3635	4.8980	5.4924
14	2.9372	3.3417	3.7975	4.3104	4.8871	5.5348	6.2613
15	3.1722	3.6425	4.1772	4.7846	5.4736	6.2543	7.1379
16	3.4259	3.9703	4.5950	5.3109	6.1304	7.0673	8.1372
17	3.7000	4.3276	5.0545	5.8951	6.8660	7.9861	9.2765
18	3.9960	4.7171	5.5599	6.5436	7.6900	9.0243	10.5752
19	4.3157	5.1417	6.1159	7.2633	8.6128	10.1974	12.0557
20	4.6610	5.6044	6.7275	8.0623	9.6463	11.5231	13.7435
21	5.0338	6.1088	7.4002	8.9492	10.8038	13.0211	15.6676
22	5.4365	6.6586	8.1403	9.9336	12.1003	14.7138	17.8610
23	5.8715	7.2579	8.9543	11.0263	13.5523	16.6266	20.3616
24	6.3412	7.9111	9.8497	12.2392	15.1786	18.7881	23.2122
25	6.8485	8.6231	10.8347	13.5855	17.0001	21.2305	26.4619
26	7.3964	9.3992	11.9182	15.0799	19.0401	23.9905	30.1666
27	7.9881	10.2451	13.1100	16.7386	21.3249	27.1093	34.3899
28	8.6271	11.1671	14.4210	18.5799	23.8839	30.6335	39.2045
29	9.3173	12.1722	15.8631	20.6237	26.7499	34.6158	44.6931
30	10.0627	13.2677	17.4494	22.8923	29.9599	39.1159	50.9502
31	10.8677	14.4618	19.1943	25.4104	33.5551	44.2010	58.0832
32	11.7371	15.7633	21.1138	28.2056	37.5817	49.9471	66.2148
33	12.6760	17.1820	23.2252	31.3082	42.0915	56.4402	75.4849
34	13.6901	18.7284	25.5477	34.7521	47.1425	63.7774	86.0528
35	14.7853	20.4140	28.1024	38.5749	52.7996	72.0685	98.1002
36	15.9682	22.2512	30.9127	42.8181	59.1356	81.4374	111.8342
37	17.2456	24.2538	34.0039	47.5281	66.2318	92.0243	127.4910
38	18.6253	26.4367	37.4043	52.7562	74.1797	103.9874	145.3397
39	20.1153	28.8160	41.1448	58.5593	83.0812	117.5058	165.6873
40	21.7245	31.4094	45.2593	65.0009	93.0510	132.7816	188.8835
41	23.4625	34.2363	49.7852	72.1510	104.2171	150.0432	215.3272
42	25.3395	37.3175	54.7637	80.0876	116.7231	169.5488	245.4730
43	27.3666	40.6761	60.2401	88.8972	130.7299	191.5901	279.8392
44	29.5560	44.3370	66.2641	98.6759	146.4175	216.4968	319.0167
45	31.9204	48.3273	72.8905	109.5302	163.9876	244.6414	363.6791
46	34.4741	52.6767	80.1795	121.5786	183.6661	276.4448	414.5941
47	37.2320	57.4176	88.1975	134.9522	205.7061	312.3826	472.6373
48	40.2106	62.5852	97.0172	149.7970	230.3908	352.9923	538.8065
49	43.4274	68.2179	106.7190	166.2746	258.0377	398.8813	614.2395
50	46.9016	74.3575	117.3909	184.5648	289.0022	450.7359	700.2330

PRESENT VALUE OF ANNUITY FACTORS
CHART B

Periods	1%	2%	3%	4%	5%	6%	7%
1	0.9901	0.9804	0.9709	0.9615	0.9524	0.9434	0.9346
2	1.9704	1.9416	1.9135	1.8861	1.8594	1.8334	1.8080
3	2.9410	2.8839	2.8286	2.7751	2.7232	2.6730	2.6243
4	3.9020	3.8077	3.7171	3.6299	3.5460	3.4651	3.3872
5	4.8534	4.7135	4.5797	4.4518	4.3295	4.2124	4.1002
6	5.7955	5.6014	5.4172	5.2421	5.0757	4.9173	4.7665
7	6.7282	6.4720	6.2303	6.0021	5.7864	5.5824	5.3893
8	7.6517	7.3255	7.0197	6.7327	6.4632	6.2098	5.9713
9	8.5660	8.1622	7.7861	7.4353	7.1078	6.8017	6.5152
10	9.4713	8.9826	8.5302	8.1109	7.7217	7.3601	7.0236
11	10.3676	9.7868	9.2526	8.7605	8.3064	7.8869	7.4987
12	11.2551	10.5753	9.9540	9.3851	8.8633	8.3838	7.9427
13	12.1337	11.3484	10.6350	9.9856	9.3936	8.8527	8.3577
14	13.0037	12.1062	11.2961	10.5631	9.8986	9.2950	8.7455
15	13.8651	12.8493	11.9379	11.1184	10.3797	9.7122	9.1079
16	14.7179	13.5777	12.5611	11.6523	10.8378	10.1059	9.4466
17	15.5623	14.2919	13.1661	12.1657	11.2741	10.4773	9.7632
18	16.3983	14.9920	13.7535	12.6593	11.6896	10.8276	10.0591
19	17.2260	15.6785	14.3238	13.1339	12.0853	11.1581	10.3356
20	18.0456	16.3514	14.8775	13.5903	12.4622	11.4699	10.5940
21	18.8570	17.0112	15.4150	14.0292	12.8212	11.7641	10.8355
22	19.6604	17.6580	15.9369	14.4511	13.1630	12.0416	11.0612
23	20.4558	18.2922	16.4436	14.8568	13.4886	12.3034	11.2722
24	21.2434	18.9139	16.9355	15.2470	13.7986	12.5504	11.4693
25	22.0232	19.5235	17.4131	15.6221	14.0939	12.7834	11.6536
26	22.7952	20.1210	17.8768	15.9828	14.3752	13.0032	11.8258
27	23.5596	20.7069	18.3270	16.3296	14.6430	13.2105	11.9867
28	24.3164	21.2813	18.7641	16.6631	14.8981	13.4062	12.1371
29	25.0658	21.8444	19.1885	16.9837	15.1411	13.5907	12.2777
30	25.8077	22.3965	19.6004	17.2920	15.3725	13.7648	12.4090
31	26.5423	22.9377	20.0004	17.5885	15.5928	13.9291	12.5318
32	27.2696	23.4683	20.3888	17.8736	15.8027	14.0840	12.6466
33	27.9897	23.9886	20.7658	18.1476	16.0025	14.2302	12.7538
34	28.7027	24.4986	21.1318	18.4112	16.1929	14.3681	12.8540
35	29.4086	24.9986	21.4872	18.6646	16.3742	14.4982	12.9477
36	30.1075	25.4888	21.8323	18.9083	16.5469	14.6210	13.0352
37	30.7995	25.9695	22.1672	19.1426	16.7113	14.7368	13.1170
38	31.4847	26.4406	22.4925	19.3679	16.8679	14.8460	13.1935
39	32.1630	26.9026	22.8082	19.5845	17.0170	14.9491	13.2649
40	32.8347	27.3555	23.1148	19.7928	17.1591	15.0463	13.3317
41	33.4997	27.7995	23.4124	19.9931	17.2944	15.1380	13.3941
42	34.1581	28.2348	23.7014	20.1856	17.4232	15.2245	13.4524
43	34.8100	28.6616	23.9819	20.3708	17.5459	15.3062	13.5070
44	35.4555	29.0800	24.2543	20.5488	17.6628	15.3832	13.5579
45	36.0945	29.4902	24.5187	20.7200	17.7741	15.4558	13.6055
46	36.7272	29.8923	24.7754	20.8847	17.8801	15.5244	13.6500
47	37.3537	30.2866	25.0247	21.0429	17.9810	15.5890	13.6916
48	37.9740	30.6731	25.2667	21.1951	18.0772	15.6500	13.7305
49	38.5881	31.0521	25.5017	21.3415	18.1687	15.7076	13.7668
50	39.1961	31.4236	25.7298	21.4822	18.2559	15.7619	13.8007

PRESENT VALUE OF ANNUITY FACTORS
CHART B

Periods	8%	9%	10%	11%	12%	13%	14%
1	0.9259	0.9174	0.9091	0.9009	0.8929	0.8850	0.8772
2	1.7833	1.7591	1.7355	1.7125	1.6901	1.6681	1.6467
3	2.5771	2.5313	2.4869	2.4437	2.4018	2.3612	2.3216
4	3.3121	3.2397	3.1699	3.1024	3.0373	2.9745	2.9137
5	3.9927	3.8897	3.7908	3.6959	3.6048	3.5172	3.4331
6	4.6229	4.4859	4.3553	4.2305	4.1114	3.9975	3.8887
7	5.2064	5.0330	4.8684	4.7122	4.5638	4.4226	4.2883
8	5.7466	5.5348	5.3349	5.1461	4.9676	4.7988	4.6389
9	6.2469	5.9952	5.7590	5.5370	5.3282	5.1317	4.9464
10	6.7101	6.4177	6.1446	5.8892	5.6502	5.4262	5.2161
11	7.1390	6.8052	6.4951	6.2065	5.9377	5.6869	5.4527
12	7.5361	7.1607	6.8137	6.4924	6.1944	5.9176	5.6603
13	7.9038	7.4869	7.1034	6.7499	6.4235	6.1218	5.8424
14	8.2442	7.7862	7.3667	6.9819	6.6282	6.3025	6.0021
15	8.5595	8.0607	7.6061	7.1909	6.8109	6.4624	6.1422
16	8.8514	8.3126	7.8237	7.3792	6.9740	6.6039	6.2651
17	9.1216	8.5436	8.0216	7.5488	7.1196	6.7291	6.3729
18	9.3719	8.7556	8.2014	7.7016	7.2497	6.8399	6.4674
19	9.6036	8.9501	8.3649	7.8393	7.3658	6.9380	6.5504
20	9.8181	9.1285	8.5136	7.9633	7.4694	7.0248	6.6231
21	10.0168	9.2922	8.6487	8.0751	7.5620	7.1016	6.6870
22	10.2007	9.4424	8.7715	8.1757	7.6446	7.1695	6.7429
23	10.3711	9.5802	8.8832	8.2664	7.7184	7.2297	6.7921
24	10.5288	9.7066	8.9847	8.3481	7.7843	7.2829	6.8351
25	10.6748	9.8226	9.0770	8.4217	7.8431	7.3300	6.8729
26	10.8100	9.9290	9.1609	8.4881	7.8957	7.3717	6.9061
27	10.9352	10.0266	9.2372	8.5478	7.9426	7.4086	6.9352
28	11.0511	10.1161	9.3066	8.6016	7.9844	7.4412	6.9607
29	11.1584	10.1983	9.3696	8.6501	8.0218	7.4701	6.9830
30	11.2578	10.2737	9.4269	8.6938	8.0552	7.4957	7.0027
31	11.3498	10.3428	9.4790	8.7331	8.0850	7.5183	7.0199
32	11.4350	10.4062	9.5264	8.7686	8.1116	7.5383	7.0350
33	11.5139	10.4644	9.5694	8.8005	8.1354	7.5560	7.0482
34	11.5869	10.5178	9.6086	8.8293	8.1566	7.5717	7.0599
35	11.6546	10.5668	9.6442	8.8552	8.1755	7.5856	7.0700
36	11.7172	10.6118	9.6765	8.8786	8.1924	7.5979	7.0790
37	11.7752	10.6530	9.7059	8.8996	8.2075	7.6087	7.0868
38	11.8289	10.6908	9.7327	8.9186	8.2210	7.6183	7.0937
39	11.8786	10.7255	9.7570	8.9357	8.2330	7.6268	7.0997
40	11.9246	10.7574	9.7791	8.9511	8.2438	7.6344	7.1050
41	11.9672	10.7866	9.7991	8.9649	8.2534	7.6410	7.1097
42	12.0067	10.8134	9.8174	8.9774	8.2619	7.6469	7.1138
43	12.0432	10.8380	9.8340	8.9886	8.2696	7.6522	7.1173
44	12.0771	10.8605	9.8491	8.9988	8.2764	7.6568	7.1205
45	12.1084	10.8812	9.8628	9.0079	8.2825	7.6609	7.1232
46	12.1374	10.9002	9.8753	9.0161	8.2880	7.6645	7.1256
47	12.1643	10.9176	9.8866	9.0235	8.2928	7.6677	7.1277
48	12.1891	10.9336	9.8969	9.0302	8.2972	7.6705	7.1296
49	12.2122	10.9482	9.9063	9.0362	8.3010	7.6730	7.1312
50	12.2335	10.9617	9.9148	9.0417	8.3045	7.6752	7.1327

FUTURE VALUE OF ANNUITY FACTORS
CHART C

Periods	1%	2%	3%	4%	5%	6%	7%
1	1.0000	1.0000	1.0000	1.0000	1.0000	1.0000	1.0000
2	2.0100	2.0200	2.0300	2.0400	2.0500	2.0600	2.0700
3	3.0301	3.0604	3.0909	3.1216	3.1525	3.1836	3.2149
4	4.0604	4.1216	4.1836	4.2465	4.3101	4.3746	4.4399
5	5.1010	5.2040	5.3091	5.4163	5.5256	5.6371	5.7507
6	6.1520	6.3081	6.4684	6.6330	6.8019	6.9753	7.1533
7	7.2135	7.4343	7.6625	7.8983	8.1420	8.3938	8.6540
8	8.2857	8.5830	8.8923	9.2142	9.5491	9.8975	10.2598
9	9.3685	9.7546	10.1591	10.5828	11.0266	11.4913	11.9780
10	10.4622	10.9497	11.4639	12.0061	12.5779	13.1808	13.8164
11	11.5668	12.1687	12.8078	13.4864	14.2068	14.9716	15.7836
12	12.6825	13.4121	14.1920	15.0258	15.9171	16.8699	17.8885
13	13.8093	14.6803	15.6178	16.6268	17.7130	18.8821	20.1406
14	14.9474	15.9739	17.0863	18.2919	19.5986	21.0151	22.5505
15	16.0969	17.2934	18.5989	20.0236	21.5786	23.2760	25.1290
16	17.2579	18.6393	20.1569	21.8245	23.6575	25.6725	27.8881
17	18.4304	20.0121	21.7616	23.6975	25.8404	28.2129	30.8402
18	19.6147	21.4123	23.4144	25.6454	28.1324	30.9057	33.9990
19	20.8109	22.8406	25.1169	27.6712	30.5390	33.7600	37.3790
20	22.0190	24.2974	26.8704	29.7781	33.0660	36.7856	40.9955
21	23.2392	25.7833	28.6765	31.9692	35.7193	39.9927	44.8652
22	24.4716	27.2990	30.5368	34.2480	38.5052	43.3923	49.0057
23	25.7163	28.8450	32.4529	36.6179	41.4305	46.9958	53.4361
24	26.9735	30.4219	34.4265	39.0826	44.5020	50.8156	58.1767
25	28.2432	32.0303	36.4593	41.6459	47.7271	54.8645	63.2490
26	29.5256	33.6709	38.5530	44.3117	51.1135	59.1564	68.6765
27	30.8209	35.3443	40.7096	47.0842	54.6691	63.7058	74.4838
28	32.1291	37.0512	42.9309	49.9676	58.4026	68.5281	80.6977
29	33.4504	38.7922	45.2189	52.9663	62.3227	73.6398	87.3465
30	34.7849	40.5681	47.5754	56.0849	66.4388	79.0582	94.4608
31	36.1327	42.3794	50.0027	59.3283	70.7608	84.8017	102.0730
32	37.4941	44.2270	52.5028	62.7015	75.2988	90.8898	110.2182
33	38.8690	46.1116	55.0778	66.2095	80.0638	97.3432	118.9334
34	40.2577	48.0338	57.7302	69.8579	85.0670	104.1838	128.2588
35	41.6603	49.9945	60.4621	73.6522	90.3203	111.4348	138.2369
36	43.0769	51.9944	63.2759	77.5983	95.8363	119.1209	148.9135
37	44.5076	54.0343	66.1742	81.7022	101.6281	127.2681	160.3374
38	45.9527	56.1149	69.1594	85.9703	107.7095	135.9042	172.5610
39	47.4123	58.2372	72.2342	90.4091	114.0950	145.0585	185.6403
40	48.8864	60.4020	75.4013	95.0255	120.7998	154.7620	199.6351
41	50.3752	62.6100	78.6633	99.8265	127.8398	165.0477	214.6096
42	51.8790	64.8622	82.0232	104.8196	135.2318	175.9505	230.6322
43	53.3978	67.1595	85.4839	110.0124	142.9933	187.5076	247.7765
44	54.9318	69.5027	89.0484	115.4129	151.1430	199.7580	266.1209
45	56.4811	71.8927	92.7199	121.0294	159.7002	212.7435	285.7493
46	58.0459	74.3306	96.5015	126.8706	168.6852	226.5081	306.7518
47	59.6263	76.8172	100.3965	132.9454	178.1194	241.0986	329.2244
48	61.2226	79.3535	104.4084	139.2632	188.0254	256.5645	353.2701
49	62.8348	81.9406	108.5406	145.8337	198.4267	272.9584	378.9990
50	64.4632	84.5794	112.7969	152.6671	209.3480	290.3359	406.5289

FUTURE VALUE OF ANNUITY FACTORS
CHART C

Periods	8%	9%	10%	11%	12%	13%	14%
1	1.0000	1.0000	1.0000	1.0000	1.0000	1.0000	1.0000
2	2.0800	2.0900	2.1000	2.1100	2.1200	2.1300	2.1400
3	3.2464	3.2781	3.3100	3.3421	3.3744	3.4069	3.4396
4	4.5061	4.5731	4.6410	4.7097	4.7793	4.8498	4.9211
5	5.8666	5.9847	6.1051	6.2278	6.3528	6.4803	6.6101
6	7.3359	7.5233	7.7156	7.9129	8.1152	8.3227	8.5355
7	8.9228	9.2004	9.4872	9.7833	10.0890	10.4047	10.7305
8	10.6366	11.0285	11.4359	11.8594	12.2997	12.7573	13.2328
9	12.4876	13.0210	13.5795	14.1640	14.7757	15.4157	16.0853
10	14.4866	15.1929	15.9374	16.7220	17.5487	18.4197	19.3373
11	16.6455	17.5603	18.5312	19.5614	20.6546	21.8143	23.0445
12	18.9771	20.1407	21.3843	22.7132	24.1331	25.6502	27.2707
13	21.4953	22.9534	24.5227	26.2116	28.0291	29.9847	32.0887
14	24.2149	26.0192	27.9750	30.0949	32.3926	34.8827	37.5811
15	27.1521	29.3609	31.7725	34.4054	37.2797	40.4175	43.8424
16	30.3243	33.0034	35.9497	39.1899	42.7533	46.6717	50.9804
17	33.7502	36.9737	40.5447	44.5008	48.8837	53.7391	59.1176
18	37.4502	41.3013	45.5992	50.3959	55.7497	61.7251	68.3941
19	41.4463	46.0185	51.1591	56.9395	63.4397	70.7494	78.9692
20	45.7620	51.1601	57.2750	64.2028	72.0524	80.9468	91.0249
21	50.4229	56.7645	64.0025	72.2651	81.6987	92.4699	104.7684
22	55.4568	62.8733	71.4027	81.2143	92.5026	105.4910	120.4360
23	60.8933	69.5319	79.5430	91.1479	104.6029	120.2048	138.2970
24	66.7648	76.7898	88.4973	102.1742	118.1552	136.8315	158.6586
25	73.1059	84.7009	98.3471	114.4133	133.3339	155.6196	181.8708
26	79.9544	93.3240	109.1818	127.9988	150.3339	176.8501	208.3327
27	87.3508	102.7231	121.0999	143.0786	169.3740	200.8406	238.4993
28	95.3388	112.9682	134.2099	159.8173	190.6989	227.9499	272.8892
29	103.9659	124.1354	148.6309	178.3972	214.5828	258.5834	312.0937
30	113.2832	136.3075	164.4940	199.0209	241.3327	293.1992	356.7868
31	123.3459	149.5752	181.9434	221.9132	271.2926	332.3151	407.7370
32	134.2135	164.0370	201.1378	247.3236	304.8477	376.5161	465.8202
33	145.9506	179.8003	222.2515	275.5292	342.4294	426.4632	532.0350
34	158.6267	196.9823	245.4767	306.8374	384.5210	482.9034	607.5199
35	172.3168	215.7108	271.0244	341.5896	431.6635	546.6808	693.5727
36	187.1021	236.1247	299.1268	380.1644	484.4631	618.7493	791.6729
37	203.0703	258.3759	330.0395	422.9825	543.5987	700.1867	903.5071
38	220.3159	282.6298	364.0434	470.5106	609.8305	792.2110	1,030.9981
39	238.9412	309.0665	401.4478	523.2667	684.0102	896.1984	1,176.3378
40	259.0565	337.8824	442.5926	581.8261	767.0914	1,013.7042	1,342.0251
41	280.7810	369.2919	487.8518	646.8269	860.1424	1,146.4858	1,530.9086
42	304.2435	403.5281	537.6370	718.9779	964.3595	1,296.5289	1,746.2358
43	329.5830	440.8457	592.4007	799.0655	1,081.0826	1,466.0777	1,991.7088
44	356.9496	481.5218	652.6408	887.9627	1,211.8125	1,657.6678	2,271.5481
45	386.5056	525.8587	718.9048	986.6386	1,358.2300	1,874.1646	2,590.5648
46	418.4261	574.1860	791.7953	1,096.1688	1,522.2176	2,118.8060	2,954.2439
47	452.9002	626.8628	871.9749	1,217.7474	1,705.8838	2,395.2508	3,368.8380
48	490.1322	684.2804	960.1723	1,352.6996	1,911.5898	2,707.6334	3,841.4753
49	530.3427	746.8656	1,057.1896	1,502.4965	2,141.9806	3,060.6258	4,380.2819
50	573.7702	815.0836	1,163.9085	1,668.7712	2,400.0182	3,459.5071	4,994.5213

Retirement Building Blocks

Social Security is designed to be a level of income for your basic necessities. It is not intended to be your sole source of income. To qualify for Social Security, you need to have worked forty quarters, or the equivalent of ten years. If you have not worked outside the home and are married to a spouse who works, you are entitled to receive a benefit equal to about half that of your spouse. You may claim half of the benefit of your former spouse, too, if you were married for at least ten years and are not remarried, even if he has remarried. (As many of his former spouses as qualify can collect simultaneously.) The amount of the benefits you will receive depends on your age—whether you start collecting at age sixty-two or at age sixty-five—and on your earnings. You can call the Social Security Administration and ask for your Social Security statement—Form 7004. You'll receive a record of reported earnings and an estimate of your current and future Social Security benefits. In 2000, the maximum monthly retirement benefit at age sixty-five was $1,433, or $17,196 per year.

Other building blocks for retirement income include personal savings, such as savings accounts, IRAs, 401(k)s, equity in real estate, and employer-sponsored or employer-paid pensions.

Retirement Accounts

Retirement accounts have special regulations under the tax code. In many cases, your deposits to these accounts are tax deductible, while growth in the accounts is not taxed until you withdraw the funds. Since they are meant to hold assets you'll use in retirement, many accounts require that you start withdrawing your money by age seventy and one-half. And if you withdraw your money before fifty-nine and one-half, you may incur an extra 10 percent penalty.

What follows is an overview of the most common retirement accounts used as of this writing. Please keep in mind that there are many intertwined tax, investment, and estate planning issues to consider when choosing an account. And, as tax laws and regulations can change, please consult your tax or financial adviser before taking any action.

The retirement plans discussed here create "qualified money." Money is considered qualified when it's been given the tax advantages of a retirement account. Once qualified, the money takes on several restrictions and benefits. In the interest of simplicity, we present the most common benefits and restrictions here. Please check with a professional for information about any exceptions.

The most significant retirement account restriction requires that the funds remain within an account until the participant reaches age fifty-nine and one-half. Also, withdrawals from these accounts must begin by the April 1 following the participant's reaching the age of seventy and one-half. Moneys withdrawn from a retirement account before the participant reaches age fifty-nine and one-half are assessed a 10 percent penalty and usually are taxed as income in the year distributed. This penalty is waived if the participant dies, becomes disabled, or uses the funds to pay for medical expenses or to comply with a qualified domestic relations order (QDRO) after a divorce.

The biggest benefit of many employer-sponsored retirement plans is that the money deposited in the account isn't currently taxed to you, the employee. This helps you save because you don't have the added expense of paying income taxes on the deposits to your account. Also, any interest, dividends, or capital gains generated in the account are not taxed so long as the money stays in the account. This is a very helpful benefit because money that would have been used for taxes can be used for living expenses or can stay in savings.

Employer-Sponsored Plans

Many employers will provide an account into which either the employer or the employee can make a contribution. These plans are called "defined contribution plans" to distinguish them from the old standby, "defined benefit plans," which provide a specific benefit over time. With a defined contribution plan, the employee's retirement benefit is based on the accumulated value of the account rather than a specific service- or age-related formula.

The most common of these plans are profit-sharing plans and special IRAs called simplified employee pensions (SEPs) and savings incentive match plans for employees (SIMPLE) retirement plans. Also, in some cases, employees are allowed to participate by deferring some of their own pay. The rules regulating this type of benefit are found in paragraphs 401 and 403 of the tax code, therefore, they are often called 401(k) and 403(b) plans.

If you change employers, many companies may allow your account to remain in their plan if it has a significant balance—usually more than $5,000. You'll also be given the option of moving your account to your new employer or to your own individual retirement account. There are several ways to make this transfer, the easiest of which is called a direct rollover. In this case, you give written instruction to your former employer to send a check directly to your new account. If

your new employer doesn't have a plan but you're careful to register your new personal account as a "rollover IRA," you'll be able to move this money back into an employer-sponsored plan when it becomes available.

Profit-sharing plans

Employers with this type of plan make regular, usually annual, deposits to their employees' accounts. Although the name of the plan implies business success, a company may choose to make contributions even in years when there is no profit. Employers may restrict the amount of the account that a departing employee can take with her when she separates from the company. This is called a vesting schedule and can stretch up to seven years. If an employee leaves the company without being "fully vested," the part of her account that she couldn't transfer is divided among the remaining plan participants.

401(k) plans

This provision is most often offered as part of an employer-sponsored profit-sharing plan. In this case, the employee may deposit some of her own pay into the employer's retirement plan. Oftentimes, an employer will "match" part of the employee's deferral by adjusting its contributions depending on the amount contributed by the employee. This is an advantage, in many cases, because it reduces the employee's current income tax by reducing her taxable income.

Under this type of plan, all deposits made by the employee are 100 percent vested immediately. This means that if she leaves the employer, she will not forfeit any of her own deposits even though she may not be able to transfer all of her employer's contributions to her new account.

After the waiting period, all eligible employees must be allowed to participate in this type of account, although some highly compensated employees may be restricted as to the amount that they can contribute.

With this type of plan, employees are given a choice of investment funds. It's very important that you research these accounts by requesting a prospectus from the plan sponsor and discussing your choices with either a private or company-provided investment representative. As of 2000, the maximum amount that an employee may contribute to a 401(k) plan in any one year is $10,500, with some exceptions.

403 (b) plans

This type of plan is offered to employees of nonprofit organizations or public schools in place of 401(k) provisions. These types of plans work basically the same way that 401(k) plans do for employees of for-profit companies.

Self-employed Plans

If you are self-employed or you work for a small company, you may participate in one of the most common self-employed plans.

Keogh

This is the original self-employment plan and works similarly to the profit-sharing plan described above. With the advent of the new "special" individual retirement accounts, however, most self-employed people are opting away from these plans.

SEP

The simplified employer pension account (SEP) is a program in which the employer makes contributions to each employee's individual retirement account (IRA). In practice, the employer generally will open a separate IRA for each

TEN COMMON OBJECTIONS TO SAVING IN RETIREMENT ACCOUNTS

- **I need the money now for current expenses.**
- **Retirement is a long way away.**
- **Only misers save for retirement.**
- **Withdrawing money before age fifty-nine and one-half incurs penalties.**
- **I need to reserve my money for emergencies.**
- **I'm saving for my children's education.**
- **"Greener investment pastures" elsewhere.**
- **I'm funding a life insurance policy with a cash value instead.**
- **I'm saving for a home down payment.**
- **I love my job and will work forever.**

employee and suggest investments for that account.

Contributions must be made for any employee who has reached age twenty-one, has worked for the employer for at least three of the last five years, and has earned a specific amount of income. In 2000, this amount was $450.

The employer's deduction for contributions to the plan may not exceed 15 percent of the employee's compensation, up to $170,000 in 2000. Since employer contributions are made directly to the employee's IRA account, the employee is always 100 percent vested in the balance. Employees no longer are allowed the option of deferring part of their income to a new SEP account.

SIMPLE

If you work for a company with fewer than one hundred employees (who earn at least $5,000 annually), your employer may offer savings incentive match plans for employees, or SIMPLE. Generally, the employer may not maintain any other type of retirement plan while providing a SIMPLE. With this type of plan, a special IRA is established for each eligible employee. The employer then makes deposits to the employee's account on a fair basis. Employees may choose the investments within the account, and may maintain the account after leaving the employer.

In some cases, the employer may opt to provide 401(k) privileges with this account, in which case the employee may deposit some of her pay, before-tax, into the account. These plans are called SIMPLE 401(k) plans.

Personal Retirement Plans

To be eligible for a personal retirement plan, a worker must have earned income for the year or be married to a person who had earned income during that year. Both the worker and the worker's spouse may open an account and may deposit up to $2,000 or 100 percent of their combined income, whichever is less. For example, if your daughter has a paper route that paid her $1,100 this year, she can make a deposit of $1,100 to her IRA. If you're a stay-at-home mom and your spouse earned more than $4,000 this year, you both would be able to put $2,000 into your separate accounts.

There are basically two types of individual retirement accounts.

Traditional IRA

Contrary to a popular misconception, everyone is eligible for a traditional individual retirement account (IRA). Even people who have employer-sponsored plans may open or contribute to an account. However, depending on income, they may not be able to deduct their contribution on their tax return.

An IRA account can be opened at any number of financial institutions—from banks to brokerage houses, mutual funds and credit unions. The worker, and, if she's married, the worker's spouse, may contribute up to the lesser of $2,000 each or the amount of their total earned income in that year.

In 1999, if you were eligible to participate in an employer-sponsored plan, you'd be able to deduct your IRA contribution in full if you were married (filing jointly) and had a combined adjusted gross income (AGI) less than $52,000. If you were single, you'd be able to make this deduction if your AGI was less than $32,000. If you made less than $10,000 over those limits, you would be able to deduct part of your contribution.

If you work for an employer who doesn't offer a retirement plan, then you may deduct the entire contribution regardless of your income. If your spouse's employer offers a plan, your deduction phases out for incomes between $150,000 and $160,000.

You can take taxable distributions from your IRA without paying the 10 percent extra penalty if you withdraw money to pay medical insurance premiums while unemployed, "qualified higher education expenses" for the owner or the owner's immediate family, or for up to $10,000 of "qualified first-time home buyer expenses."

Roth IRA

Created in the 1998 tax year, the Roth IRA has become very popular. Unlike other retirement plans, contributions never are deductible and withdrawals after fifty-nine and one-half also never are taxed.

Let's mention that again for emphasis. The growth in the account is never taxed if withdrawn after the account is aged five years and the participant is past fifty-nine and one-half years old!

Needless to say, Roth IRAs are great accounts and should at least be considered by everyone who is eligible to participate. Like the traditional IRA, the maximum annual contribution to a Roth is $2,000 per person. This maximum contribution is phased out for single people making between $95,000 and $110,000 and for married couples filing jointly with incomes between $150,000 and $160,000. Married couples filing separately only are allowed to contribute if their combined income is less than $100,000.

Roth IRAs also are excluded from the required distribution rules that affect participants who have reached seventy and one-half.

You can withdraw assets from a Roth IRA without paying the 10 percent penalty or taxes on the distribution if the owner of the account dies or is disabled, or to pay "qualified first-time home buyer expenses." If the Roth IRA, or the owner's first Roth IRA account if this is a different account, passed the waiting period, then you won't need to include the withdrawal in taxable income either. Like the traditional IRA, you can take taxable distributions without paying the 10 percent

More than 50 percent of the women who live alone are sixty-five years or older. (Source: U.S. Bureau of the Census)

The average age of retirement for both men and women is 62.1. (Source: U.S. Department of Labor)

With life expectancy nearing ninety, women can anticipate living in retirement nearly 25 percent longer than men. (Source: U.S. National Center for Health Statistics)

Only 5 percent of Americans ages sixty-five and older have annual incomes greater than $25,000. (Source: U.S. Bureau of the Census)

extra penalty if you withdraw money to pay medical insurance premiums while unemployed or to pay "qualified higher education expenses" for the owner or the owner's immediate family.

The Roth IRA is a wonderful opportunity, but like many of our tax laws, is quite complicated. Please speak with your tax or financial adviser for a more complete analysis before taking action.

Where Are You in Your Retirement Savings Process?

I have an IRA which doesn't have a whole lot of money in it. I've joined an investment club recently, which doesn't have a whole lot either.

I have an IRA and just started a 401(k) at work.

I am living on a pension. My late husband made some small investments and I get his Social Security.

I have some investments, but my husband manages all of them. As far as he's concerned, I've been retired for my whole career. A stay-at-home wife and mother just doesn't cut it in his opinion.

I haven't started yet. I guess I always thought my kids would look after me, the way I looked after my parents. That's probably a big assumption. I'd better do something about retirement, but I don't know how or where to start.

To make up for lost time, you can:

- Increase savings by cutting spending.

- Be more realistic about your retirement age.

- Use home equity to help finance retirement.

- Get aggressive with investments.

- Turn a hobby into a supplemental income.

- Invest in a tax-wise way.

- Consider jobs that offer retirement plans.

- Delay saving for children's education. Take care of yourself first.

- Stop funding cash-value life insurance plans.

Where to Get Help

More than any other part of financial planning, retirement planning requires your active participation. It's important that you regularly revisit your goals and take pains to be sure that your plan is achieving those goals.

With any part of financial planning, it's important to look for unbiased advice. The best way to recognize good advice is to be well informed yourself. Your relationship with your financial adviser should be one of shared discussion, not dictation. To start this process, look for retirement planning classes offered through your employer, association, local community college, or adult education programs. Decide to attend a new class every year or so to keep up with new developments. If you're a reader, good programs also can be found through the National Endowment for Financial Education (www.nefe.org). Through participation in a variety of programs, you'll be better informed about your own welfare and will feel more secure about your money decisions.

Financial advisers come with a variety of "designations." Certified financial planner (C.F.P.), charter financial consultant (C.H.F.C.), personal financial adviser (P.F.A.) are among the more frequently seen in the personal financial planning world. The letters after the person's name serve to show you, in most cases, that the adviser participated in an educational program to earn those letters. Ask the adviser the meaning of her designations and the amount of continuing training she needs to participate in order to retain them. Ask about her specialty, and if she has worked with people in your particular situation. Also, ask if she has had any disciplinary actions against her. If you wish, you may follow up this discussion by contacting the organizations to which she belongs, and reading about their membership requirements. If you are not sure where to find a financial adviser, ask your friends or other advisers, attend a workshop given by an adviser, or contact a referral organization for a list of names in your area. (Remember that these organizations charge a fee for inclusion in the association, so collect a couple of names and do some comparative interviews.)

Financial planning was born many years ago out of the insurance and security sales industry. For much of this time, financial advisers were compensated by the sale of the products that they recommended. Fortunately for the consumer, financial planning is outgrowing this period and now offers a variety of ways to retain professional advice. Basically, the compensation arrangements you can expect to see fall into two categories: commissions and fees.

A commissioned planner generally will not charge you for preparing a financial plan and recommendations as to the products that might fit into that plan. Since the companies providing the financial products compensate her, it's important to ask her what her compensation level is. Even though you won't be receiving a bill from her, your money still supports her activities through the expenses and sales charges in the products

she recommends. The state insurance commission regulates advisers who sell insurance. Advisers who sell securities are associated with a broker-dealer and will be supervised through the broker-dealer by the National Association of Securities Dealers (www.nasd.org).

A fee planner receives her compensation directly from you. Depending on the structure of the adviser's business, she might charge you a fee based on the amount of money she's helping you invest, or she might bill you by the hour. This type of adviser generally will present you with an advisery agreement or contract early in your discussion, outlining her fee structure and the service that she will provide. Advisers charging fees for investment advice are regulated by their state securities division or the Securities Exchange Commission (www.sec.gov) depending on the amount of client assets they handle.

Thinking About Creating Your Legacy

How and for what do you want to be remembered? What do you want to leave behind when you leave this earth? According to a Chinese adage, the way to ensure immortality is to "Have a child, write a book, plant a tree." While it is nice to think of ways to make a mark on the world, many women—so busy caring for others—simply do not have time! The later years of life can offer time for reflection—finally!—and make room for creative, intellectual, athletic, spiritual, and other pursuits, as well as opportunities to travel, pursue a long-held dream, become active in community politics or in a charitable organization. You also may wish to think about writing an ethical will, described in the section that follows, as you begin to take charge of planning for your estate.

PART II: ESTATE PLANNING

As part of your growth as a woman taking control of her financial life, add the component of attending to your legal life, and putting in place the documents that will cover your needs. You do not need to own millions to have an estate. Everyone has an estate, and, regardless of the value, everyone should participate in estate planning. As you read in chapter 3, your estate is simply your net worth at the time of your death plus the value of any life insurance. Estate planning includes planning for your financial and health needs during your lifetime, in the event that you are not able to manage them yourself, and for the disposition of your assets when you die.

Everyone needs three documents: a durable power of attorney, a health care proxy, and a will.

Durable Power of Attorney

A durable power of attorney is a written document in which you, as the principal, designate someone you trust, such as your spouse, another family member, a friend, or a professional (or any combination) as your attorney-in-fact. Your attorneys-in-fact are authorized to perform certain acts on your behalf. You may give as much or as little power to your attorney-in-fact as you desire. Generally, a durable power of attorney is very broad, intending to allow the attorney-in-fact to do anything and everything necessary to fully manage your financial affairs if you are not able to manage them.

Your attorney-in-fact is *not* your lawyer, unless you specifically choose her. The phrase "attorney-in-fact" is simply the name given to the person (agent) designated with the power to handle your affairs. The attorneys-in-fact, or "agents," are fiduciaries, meaning they must account to you for all funds or other assets in their possession, and they are liable to you for any improper actions taken, as measured against a standard for fiduciaries.

It is important to name two agents because you want to be sure that at least one of them will be available and able to act on your behalf at the time when they are needed.

It is also important to have a *durable* power of attorney. "Durable" refers to the fact that the validity of your power of attorney survives your incapacity. It does not, however, survive your change of mind (assuming you are competent), in that you may always revoke the power of attorney and create a new one naming different agents.

The durable power of attorney gives the right to named agents to handle your finances: sign your checks, pay bills, make and sell investments, sell, lease, buy real estate. The powers you give your agent become effective when the document is signed. However, the durable power of attorney is only valid when the actual document is presented to an institution (bank, investment company) by the agent. So, if you hold the original document, you control its use. But in planning for possible incompetence, you should let your agents know where the durable power of attorney is located. Needless to say, it is crucial that you name agents you completely trust!

The durable power of attorney is a *big* power. This person can take this document and go into a financial institution and wipe out your accounts. She could sell your house or anything else you own if it is just in your name alone. So if there is somebody that you trust with all of your life, then you could name that person now. A reason to do that might be if you travel a lot and might want something to be traded—for example, stocks, or if you might need accounts to be moved while you are inaccessible. You also can make it effective only upon your incapacity as attested to in writing by a licensed physician

The power granted to your agents in the durable power of attorney survives your incapacity, but not your death. This document allows your agents to handle your finances on your behalf during your lifetime only. At your death, the terms of your will (and/or trust) control and the power of attorney is no longer valid.

If you do not create a durable power of attorney and you become incapacitated and it is necessary for someone to handle your finances, they must be appointed by the probate court as either guardian or conservator of your estate (i.e., your assets). This is a time-consuming process and involves court costs and court supervision of the guardian/conservator's handling of your finances. The guardian/conservator will have to obtain court approval to sell, transfer, or mortgage assets. In addition, the guardian/conservator must file periodic accounts with the probate court and these accounts are open to public scrutiny. Anyone can examine court files.

The cheapest, easiest, and simplest way to plan for the possibility of your need for another to handle your finances is to create a durable power of attorney.

Please note: Some states have laws regarding the power of attorney, some do not. You should discuss with the attorney preparing your power of attorney how the laws in your state affect your power of attorney.

A couple came in to plan their estate. She was in her late fifties and he was in his early sixties. Shortly after, he underwent routine bypass surgery.

But he had a negative reaction to one of the drugs, and as a result was permanently institutionalized in a nursing home. That of course turned their life completely upside down and the wife was grief-stricken. She'd never handled the money. All of a sudden, she had to pay a $6,000-a-month nursing home bill. She had a vacation home and didn't know what to do with it. They were living in a condo. The condo fees were very high; she didn't know whether to stay or to sell. Early on in the process, we were successful in having the husband sign a durable power of attorney. Without it, as bad as it was for her, it would have been even worse. Many people think if there are two names on the asset you're all set and you don't need to do anything. That's true only for bank accounts. If you've got two names on the stock fund, on a brokerage account, on a mutual fund, or on real estate, it takes two signatures. So if you want to sell or refinance, you need your spouse's signature as well.

With the durable power of attorney, she was then empowered to be able to make financial decisions. She sold the vacation home; she took the proceeds and managed them so as to qualify her husband for Medicaid. She decided not to keep their condo. She bought another condo, in a place that was more accessible for her husband to come on visits. She had to transfer the ownership of his life insurance to her, because on Medicaid, he could not have more than $2,000 and the cash surrender value on that life insurance is a countable asset. So she needed his signature and she needed to use the durable power for that.

She needed to cash out his IRAs. That was very painful because of the tax ramifications. But while she could keep her own IRAs up to a modest dollar amount, he couldn't have more than $2,000 in assets in his name.

The linchpin of the plan was a durable power of attorney. The durable power enabled her to sign his name. Without it, he would have had to sign himself or the wife would have had to be appointed guardian or conservator of her husband's estate and would have had to acquire court approval for all the asset transfers.

In order to sign a power of attorney, you must be competent, mentally competent to understand the grant of power you are creating. However, if someone is physically incapacitated and cannot sign their name, they may still be able to execute a durable power of attorney if they are mentally competent to do so. If they can make any mark at all on the document, that mark can be witnessed and notarized and the document will be legally valid.

Health Care Proxy

While a durable power of attorney appoints agents to handle your financial affairs should you not be able to do so yourself, a health care proxy appoints agents to make medical decisions on your behalf in the event you cannot. A power of attorney can be used even when you are competent, a health care proxy is only used when you're unable to make your own decisions.

A health care proxy is the legal document that names the person(s) whom you authorize to make health care decisions for you if/when you are not capable of making them yourself. You should name at least two persons. Again, each state has its own laws regarding health care proxies. Some require that the agents be named in order, that is, one first, and an alternate. If that is the case, you should make sure that the document does not require you to prove that the first named agent is unavailable or unable to serve, but that in the absence of the first named agent, the alternate can act. If possible, state that the named agents may serve jointly or individually to ensure that one is available when needed.

You would need your health care agent to take over for you even if the situation does not have anything to do with terminal illness. It can be, for example, you are bumped over the head so you are unconscious; it is a nonemergency situation, but someone has to decide "yes surgery" or "no surgery."

The health care proxy gives your named agents the right to make medical decisions on your behalf, including the decision regarding life support systems, if you so state. However, this document does not state exactly what your personal choice is regarding life support systems, only that you give your agent the right to make decisions regarding life support systems. You must discuss that with your health care agent and be sure they know your wishes.

The person you name as a health care agent does not have to be a medical person at all but does have to be someone who is assertive and not intimidated by doctors and hospitals. We have had a lot of clients who prefer not to name a spouse because that person is not assertive enough. Doctors and hospitals can be quite intimidating. Your agent should be a person who will go and get a second opinion, one who will do what you would do before you made a decision.

If you are in a lesbian relationship, and your family is not supportive of your lifestyle, you should consider making your partner your health care proxy and giving her durable power of attorney. Make it effective right now. Otherwise, they could prevent her from seeing you, should you become hospitalized in an emergency.

I want to stay on life support systems until a cure is found for what ails me. Don't pull the plug on me!

You may wish to have every treatment available for as long as possible. Or you may wish not to linger at all. It is a very personal matter that you should discuss fully with your health care agent.

A problem can arise if you are without this formal health care proxy. If *anybody* objects to the plan to terminate life support systems, including a third party that's not involved with your family, say, a "right-to-life" group, they can come forward and say, "I object," which effectively sends the matter to probate court to be resolved.

With the health care proxy, the person *you* have designated is authorized to make this decision. That does not guarantee that if someone says, "I object," the hospital won't get cold feet and say "We want a court order" and make you go to probate court, but in that instance, the issue before the probate court becomes very different. Without a health care proxy, the issue before the probate court is "What would you want, what's in your best interests." With a health care proxy, the issue becomes, "Why shouldn't we follow the decision of the agent that you chose when you were able to do so?" So the burden changes and the one doing the objecting now has to overcome the presumption that the proxy person is authorized to make that decision. Reasonable people can differ on when enough is enough at one end of the spectrum.

About once every three years, I change my mind completely about donating my organs if I am in a car accident. It is important to keep your health care agent up-to-date on your wishes.

As soon as you start the process of divorce, you should see an estate planner. Otherwise, because it

is assumed that if you do not have a health care agent, your spouse would make those decisions; you could end up in the situation of someone who really is angry with you making your life-and-death decisions. And there are issues about inheritance that need to be rethought, at least.

Living Will

You also may execute a living will, which is not a legal document in all states. A living will states in rather general language that you give your agent the right to make life support system decisions on your behalf. The health care proxy should state this as well, or state that your agent does not have that authority. Again, some states have laws regulating the living will, some do not. In Massachusetts, for example, it is simply used as a document to comfort the family, that is to show that you thoughtfully gave your health care agent the right to make life support decisions on your behalf. When the time comes, it is sometimes easier for family members to know you made this choice.

I often find that the relatives who haven't had a lot of involvement with the parents are the ones who stayed away; their lives were too busy. They are the ones who, at the eleventh hour, come in and say, "No, no, no, we can't do this to Mom or Dad," and may become very obstructive. Often they are dealing with their own denial and their own guilt. They haven't evolved into the acceptance that this is the time, because they haven't really participated in the patient's care. So to be able to read what the relative would have wanted might well help assuage these feelings.

Hospital regulations now require that you be told about your right to a proxy and they will give you a form. By definition, if you are at the hospital, you aren't feeling your best. So you may not really be able to make those kinds of decisions. It is much better to handle these decisions in a contemplative atmosphere. While you are making an estate plan is a natural time to think about these issues and to make these decisions. Doing so is a way of taking care of yourself, and of your loved ones.

Will

A will is a written instrument that disposes of probate property at your death. Probate property is property owned by you alone, that is, titled in your name only. Any property held jointly with another will pass to the joint owner. This does not apply to real estate held as "tenants in common" (that is not joint ownership). In that case, each tenant's share passes through their probate estate to their heirs, but real estate held as "tenants by the entirety" (for married couples only) or as joint tenants with rights of survivorship will pass to the surviving joint owner. Joint bank accounts, security accounts, etc., pass to the joint owner.

Assets such as life insurance, pension plans, etc., which have named beneficiaries pass to the named beneficiaries at your death. Only assets held in your name alone are subject to the terms of your will.

What if you do not have a will?

If you don't have a will, everything is going to be distributed according to the laws of the state in which you reside at your time of death. Most states divide the assets between your spouse and your children in varying proportions.

I have discovered a marital law of physics: most people hold everything jointly with their spouse— the deed to the house, the bank accounts, the retirement funds. They make each other beneficiaries of the life insurance and the IRA. So, as a result, if the first spouse dies without a will, everything's going to go to the surviving spouse because of surviving joint ownership. It's pretty unusual to have to go to probate court when the first spouse dies because of this marital law of physics. But when the second spouse dies, it's time for probate court.

If you have children and no will, it is not true that your assets will go to the state. They will go to your children, *but* your probate assets are distributed to your heirs as determined by state law at your time of death in the state in which you die. If you die leaving a will, you are considered to have died testate. If you do not have a will, you are considered to have died intestate. If you die intestate, states provide for assets to be distributed to next of kin. Regardless of their age, your children will inherit some percentage (depending on state law) of your assets by intestate succession.

A problem can arise if minor children inherit real property and assets. Either the assets will be held by the probate court or a legal guardian must be appointed to receive the funds on their behalf, manage the funds until they reach majority, and file accountings with the court regarding the inheritance. The children must receive the inheritance outright when they reach majority. This could mean that when your child reaches eighteen years of age, she has control of assets that she may not use as wisely as she would when she is somewhat older. Therefore, it is advantageous to create a will and control the distribution of your estate and the timing of that distribution. In your will, you should name not only your heirs, but guardians and trustees for your minor children.

Guardians are the people who will raise your

children. You should name persons you like and trust to do a good job.

If your children are minors, you should leave your children's inheritance to them in a trust. The trustees will manage the assets for the benefit of the children until they reach a certain age, which you name in the will, at which time the child will receive their inheritance outright.

You can give the trustee full discretion to manage the money for the children's benefit. By naming an adult to handle the assets until age twenty-five or so, you are giving your children the opportunity to mature and receive the assets when they will use them wisely. If you create a trust in your will for the benefit of your children, you will also want to name the trustee of the trust as beneficiary of your life insurance instead of your children (as second or contingent beneficiaries if your spouse is named as first beneficiary). That way the life insurance proceeds, usually the largest part of an estate, will also be held until the children reach adulthood.

The benefits of a will are:

- You, the property owner, determine who will inherit your probate property and how taxes and expenses will be paid, so that distribution and taxes are not simply determined by state law.

- Because you control the disposition of assets, you create an opportunity to save on taxes.

- In your will, you choose an executor to administer the estate.

- The court monitors the actions of the executor and of any trustee of a trust created under your will (testamentary trust).

- A will may nominate guardians and trustees for minors.

However:

- An estate planning attorney is required to be sure that the will is drafted properly.

- A will provides no lifetime management of assets.

- A will itself does not address incapacity.

- A will becomes a public record at your death in that the original will is filed with the court, an issue if you wish your records never to be public.

- There are court costs associated with court supervision.

- A will must be updated periodically to account for important life events such as changes of residence, marriage, divorce, changes in beneficiaries' needs, new tax laws, etc., so that there are no unintended results.

- A will requires strict formalities in its execution (signing), including witnesses to your signature. Each state has its own requirements regarding the formalities of signing a valid will, but most require two witnesses and a notary to all signatures. In order for your will to be valid, all formalities must be strictly enforced.

Estate Planning Goals and Objectives

When planning your estate, you will want to consider five factors. Does the distribution of your assets meet your goals and objectives? Will your estate be administered as efficiently and economically as possible? Has your estate plan lowered taxes as much as possible? After taxes and expenses, will there be enough of your estate left to provide income and support for your family? Will your spouse and children (heirs) require professional asset management?

Where You Are in Life Affects Estate Planning

Like everything else in life, we go through cycles. Your estate planning process will be more or less complex and will reflect where you are in your life.

Young adult

When you're young and have minor children, you will want to make sure that provisions are made for the children in the event of your unexpected death. You will want to name a guardian to raise the children—a guardian of your choice and not the court's choice. You will want to name a trustee to manage the inheritance for the children, and hold it in trust with adult trustee discretion as to expenditures until the children are perhaps twenty-five years old, or whatever age you choose, that is, the age at which you are comfortable giving your children their inheritance outright. Again, state laws differ, but in most states, if you do not declare otherwise in your will, your children are entitled to their inheritance at age eighteen. Those of us with teenagers know that even the best-intended teenage children spend money on different things than they would at age twenty-five or so, when their perspective has matured.

The law says that when a child turns eighteen, he or she is an adult. I have an eighteen-year-old, and would really question that. He's a good kid, but the

concept of his having $10,000 with no strings attached, never mind potentially hundreds of thousands of dollars, is something I wouldn't like at all. And most people feel the same. And if you do nothing and you die early, that's what happens; they get it right when they're eighteen, and could blow it on things that seem desperately important when you're eighteen and in a couple of years, when they've woken up and decided to rejoin the human race, they wonder where it all went. By holding it in a trust for their benefit, you can protect the assets for those years while still allowing the trustee to use it for their benefit. You should pick an age when you think they will be mature enough to be responsible.

Obviously, most women don't die prematurely. Most of us make it all the way through the raising of our children, and managing our own finances. Our children only inherit in the fullness of time. But accidents happen, diseases happen, and if you don't plan for that possibility, you can leave behind both economic chaos and psychological chaos.

If you don't speak, the law will name a guardian for your children and it's typically the family member who gets to the courthouse steps first, finds the parking lot first, gets in the door first—if they're not shown to be an ax murderer there's no reason not to appoint them. The court will appoint them even though you might think they're flakes when it comes to raising children. You may have real concerns about their value system or their child-raising style. If you haven't taken action, then your wishes may not be honored and your children could end up turning out to be very different people than you would have hoped.

Middle age

Between those with minor children and the other end of the age cycle, the middle area is the quiet time. You definitely need legal documents in place; you are usually more worried about taxes at that time. But you don't have to worry about holding inheritances for children because they are probably grown and mature, and you are not yet ready to worry about chronic long-term-care issues. There are obviously exceptions.

If your health predisposes you to some particular condition or you have some chronic condition like multiple sclerosis, or if you're perfectly fine but your spouse is quite a bit older than you and his health is not so good, you may want to see your estate attorney now. There are a lot of May/December marriages where the wife is in her forties and the spouse is in his sixties. If he needs a nursing home, everything she has counts toward the payment of that care. Even if they entered into a premarital agreement, Medicaid ignores that and still will count everything that's owned by the wife as if it's owned by the husband.

Younger people with chronic illness, needing to be institutionalized in their fifties with Alzheimer's, Parkinson's, multiple sclerosis, may still have children at home, may still have those major expenses for college in front of them, and unfortunately the Medicaid program never envisioned that situation. While there are modest protections for a spouse of someone who is in a nursing home, there's no recognition of the need to set aside funds to finish raising a child to adulthood. We are finding that to be a real problem. This is an issue that needs to be addressed by the federal Medicaid program.

Elder

When you are age fifty-five to sixty or older, you have other issues to worry about. In a classic estate plan, we worry about what happens after death: taxes, probate, inheritance, things like that. Beginning fairly recently, a growing number of attorneys now practice "elder law," a more holistic approach to planning for the later years, with an emphasis on quality-of-life issues. Advance directives, incapacity, management of your affairs, putting in plan your wishes for how your funds should be used for your care, how they should be used for the support of your family, preservation of assets for the payment of nursing home costs, all are issues to address as part of your estate plan.

I get many calls from many lawyers who don't know anything about this but they're being asked by their clients—what happens to this grand plan if either my husband or I needs a nursing home? What happens is a mess.

So we're finding that estate planning attorneys are going to have to grow in this direction because their clients are demanding answers. But most don't have those answers right now, so it behooves you, the client, to be very proactive. As women, we are conditioned to some extent to be "the good little girl": to do what we're told and not to ask a lot of questions. Of course, that has changed in the medical field during the last twenty-five years, but, unfortunately, not so much in the legal field.

You have to take responsibility in the other areas of your life as well and that includes your legal health. When you ask the questions, if the answers don't seem logical to you, then getting a second or even a third opinion is vital.

Because we're living longer and longer, we increase the possibility that we are going to suffer a chronic illness that will require very expensive long-term care. And, as we've discussed in chapter 6, in this country, we haven't yet developed a plan to cover even basic preventive and emergency medical care, never mind long-term illness.

The sooner you begin to plan, the more likely you will be able to save a larger amount of assets. The earlier you are aware of your state's Medicaid regulations regarding eligibility, the more planning tools will be available to you.

Tax

The unified tax credit for the year 2000 was $675,000, and is increasing in increments to the year 2006, when it will reach $1 million. The unified tax credit is the combination of the amount gifted during your lifetime and the amount you leave at the time of your death. No tax is due on this amount. This does not include the $10,000 per year you are allowed to give as a gift to as many persons as you choose tax-free. This $10,000 per year, per person limit on gifting applies only if you have a taxable estate. If your estate is less than the unified credit amount, you may gift any amount with no tax ramifications because all of your gifts and the value of your estate at death will be less than the unified credit, therefore tax-free.

If as a couple you are worth more than $675,000—which is not difficult, since this amount includes your home and other real estate, your life insurance, your IRAs, your portfolios, your deferred comp or any other employee benefits—you have what is known as a tax problem. One of the best problems to have! And it is solvable!

Typically, married couples leave everything to

the surviving spouse. The tax rules allow a marital deduction that applies to everything that goes to a surviving spouse. So, if you leave everything to your spouse, it is all tax-free. Let's say the husband dies first. He leaves everything to his wife. Because she's the surviving spouse, there's no tax due. It doesn't matter how much—you can leave $600,000 or $600 million to your surviving spouse—it is tax-free. This sounds great. Here's the catch: the surviving spouse owns it all. When she dies, it likely will go to the children. The children are not eligible for the marital deduction because they are children, not spouse, so only the amount of the unified tax credit in the year of death passes tax-free.

The Million-Dollar Couple

Sam and Maria together are worth $1 million. Sam dies first, leaving everything to Maria tax-free. Then Maria dies. The million dollars will go to the children. The first $675,000 in value will pass tax-free, but the remaining $325,000 will be taxed. It will be taxed at 41 percent and the tax will be about $135,000.

The tax codes use a progressive rate to tax assets above the unified credit amount. The estate tax begins at 37 percent and maxes out at 55 percent. It's very high.

Now let's take that same couple. Sam and Maria set up living tax trusts with the assistance of their attorney. These trusts divide the assets: half in Maria's name, half in Sam's name. Sam sets up a trust. Sam is the trustee of the Sam trust; Maria is the trustee of the Maria trust. They are fully revocable: as trustees of their own trusts, they can fully manage their assets. So Sam has $500,000 and Maria has $500,000.

Now, when Sam dies, his $500,000 passes into two subtrusts: a credit shelter subtrust, which is funded in the amount of the unified credit at the year of his death, and a marital subtrust, which is funded with any excess. The terms of the credit shelter subtrust are that Maria has the benefit of it during her lifetime with some limitations, and when Maria dies, it goes to the children. Maria has full benefit of the marital trust.

The assets in the credit shelter trust are subject to tax, but no tax is due because it's less than the unified credit amount. The assets in the marital trust are not taxed because there is no tax on money left by one spouse to the other. When Maria dies, only the assets in her trust are subject to tax, but the assets in Sam's credit shelter trust are not taxed again.

Because the assets in Maria's trust ($500,000) are less than the credit shelter amount, no tax is due. So it is possible for a couple to pass $1.3 million (in 2000) to the children tax-free, instead of paying $135,000 to the government. The trusts allow each spouse to use their credit amount, instead of only the second spouse to die using one credit amount. The tax trust allows you to save an enormous amount of money on taxes.

A very hot topic these days is estate planning for retirement benefits. We now are seeing people who have been in professions traditionally considered low-paying, like school teaching. And then all of a sudden, thirty years later, these teachers have accumulated enormous retirement benefits: $500,000, $700,000. These are people who have had $30,000 or $40,000 salaries! They have just been good savers. And the taxes are deferred on those plans. So then they have a huge amount of money, which also will be considered an asset subject to tax by the estate tax system when they die.

Supplemental Needs Trust

If you are a single female without any children, a will becomes a higher priority because your legal heirs are your parents. If your parents are predeceased, your estate will go to your siblings. While parents inheriting is great in theory, the reality is that they are a generation older than you by definition. They are at greater risk for long-term illness; the likelihood of them needing a nursing home is higher. If they are now or might in the future be in a nursing home, an inheritance from you is simply a gift to that nursing home.

So when older people are possible recipients of inheritances, or if the possible recipient of the inheritance is currently ill or disabled—and this also applies to parents who have disabled children—the heir may lose his or her government benefits. To avoid this, you can set up a supplemental needs trust, a trust that says "this money is targeted to pay for the supplemental needs of the beneficiary": the parents, the disabled child, to improve their quality of life—buy the TV, take a trip to Disney World with the personal care attendant—without the money being used to pay the core caretaking bills. The supplemental needs trust provides that money used for the benefit of the beneficiary cannot be used to interfere with government benefits (such as Medicaid), which the beneficiary may receive.

So even if your parents are very healthy right now, you should consider alternatives. If your parents are financially comfortable, and don't need your money, consider skipping them entirely and looking at siblings, nieces, and nephews.

Life Insurance Trust

Many people think that life insurance is not taxed. Since 1976, life insurance has been taxable in an estate. When you have a significant amount of life insurance, you can remove it from your taxable estate. In the case of the million-dollar couple, Maria and Sam, if $700,000 of their estate was life insurance, they would not create the living trusts. Instead, they would remove the life insurance from their taxable estate.

> *When my kids were born, I took out small life insurance policies—$10,000 apiece on their lives. They didn't buy it, I bought it. I pay the premiums. I designate the beneficiary. I'm the owner. But I'm not the insured. So if I die, the policy does not pay because I am not the insured. If they die, the policy pays, but because they had no ownership interest in that policy, it is not taxed to their estate.*

If you want to remove life insurance from a taxable estate, you create another entity to own it and that is an irrevocable life insurance trust. There are technical requirements, but when it is created and funded correctly, at your death the proceeds will pay into the trust for the benefit of the spouse or the children and upon the death of the spouse will then go to the children and it's all tax-free. So the million-dollar couple, if their tax problems were largely driven by life insurance, should remove the life insurance from their taxable estate and then the rest of their assets can be held jointly because their estate is now below the unified credit.

If you are single, and worth more than $675,000, you should consider creating a life insurance trust. Also, look at the desirability of making annual gifts. It might be appropriate for you to give $10,000 per person, per year. If the children you want to give it to are not old enough to be responsible to receive it, you can create a trust to hold it for them. Resist the temptation to cre-

ate Uniform Transfer (or Gift) to Minors Act accounts, for reasons explained below.

Uniform Gift to Minors Act

The Uniform Gift to Minors Act (UGMA) account is an account created by an adult for the benefit of a minor. The proceeds in the account are distributed to the child directly when he or she reaches age twenty-one, which is still a very young adult. These accounts are very easy to set up, but can create enormous problems.

If you name yourself as the custodian of the account and you put the money into it, you have not removed it from your taxable estate. Even though for all purposes it belongs to the minor and you can never take it back, because you've retained control as the custodian of the account, the IRS says it's still taxed to your estate. It's considered to be yours under the tax code.

Another problem with a UGMA account occurs if, as custodian of the account and parent of the child, you want to use the funds in the account to pay for college. You may run afoul of your parental duty to provide support to your child. Certainly, support requires food, clothing, shelter. So you could never use the Uniform Gift to Minors Act account to pay for the weekly grocery bill, for example, because you have a parental obligation to feed that child under your duty to support. Nobody really wants to use the money for everyday support; they really want to use it for college. Do you have a duty to contribute toward college? It's a gray area of the law.

In the event that you use the child's money first, two bad things happen—the child can make you put it back, and the IRS will tax it to you on your income tax because you used it to discharge a support obligation. If you must have UGMA accounts, the giver of the gift should not be the custodian, and the parent of the child should not be the custodian.

Let's say that your sibling—the aunt or uncle of the child—is the custodian. She or he then has no duty to support, so now you could use it for college tuition. Also remember, as described in chapter 5, when you apply for financial aid, those accounts are considered the child's, and the college will expect that 35 percent of the child's assets be used for her education, a much higher percentage than yours.

If an older child becomes adversarial, she can sue you for reimbursement of moneys that were expended for her support. The cases are equivocal on whether or not you as a parent have a duty to contribute toward college. But they are not clear that you do not. And there is an increasing trend in divorce law that if you have the ability to contribute, you are expected to do so. And it's a very small step from there to saying that using a child's money to pay toward college before you yourself have contributed, given that you are in charge of that money, is a breach of your obligation in managing the money.

It is best to keep less than $30,000, or a relatively small amount of money, in your own name, just mentally earmark it for your child's needs. That way it remains yours. If a lot of money is involved, it is best to establish a children's gift trust to receive it. Then you can designate the proper person as the trustee and you can indicate an older age at which the child receives the funds. The trust will say that any distributions before the designated age, say, twenty-five, are made at the discretion of the trustee. So for college financial aid purposes, a child under the age of twenty-five has zero interest in the trust, because she has no legal right to anything until she reaches the designated age, unless the trustee chooses to make it available.

I heard of an interesting trust. I had never thought of this. A friend of mine was going to leave his money for the education of his several adult children and lots of grandchildren. He does not have so much money. The stipulation is—they get money for their education, but they have to pay it back. They have to pay it back because he feels that money without any ties is too easy. Essentially, he is providing them all with no-interest student loans.

Charity

You also may wish to consider leaving your estate to one or more charities. We often tell our clients, who already know about the bigger charities, such as the American Cancer Society, the United Way, and the Heart Association, also to look at the small charities. For example, you might think about making a gift to your local park and recreation department, often one of the first budgets to be cut in hard times. Think about giving to your local Girl Scouts Council or to the animal rescue league, or to a battered women's shelter. Even a very modest bequest to a small charity can have a tremendous effect. And the smaller organizations are always the ones that are really struggling for operating support. When you have no direct heirs, or if you have plenty to share, then this is a very reasonable way to go.

You will read more about vehicles for charitable giving in chapter 10.

Posthumous Wishes

Sometimes we are asked if there is anything you can put in writing that would legally bind the executor of your will to the decisions that you have made.

Is there some sort of document similar to a living will that can express your wishes on what to do with your body after you die, such as "I do not wish to have an autopsy," or "Please do an autopsy for my family"? Or "Take my organs," or "Do not take my organs"? "I want to be buried in such and such a way." "I want to be cremated." Is there some document that is legally binding? Does my executor have to go along with what I want once I am dead?

Organ donation is done via the anatomical gift instrument. It is the same law that enables you to put a little sticker on your license and give organs. But if you want to donate your organs for transplants or therapy—which is what the statute is about; it is not about ending up in a medical lab for research, although you can do that, too—we recommend that you execute a document as well as putting it on your license.

In a memorandum separate from your will, you can designate to whom specific favorite items should be given. You may wish, for example, to leave a special photo album to a granddaughter, or a silver teapot to a nephew. This memorandum, although not legally binding, will be very helpful to your executor, so he or she knows and can carry out your wishes. Also, since it is not part of your will, you have the option to change it easily any time your wishes change.

Personal Records

As you read in chapter 3, as far as your personal records go, if you have your own system of record keeping that works for you, that's fine. But *please* be kind to your loved ones. Should you become incapacitated, or when you die, those closest to you will greatly appreciate your kindness in making your records accessible.

When my grandfather died, my grandmother had a mess to deal with. She knew he had bank accounts,

but couldn't find the books, and many of the banks had merged. She knew there was a safe deposit box somewhere, but couldn't find the key. He did leave insurance, which she found eventually, but in all it took her about a year to sort out all his papers. She definitely did not need that added burden while mourning the death of her husband.

You can use the following as a worksheet and then make your own. Keep a notebook, and either leave it in your files, or put it somewhere safe and accessible. Tell someone you trust where it can be found. Obviously, there are items on this list that you may not want your relatives to know before you are dead, like your credit card numbers, or the contents of your will.

I picked my youngest brother, who lives out of state. He has the copy of my safe deposit box key, and knows where my notebook is kept.

I keep a little cash in my basement in a coffee can. I don't want it to get thrown out with the nails. Somebody needs to know this information. My kids know. They know that if they are at a party and somebody's been drinking, they can take a cab home, go down and get the cash to pay the driver. I don't keep much money, but someone needs to know. When I die, who is going to open every single box and bag in my cupboard?

Indicate whom you want to be notified of your death. You shouldn't leave it to your next of kin to have to go through your address book and wonder, "Is she still talking to this person?" "Is this a friend or colleague, or is this someone she called once to fix the plumbing?" You might want to update this list once a year, say, on your birthday or on New Year's Day.

With these records, we suggest that everyone write an ethical will. An ethical will is a letter you write to your loved ones, to be read after you are gone. Some churches and synagogues have workshops in writing an ethical will, but you surely can do it on your own. It may contain what you want the people who are left after you to know. Some people like to talk about their own history: where they were born, how they grew up, the lessons they learned during their lives. Others want to give advice to their children, their nieces and nephews, their grandchildren. In any case, it is a very special and important legacy you can leave your heirs.

LOCATION OF PERSONAL RECORDS

Will*

(original with attorney, leave a copy with relative)

Notebook containing the following

(leave with a relative):

Your social security number

Date and place of birth

Mother's maiden name

List of assets:

all bank accounts, brokerage accounts, insurance policies, safe deposit box, location and location of key

Name, address, and telephone number of:

Attorney

Accountant

Financial planner

Brokers

Clergyperson

Doctors

Dentists

Other professionals

Location of:

Safes and combination to locks or safe

Military papers

Marriage license

Divorce decree

Birth certificates

Driver's license

Traveler's checks

Mortgages

Titles to cars

Deeds to property

Stock certificates

Passport

Cash

List of home repair and maintenance help:

Plumber

Electrician

Cleaning service

Septic tank service

List of credit cards and phone numbers of issuing company

List of those you wish to be informed of your death, with phone numbers

Ethical will

(copies with a relative and your clergyperson)

Health care directives

(copies with a relative and your clergyperson)

Durable power of attorney*

(copies with a relative and your clergyperson)

Burial information and instructions

(copies with a relative and your clergyperson)

Disposal of home and contents instructions other than as described in will

(copy with a relative)

*Will and durable power of attorney drafted by an estate lawyer.

9: Negotiation, or Use What You've Got to Get What You Need

Contributing Author:

Rose Ellen McCaig

"People who earn the money have the power, which has a tremendous impact on the family home front for at-home mothers. We need a successful model for shared financial decisions regardless of who is bringing home the pay check."

—LAUREL DOGGETT, MOTHER

WHAT IS NEGOTIATION?

Negotiation is a resolution-oriented dialogue between two or more parties with different positions with regard to a specific issue or issues. Negotiations happen on a daily basis between parents and children, between friends, between spouses and partners, between client and salespersons. Negotiation may be simple:

Denise, a customer, asks the store manager if he will discount a suit $10 because a button is missing from the suit Denise wishes to purchase.

Or more complex:

Homeowner Francine believes she is owed $5,000 back from general contractor Gertrude, who may have been negligent while putting on a new roof.

There also are more formal negotiations, with attorneys present, such as those scheduled toward the end of contract agreements or divorce proceedings.

Most negotiations are complex because the situation, whatever it may be, involves much more than two conflicting positions. The traditional ex-

amples of negotiation presume equality between the negotiating parties. The truth is, however, that equality rarely exists. On the surface, even when both parties appear to be of equal educational and financial stature, each comes to the negotiation with his or her own unique dynamic: underlying needs, fears, patterns, and issues that may either help or hinder both personal power and the ability to get what it is he or she really wants from the negotiation process.

Twenty years ago, Roger Fisher and William Ury of the Harvard Negotiation Project wrote what would become the national best-seller and classic negotiation text, *Getting to Yes*.[1] Fisher and Ury first described the two traditional styles of negotiation: "soft" negotiation ("avoid personal conflict and readily make concessions") and "hard" negotiation ("any situation is a contest of wills"). They then offered a third method: "principled" negotiation, which is "to decide issues on their merits" rather than through a haggling process focused on what each side says it will and won't do. This technique suggests that you "look for mutual gains wherever possible, and that where your interests conflict, you should insist that the result be based on some fair standards independent of the will of either side."

Allie and Jim are recently divorced parents of six-year-old Peter. Allie has physical custody of Peter. This summer will be the first that Allie, Peter, and Jim have lived apart. The divorce agreement provides that during the school year, Peter spends Tuesday and Thursday evenings and alternate weekends with Jim. The agreement states that the parents will negotiate a mutually acceptable summer arrangement that is in the child's best interest. Jim wants to continue the regular school-year visitation schedule because it gives him freedom to develop a relationship with a new woman, while allowing him to see his son at frequent intervals. Allie wants to change the schedule for the summer: she would like Jim to take Peter for the entire month of July so that she can take an intensive computer training course, and she would like Peter with her for the entire month of August because she and the mother of Peter's best friend have an opportunity to rent a place on a nearby island for the month. Allie has not yet told Peter about the beach house, because she doesn't want him to be disappointed if Jim refuses. She knows how much fun the arrangement would be for her son. Finances are not at issue. Furthermore, Jim is self-employed as a psychotherapist with an office in his home.

In Example 1 below, Allie is a "soft" negotiator, and in Example 2, she is a "hard" negotiator. After you have read both, can you give an example of Allie as a "principled" negotiator?

Example 1: Allie explains her position and Jim says, "No. I cannot manage with Peter at my house for a solid month. What will he do all day while I am seeing patients? And what about my social life? And then I'll miss him too much all of August. I

can't believe you'd think of taking him away from me for a month!"

Allie focuses in on Jim's discomfort, his pain at the thought of missing his son, and at his dilemma regarding arrangements to keep Peter happy and cared for during the workday. Rather than discussing solutions to these obstacles, she lets her emotions take over, and she concedes to Jim's wishes.

Example 2: Jim says the same thing as in Example 1. Instead of conceding, Allie tells Jim, "Look. You drop Peter off at the day camp he loved last year. You pick him up at four. You limit your social life. You can fly down to the island to visit Pete if you miss him. This will work. If you don't like it, call my attorney and we'll go to court to resolve this."

How would Allie reply if she were a "principled" negotiator? You can try writing what she might say to Jim here:

_____
_____
_____

An intellectual grasp of the concept and the construct of "principled" negotiation may not always be enough to help us when we find ourselves in a position in which we need or want to negotiate. We all have underlying patterns and dynamics that alter or control our voices. Women, especially those who have been influenced greatly by a society that shapes our ability to assert our needs and get those needs met, first must recognize these inner agendas in order to then become more effective negotiators. In any negotiation, we must believe that we are entitled to ask for what it is that we want. Some women tend to be nervous and fearful of asserting themselves, or of asking for too much. We then tend to act apologetic. To unlearn this self-defeating behavior, we must practice. The first few times we assert ourselves, we may be afraid, and feel as if we have gone too far.

If we are practicing what I call "clean" negotiation, then we do not learn to be simply pushy. We learn to stand up for ourselves and to feel good no matter what the outcome. The idea isn't to learn to make demands and to push and bully others into giving us what we want. The goal is to understand what we want, and to ask for it and to hold on to the goal while at the same time listening to the other person. The goal is to stay grounded in who we are, to feel as if we are our own anchors and our own strength. What is most important is not who wins the game, but that you feel good about the way you played it!

There are many different reasons to negotiate and many varying types of negotiations. Still, there are common themes and basic skills that can be recognized and learned. Below is an exercise that presents a seemingly simple negotiation between two roommates.

ANN, BETTY, AND RAFFLES

Ann and Betty are roommates. Ann wants to get a dog to keep at the apartment. Betty says "No way!" Can this situation be resolved through negotiation? See if you can:

- Think about questions you want to answer in order to determine a "fact pattern" for your negotiation

- Think about some objective criteria that might influence or determine the outcome of your negotiation

- Spot the basic issues in your fact pattern

- Spot the possible underlying issues, and

- Come up with possible solutions in a role-play

Try this exercise with a partner or with a small group before reading on. Some sample questions to establish what we call a "fact pattern":

- How old is Ann? _____

- How old is Betty? _____

- How long have they been roommates? _____

- Are they friends as well? _____

- Do they have a lease? _____

- Can they keep a dog in the apartment? _____

- If so, is there an extra charge? _____

- What kind of dog is it? _____

- Is Betty opposed to all types of dogs? To all pets? _____

- Would Ann consider another type of pet? _____

- Why does Ann want a dog? Why does Betty not? _____

- Does either Ann or Betty care if they continue to be roommates and/or friends? _____

- How have the two women resolved differences between them in the past? _____

- How has each resolved conflict with others? _____

Some objective criteria might be the existence of a lease and the legality of keeping a dog in the apartment, medical reasons to have or not to have a dog, whether there had been a discussion between the women regarding pets prior to their signing the lease.

Sample underlying issues might be power struggles, underlying anger, a need to please, fear, or control.

Before reading the example below, try to come up with a solution(s) based on your own criteria. You might experiment with role-playing, based upon the questions and answers you provided above. List your possible outcomes here:

_____

_____

_____

_____

Now imagine that Ann and Betty's conversation continues along the following lines:

ANN: I am so excited! My brother is being transferred to Europe for a year and wants me to take Raffles, his wirehaired terrier. You've met him a few times, so it's not like he's a strange dog. I already checked it out with our landlady and she said it would be fine to have him. I already asked Mary, the teenager downstairs, and she said she'd walk and feed Raffles after school and whenever I'm not home. I'll pay for his care. Betty, you won't have to do anything extra. You have to say "Yes"! Remember how I took care of you when you broke your leg last year?

BETTY: I don't know. You know I don't really like Raffles. He kind of makes me itch or something. Maybe after I consult an allergist . . . [Her voice fades out.]

What do you think of the negotiation thus far between Ann and Betty? What "techniques" does Ann employ? Which are principled and which are not? What is happening to Betty? Is she taking care of herself? What about Ann? Do you think she will get what she really wants from Betty? How about if you change some of the facts and/or dynamics? What if Ann were a man? What if Ann and Betty were partners? What if both women were men? Remember that men also experience societal and cultural pressures to act in a certain way!

Is either woman a "soft" negotiator? A "hard" negotiator? What do you think are some of the societal and/or personal influences or reasons that would make a woman a "soft" negotiator or a "hard" negotiator?

Sometimes, given advance warning and enough time, we can call upon our intelligence and our organizational skills in order to diligently prepare for a negotiation in which we will be successful. For example, Susan would like to take an out-of-town seminar but she doesn't have a great deal of money to spend on accommodations. Since it is the off-season, Susan thinks that perhaps an innkeeper might rather make some money than none at all so she researches smaller inns as well as any discounts to which she may be entitled, such as Triple A, AARP, government rate, corporate or group rate, and she knows she will ask, "What is the lowest rate you can offer?" and "Are there any special deals?"

Most negotiations, however, are integrated into the fabric of our everyday lives. Situations occur in which we must learn to be strong enough to react in a manner that best serves our goal and to take care of ourselves without any advance practice. How can we learn this strength? So many of us hear our own voices fading out when we are confronted with an uncomfortable situation, whether expected or unexpected, or when we need to ask for something, no matter how reasonable it is.

NEGOTIATION—BEYOND THE DEFINITION

That which we bring to the negotiating "table"—whether that table is in a formal setting such as an attorney's or mediator's office, at the mall, or in our own kitchen—is more than a set of objective facts or discernible positions. We bring our underlying and often unrecognized agendas and attitudes to each negotiation. The better we can learn to uncover and understand these often-unconscious motivations, the more successful we will be at "principled" negotiation, or a "clean" transaction.

Think again about Ann and Betty. The first mention of them told you that Ann wants a dog and Betty does not. The underlying issues that each woman brings to a negotiation of the subject may turn the negotiation into something other than a "clean" transaction. Examine the fact pattern that you developed. If you decided that there was a "no-pet" clause in the lease, or that Betty was extremely allergic to dogs, then you probably need to go no further. Ann's desire to have a dog may have been precluded by what principled negotiation seeks: objective criteria. If, however, you eliminated any legal or medical reason not to keep a dog at the apartment, and you came up with ready defenses for Ann, you then needed to look at the negotiating styles of the two roommates and what possible underlying issues and motivating forces exist for them. How do Ann and Betty resolve the situation? What are some possible outcomes? What do you think is the best outcome?

_____

_____

_____

WHY WE HAVE TROUBLE "GETTING TO YES"

As an attorney involved in many domestic relations and other types of cases, I have noticed that women often know exactly what they want, but because of certain general factors do not stand their ground. Some of these factors are the need to please others, a need to "get it over with," and a need to keep everything "nice" or "friendly."

These three basic factors are relatively easy to understand. As women, we often give up what we want in order to please someone else. Then we defend our actions and exclaim that we are just being "nice"! We also may be uncomfortable in a situation that calls for us to stand up for ourselves. So we try to alleviate our discomfort by ending the transaction as quickly as possible—often to our own short- and long-term detriment. But what happens down the road? Here is a story that illustrates what may happen when we are less than honest.

Jane and Kendall are going out to dinner. Jane is starving. Kendall wants to go to her favorite pizza place, one that serves only pizza. Jane does not like pizza at all. Jane doesn't say anything and just agrees to go for pizza because she is eager to talk to Kendall about a problem she is having at work. When the two friends arrive at the pizza place, Kendall spends the entire time ogling Chris, the manager, and talking about how much she would like to meet Chris.

Jane's needs were not met. Jane didn't satisfy her hunger—for food or for comfort. And what about Kendall? It is probable that she had no idea Jane hated pizza or that Jane had a problem she wished to share with Kendall that night! What Jane did was not "clean." She tried to please Kendall, to not make waves, to keep everything nice, so she, in turn, would be rewarded with the attention she craved. How could Jane have acted differently? You can try writing your own script before reading the one below:

JANE: _____

_____

KENDALL: _____

_____

JANE: _____

_____

KENDALL: _____

_____

JANE: _____

_____

KENDALL: _____

_____

JANE: I am really looking forward to seeing you for dinner tonight. Do you mind, though, if we don't go to Pat's Pizza?

KENDALL: Oooh . . . I have been craving pizza all day!

JANE: How about we go to Party Pizza instead? It's in the same neighborhood. You can get pizza and I can order the grilled chicken salad I like.

KENDALL: Oh.

JANE: What's wrong?

KENDALL: Well, the truth is . . . I want to go to Pat's because I have kind of a crush on the manager, Chris. I was hoping . . .

JANE: Oh. Well, how about we go to Pat's afterward and pick up some take-out menus or some sodas? Besides, I want to discuss something important with you over dinner.

The negotiation between Jane and Kendall could have taken many different turns. In the example above, however, Jane was direct and honest and her honesty made Kendall react honestly with regard to the real reason she wanted to go to Pat's Pizza.

What might prevent Jane, or you, or anyone who does not make her needs known from being honest and direct?

Often the answer is "fear." Of what are we afraid? Why might we have such difficulty stating our needs? Sometimes, we may have no problem being honest, direct, strong, and assertive. If asked where we want to have dinner, we respond with: "I'd love to go to Party Pizza because there is a great grilled chicken salad on the menu and that's exactly what I'm in the mood for tonight!" But what happens to us when the question is posed in a slightly different way? For example:

Kendall telephones Jane and asks, "Do you want to go to Pat's Pizza tonight? I've been craving pizza all day!"

Jane may be able to state her needs if no other dialogue has been written yet: she is "speaking on a blank page." She may not be able to do so when the stakes have been raised, that is, someone else's needs already are "spoken on the page." Or Jane may not be able to state her needs even when she is given a completely blank page upon which to speak. Some of us need practice just saying our needs out loud to another person! Have you ever been in a situation such as the following?

KENDALL: Where do you want to eat tonight?

JANE: I don't care. Wherever you want.

It may be true that Jane doesn't care—that particular evening for that particular meal. But you may have a friend like Linda, who *never* seems to care. You may think of someone like Linda as laid-back, easygoing, or relaxed. But the truth is, Linda *does* care where she dines, what movie she sees, and that you were twenty minutes late the last two times you were to meet with her.

What would it take for Jane to give Kendall an honest answer? List all the reasons Jane might be afraid to state her needs:

_____

_____

_____

_____

What would you do in this situation?

You can practice answering questions honestly and stating your needs in a direct fashion—first in situations where there is a "blank page," and then when someone else has first stated her own needs and her needs are different or in contradiction to yours.

In negotiation, we cannot be afraid of anything. It is much more useful to be brave enough to state important needs, to be able to face any potential outcome.

TAKE GOOD CARE OF YOURSELF IN ANY NEGOTIATION

What do these scenarios have to do with your divorce negotiation scheduled for next week? Or with the fact that you want to buy a car but think you need a male friend or relative to go with you so you do not feel intimidated? In order to be able to take good care of yourself in any negotiation, you need to be able to follow these steps:

- Assess your underlying fears.

- Know what it is you really want.

- State what it is you really want.

- Listen to the other person(s).

- Pay attention to your feelings every moment of the transaction.

- Call for time-out to reconnect and recenter yourself if you feel overwhelmed by your underlying fears.

- Return and continue—try to make the transaction a clean one.

Look again at the Jane and Kendall situation, imagining that you are Jane. Let's go through these steps, one by one.

Assess your underlying fears

What are you afraid will happen? Imagine the worst-case scenario. You tell Kendall you don't want to go to Pat's Pizza. You will feel selfish. You will not be a good friend. She yells at you. She cries. She doesn't want to have dinner with you. She calls you names. She'll get a new best friend. You will be alone.

It is important to remember that if you keep quiet and stuff down your true feelings, you are alone anyway—you are not really fully present in the relationship with Kendall. If you are too afraid to be yourself, who is there with Kendall at Pat's Pizza?

Know what it is you really want

Does Jane know what it is she really wants? Does she want to please Kendall more than she wants to eat a dinner she enjoys? If she understands what she really wants, and her wants are healthy, adult, and grounded in present reality rather than based in deep, dark fears, she will be able to express herself in a way that will be good for her and most likely good for Kendall as well.

State what it is you really want

What happens when Jane knows what it is she really wants, but the words won't come out? Getting dressed in the privacy of our bedrooms, we know exactly what we want and what we want to say, but when the doorbell rings and the friend, colleague, in-law, or vacuum salesperson comes in, we sometimes lose our voice.

Jane knows she wants to please Kendall. Jane also knows that she is going to tell Kendall that she would like to have dinner somewhere that serves salad. Jane also knows that she wants to talk to Kendall about a personal problem. Somehow, Jane winds up at Pat's Pizza drinking a diet soda and eating a roll and listening to Kendall launch a plan to meet the manager. Jane comes home later that night and mentally kicks herself—"Why didn't I say . . . ?" she groans to herself. In order to take care of ourselves, we need to hold on to our voices—not just before and after, but *during* any given transaction.

Listen to the other person(s)

When we are preoccupied with our own fears, we are not really listening to the needs of others. In order to fully participate in any negotiation and make that negotiation a productive one, each participant must truly acknowledge the others. Jane, for example, may one day become secure in her ability to hold on to her voice no matter what happens in the negotiation. This security, or trust, that Jane has in herself will free her to be able to really listen, appreciate, and objectively assess the point of view of another.

Pay attention to your feelings every moment of the transaction

In order to develop such a trust in herself, Jane needs to practice being aware of her own feelings at any given moment. This is more difficult than it sounds. It is a very individual, personal, and valuable skill that cannot be taught—it must be experienced, practiced, and learned by each of us.

Call for time-out to reconnect and recenter yourself if you feel overwhelmed by your underlying fears

When Kendall tells Jane how much she wants to go to Pat's Pizza, Jane feels her own voice fading. Jane feels herself becoming invisible. If Jane is aware of these feelings but cannot stop them, she needs to be able to reconnect with herself. If they are speaking in person, Jane can say, "Hang on, Kendall. I'm going to the rest room." Or if they are speaking on the telephone, Jane can say, "I need to call you back in a minute." In neither case did Jane tell a lie. She simply removed herself temporarily from a situation in which she felt she was losing her own voice. Jane can take a deep breath and find her voice.

Return and continue—try to make the transaction a clean one

Jane returns from her time out with restored strength. Jane has taken a moment to reconnect with her own feelings. She trusts herself enough to return to Kendall. Jane doesn't need to demand that Kendall eat dinner where Jane wants to eat. Jane trusts herself to listen to what Kendall wants, to carefully consider how Kendall's wants feel to Jane, and to express her own needs. At the restaurant, Jane can directly ask Kendall for her attention—that Jane has a problem with her boss and she'd like to discuss it with Kendall. This time, Jane won't have to go home at the end of the evening and ask herself, "Why didn't I say . . . ?" Nor will Jane resent Kendall. Nor will Jane want to call up Kendall the next day and say, "You know, last night when we were at Pat's and you were busy looking at Chris, I really wanted to talk to you, but you were too busy . . ."

TECHNIQUES TO MAKE EVERY NEGOTIATION SUCCESSFUL

If you are true to yourself, you will feel good about yourself at the close of any transaction!

On their first date, Richard takes Anna, whom he met at the gym, to dinner. During the evening, he mentions how much he likes home-cooked food. Anna doesn't really like to cook but she does like Richard. For their next date, Anna invites Richard to her condo for dinner. In preparation for the date, Anna agonizes over recipes and gives up a meeting of her Thursday-night book club in order to clean house and food-shop. Anna is excited about seeing Richard but wishes they were meeting at an interesting ethnic restaurant instead! Richard arrives at

Anna's place. He seems to enjoy the dinner. At the end of the evening, he says he will call her. He never calls. When Anna runs into him at the gym a couple of weeks later, Richard is friendly but casual.

How would you feel if you were Anna? Anna was not true to herself when she gave up her club meeting and when she did something that she really did not want to do to get a reward. Not only did Anna lose her voice, she also didn't get the reward! And what kind of a reward would such a relationship be, if Anna could not be herself? How can Anna feel good about her two dates with Richard? Can you think of another possibility? Here's one:

Anna gets together with Richard, a guy she met at the gym. On their first date, Richard takes her to dinner and mentions how much he likes home-cooked food. Anna doesn't like to cook, but she does like Richard. So her response to his statement is (1) a smile, (2) that she does, too—her mom is a wonderful cook (if true!) (3) she's not a cook, but take-out is fun. On their second date, Richard takes Anna to a movie they both wanted to see. Then, Richard does not call her back. When Anna sees him at the gym two weeks later, he is friendly but casual. Although Anna is disappointed, she feels okay because she knows she was true to herself. She can look back on the two dates with Richard for what they were—two pleasant evenings.

Here is another example:

Sandy works part time as the assistant manager of a small dress shop. She plans to ask the owner for an extra week off after Christmas so she can be home with her children. The week of Thanksgiving, Sandy's best friend comes to town for the holiday. The only time they can get together is the day after

Thanksgiving. Sandy is happy because the shop will be closed and she has the day off. Sandy and her friend make plans to go to the theater. The morning after Thanksgiving, the owner calls Sandy. Could she please come in, as she thinks she will open the shop after all? Sandy, hoping that the owner will remember the favor come Christmas, replies, "Certainly." When Christmas comes, the owner says the shop is "too busy" for Sandy to take off the week. Sandy then reminds her of the "special favor" at Thanksgiving. "What special favor?" wonders the owner. "You agreed so readily."

What do you imagine the next part of their conversation will be?

Role-playing can be helpful in exploring reactions to certain situations. Other techniques to strengthen your sense of self, your confidence, and your ability to take care of yourself in any type of negotiation are:

- Using imagery (future)

- Drawing on your own experiences and feelings (past)

- Creating positive situations (present)

Tracy says she is able to accomplish new and challenging goals by first envisioning herself in the act of accomplishing them. For several days before her meeting with a divorce mediator, Tracy imagined herself driving to the meeting, the confidence with which she would present her position and her goals, and on the parts where she would be comfortable making compromises. Tracy didn't simply think about the upcoming meeting—she closed her eyes and she saw it!

I have developed another technique[2] that you can use when faced with a tough situation, for example, at a job interview: Draw a line down the center of a piece of paper, labeling the left-hand column: "If the interviewer (or my opponent) says/does . . ." and labeling the right-hand column: "Then I will do/say . . ." If you have difficulty trusting your own instincts at the moment something is happening, you may want to think ahead and to practice. This is not the same as a rehearsal, and certainly many encounters are unpredictable. However, this technique is one that may help you to focus on some of the potential situations that might occur and to practice acting on your own instincts.

Martha wants to have work done on her property and she is scheduling interviews with potential landscape architects. She is nervous because this is something her late husband would have taken care of. If Martha thinks back, however, a month ago she bought a new car for the first time all by herself. She had done research, bargained well, enjoyed the respect of the salesperson, and she drove away with a nice deal. She felt great! If Martha can draw on her past success, she will be able to feel the same confidence in negotiations with the potential architect.

Marissa is the building manager of ABC Properties. She is responsible for collecting the rents due on the first of the month. If ABC has not received a tenant's rent check on or before the tenth of each month, Marissa must contact the tenant. The Wilsons in Apartment 22 never pay by the tenth but do pay when Marissa confronts them. They make her wait, however, in their smoke-filled apartment and Mr. Wilson often greets her in his underwear. Marissa is very uncomfortable.

How can Marissa use the chart to prepare herself for her monthly encounters with the Wilsons? Should Marissa also discuss this situation with her superior at ABC? How can she prepare herself for that conversation or confrontation? Also, Marissa believes she deserves a raise from ABC. Does her belief alter her behavior in the above scenarios?

Each time we create a positive situation, we are stronger when we are faced with the next new situation.

In the case of Sandy, the dress shop assistant manager, she could have spoken up when the owner asked her to work on her day off. She could have said she had important plans but might consider changing them if the owner would consider giving her some extra time off at New Year's. Whatever the outcome, Sandy will feel good about herself. And she will be even stronger the next time. We have so many opportunities in our everyday lives to learn and to grow—we just need to make each transaction count!

NEGOTIATING WELL MEANS KEEPING GOOD BOUNDARIES

If we have "good boundaries," we know where we begin and end. Pia Mellody calls boundary systems "invisible and symbolic fences."[3] If our boundaries are healthy, we don't allow someone else's needs to come before our own. We don't get absorbed by another's need, desire, or pain nor, on the other extreme, do we feel nothing because we are wearing a heavy coat of protection. Rather, we trust ourselves enough to let others' ideas in and out of us in a healthy, satisfying way. Good boundaries are essential to being a good negotiator. We can enter into any situation and know that we can take care of ourselves.

When you are true to yourself, you will feel positive no matter what the outcome of the negotiation. Being true to yourself does not mean you cannot recognize, understand, and even empathize with another's position. Often we have trouble holding on to our identities when we are nervous or we feel as if someone won't like us if we stand our ground. It is important for us to be aware of where we are comfortable negotiating, and how far we are willing to go to reach a settlement of the issue. It is important to stay in the present, and not to negotiate only in our own minds. We can learn techniques that will enable us to better negotiate through role-play, imagery, from drawing on past experiences and feelings, and, finally, from continuing to create positive situations from which we can find strength.

10: Around the Glass Ceiling: The Collective Power of Women's Philantrophy

Contributing Authors:

Nancy A. Haverstock and Gail R. Shapiro

"Find a cause or causes that you feel passionate about and start early asking people with substantial wealth to donate to these causes. Getting comfortable with asking others to support our various projects has been key to our ongoing success."
—JUDY NORSIGIAN, BOSTON WOMEN'S HEALTH BOOK COLLECTIVE

IN THIS CHAPTER, YOU WILL LEARN:

- The great personal and financial benefits of charitable giving

- Why creating a plan for your charitable giving is so important

- Why funding is so critical for programs for women and girls

- How women's funds help address issues important to women and girls

- About women as philanthropists

- The potential power of our collective philanthropy

You have read about how to set goals, how to budget, how to save, invest, buy insurance, homes, and cars; you have read about creating a feasible plan for your later years, and perhaps leaving a legacy to your heirs.

Now that you have done everything prudent to protect yourself and ensure financial security, how can you be sure that money keeps on flowing your way? You can give it away!

"Philanthropy" or "charitable giving" are names usually used interchangeably to describe gifts made by individuals and organizations to aid the needy, solve a problem, or enhance the community, the nation, or the world. From the Greek, "love of (wo)mankind," philanthropy is "altruistic concern for human beings, especially as manifested by donations of money, property, or work to needy persons or to institutions advancing human welfare." "Charity," or "donations or generous actions to aid the poor, ill or helpless," is derived from the Latin word *caritas*, meaning "dear."

Charitable giving shows our support for those people and causes we consider dear or worthy. We can give cash, goods, or our time. Charitable giving is a very personal response to human needs, which can help to improve the quality of our life and the lives of those around us. Giving in every form also helps to set an example for our children and our friends:

"When people begin volunteering young," said Charlotte Lunsford, former Red Cross national chair of volunteers, "normally they volunteer throughout their lives."[1]

Why do people give? Why do you give? Our students say:

Personal gratification

When you give, you know that no matter how poor you are, someone else is needier.

Because the world is such a mess, it's the least I can do.

You feel rich when you give money away.

Guilt.

Giving helps me feel better about myself.

A conditioned reflex—like dropping a quarter in the box for the Salvation Army.

A deep yearning: You've done well and now you want to do good.

To be involved with a community of like-minded individuals.

It's great to volunteer at the museum: I've met wonderful people, learned so much more about art, and gained skills which will help me when I graduate and go to work someday.

People give because they are asked. Pressure from peers, like collecting for their kids' candy drive. Pressure from superiors at work, such as to give to the United Way. Or asked by a friend to support his or her special cause.

I give to causes with personal meaning, such as research for a disease a relative has.

Gratitude: to give back to the community

My husband and I have had many advantages, and we are proud of our success. We feel it is our social obligation to respond to important human needs in the same community that supported our business these many years, and fostered our achievements.

When my son was born, I was alone and I didn't have a dime. I'll never forget the kindness of the folks at the Visiting Nurses Association in the town where we lived. They did so much for me! Even though I now live in another state, I send them a check every Christmas.

To be recognized as a philanthropist or to leave a legacy

It's an ego thing—look at me—I've done so well, I can afford to give big bucks and get my name on a bench/building/in a program, etc.

Desire to be looked up to as a leader in the community.

To promote a cause or philosophy

Our nation depends upon the independent sector to fill the gap in social services. I do not believe that our government should be in the welfare business. Communities need to look after their own.

I want to support the causes I believe in: home schooling, animal rights, and protecting the environment.

Philanthropy ensures democracy. Because of my community and political work in the sixties I'd always felt like a subversive. Now that I see things differently, I feel like a patriot!

I believe strongly in the right of citizens to bear arms, and I support organizations that work for that freedom.

To teach our children about giving

Giving together as a family unites the family with a shared purpose.

To show my kids that they have enough, and that it's right to give to those who don't.

I grew up in a family that didn't have much to give. We were encouraged to volunteer, to give our time, to help those not as fortunate.

We want to model philanthropy for our children. In our family, we vote every month about where to give donations. Sometimes, the gifts go to places I wouldn't necessarily pick: the Rock and Roll Hall of Fame, for example!

To honor or remember a loved one

When my friends started turning forty, I figured they didn't need any more stuff. I started making gifts to organizations they support, in their honor. It's a win-win thing.

My mother passed away last year. We established a scholarship fund in her memory at her alma mater. Instead of sending flowers, her friends sent gifts. Mother would be so happy to think that a needy student can attend the school she loved so well!

For tax advantages

The tax deduction for gifts of cash to charity can be up to 50 percent of your adjusted gross income for the year.

You can set up a charitable foundation that is exempt from federal income tax on its income, and your gifts to the foundation are tax-advantaged. I have heard that you can deduct up to 30 percent of your annual adjusted gross income for cash donations.

To fulfill a religious obligation

Why give? Because the Bible commands us to do so.

As far back as I can remember, my family always has tithed—giving 10 percent of income to charity. Giving the first 10 percent not only makes you feel good, it keeps the money flowing. It does take an awful lot of trust the first few times, but after that, you see that when you tithe, it works. It's very empowering and very practical.

When you give money away freely, it comes back to you tenfold. It is especially important to give generously at the times you feel the most broke!

The IRS says that you can give up to 50 percent of your income to charity and receive a tax benefit. My friend lives in an ashram, and he gives a lot more. He was called in for an audit. He was asked, "Why are you giving all this money away?" He said, "Well, I have enough. I take what I need and I don't need any more."

Consider giving as a regular part of your fiscal and spiritual practice.

WHY CREATING A PLAN FOR YOUR CHARITABLE GIVING IS SO IMPORTANT

When you have money to give away on a large scale, you are apt to spend a lot more time thinking about it. If you are like most women, you give without a plan, goal, or objective. And just as with other aspects of your financial life, if you don't know where you are going, it's unlikely you'll get there. What do you want your charitable dollars to do? To make you feel good? To help make a difference in your community? To honor a friend or relative? To show publicly that you are a philanthropist? To start or replicate a good program for a cause you care about deeply?

Here are nine questions to encourage thoughtful giving. We strongly suggest you discuss these in a group or with your family:

1. What did you learn about charitable giving as you grew up? Who in your family decided how gifts were made? What family traditions, if any, did your family have regarding charitable giving?
2. For you now, as an adult, what are the benefits of giving? What do you want/expect in return for your gift?
3. How do you decide which charities to support, and at what level?
4. Do you tend to give in response to a person or to a cause?
5. Are you more or less likely to encourage a friend to give to your favorite charity?
6. Do you make charitable gifts instead of/in addition to more tangible gifts to honor friends' birthdays, other events?
7. Do you have a plan for charitable giving (i.e., a predetermined percent of your income, a regular time of the year to give, or a fixed amount of time you volunteer each week) or do you give "as the spirit moves you"?
8. What factors might influence your giving?
9. Are you comfortable with your charitable giving practice? If not, what would you like to improve? What do you need to do so?

HOW TO DECIDE WHERE TO GIVE

I appreciate that in the phrase "cash flow" the emphasis is on the word "flow." If you hoard money, you end up only with the money you hoard. If you spend, give away, invest, or otherwise use your money, you keep it in circulation, and it comes back to you in a positive way.

Research on women's philanthropy shows that most women do not define ourselves as philanthropists, nor do we think strategically about donations. So how then do we begin to choose from among requests and causes, and support those that move us in some way?

If your house is typical, starting in November, you get a huge number of requests from organizations asking for every good cause: those you care about, those you don't care about, those you used to care about but don't anymore, those you are forced to care about—like the fund-raisers your coworkers' children are collecting for.

Thoughtful giving takes some work. How do you decide where to give, how much to give? Should you give money, time, or things? How often should you give? Should you give to women's causes, or should you give to general causes? Should you give locally, nationally, or globally? Should you choose individual organizations to support, or give one larger gift to your local community foundation, a women's fund, or to a program that distributes money to many groups, such as Community Works or United Way? And how do you make those decisions?

Obviously, there are no right or wrong answers here; the choice is yours. No one should tell you that you should give money only to your church, or only to your school. Of course, if you live with a partner, you will need to make some joint decisions about giving. Who in your household currently makes those decisions? You, your partner, both of you, the whole family, if you live with children? And what informs those decisions?

Your gift is never too small to matter. Here's why. Our nonprofit organization is relatively new and fairly small. Last week, we applied for a grant, and we were asked, "How many donors do you have?" The funder wanted to see that we had a lot of support in the community, not that we had a lot of money. Many of the gifts we'd received were $35, $50, $100. Some were only $10. In this case, the size of the gifts didn't matter; the size of the donor base did. What's very interesting about that is that as you look at statistics of philanthropy, people with incomes under $15,000 give a far higher percentage of their income than do people with incomes greater than $100,000.

We have found that in most households, women are active participants in the giving decisions. This participation reflects the nature of our values, as we discussed in chapter 1. We tend to value relationships with people and how they interact for the betterment of all. We are expert at giving of ourselves and our time—now we must become as expert in the giving of money. Thinking about where and how much to give leads to questions of how to give. Here are some options. For any other than cash gifts, you will want to consult with your financial adviser, your attorney, and/or an independent charitable giving adviser, who can help you make sound decisions.

In the Jewish tradition, everyone is expected to engage in service and charity to benefit the needy. There are different levels of giving, here arranged according to Maimonides's Ladder of Giving, from best to least good:

Give the recipient the wherewithal to become self-supporting.

Neither the donor nor the recipient knows the other.

The donor knows the recipient but the recipient is unaware of the donor.

The recipient knows the donor but the donor does not know the recipient.

The donor gives without being solicited.

The donor gives after being solicited.

The donor gives less than he should but does so cheerfully.

The donor is pained by the act of giving.

LOOK BEFORE YOU GIVE!

If you are not familiar with a particular charity, you can get more information from the National Charities Information Bureau (212-929-6300) or the Council of Better Business Bureaus (703-276-0100). Your state attorney general's office is also a source of information. All 501(c)(3) organizations are required to file federal tax form 990, and these forms are public records. For more information, GuideStar is a searchable database of more than 620,000 nonprofit organizations in the United States, at www.guidestar.org.

VEHICLES FOR CHARITABLE GIVING

Give directly to the charity of your choice

For most of us, the most familiar way to give is to donate directly to the charity of choice. Gifts can be made in cash—such as the dollar you drop into the Salvation Army kettle—by check, or by credit card. Or you can give property, such as clothes to Goodwill or furniture to the veterans' association. If you are interested in receiving a tax deduction for your gift, you can ask the organization directly whether it has received the 501(c)(3) tax-exempt status from the Internal Revenue Service. You also may make donations of property, including real estate, mutual funds, stocks, and other securities. A different tax structure applies to these gifts.

If you own some stock that your grandfather gave you, in Standard Oil, now Exxon, and sell it, you'd almost surely have to give away 20 percent in capital gains to the feds because they would trace the cost basis back not to when Grandpa gave it to you, but to when Grandpa bought it. So if you just give it to your alma mater you get an enormous tax deduction; they'll throw a dinner in your honor, no capital gains. Giving can make much more sense than selling.

Give to or through a federated fund, community foundation, or other public foundation

Federated funds, like the United Way, the Black United Fund, Community Works, and others, participate in annual workplace giving campaigns that raise funds for distribution to local, state, and national nonprofit organizations.

Community foundations are local charitable entities that may administer a number of endowed funds specifically aimed at serving local causes. Most large cities and many regions now have community foundations. Donors can make an unrestricted gift, to be used where the foundation managers think best, or a designated gift, to a particular charity or field of interest. Or you can create a donor-advised fund within a community foundation for any purpose you choose. The foundation administers the fund, usually for a small annual fee.

You also may choose to support a public foundation, a public charity established to address a particular issue, such as arts education, or to support the needs of a particular group, such as women and girls.

Set up your own foundation

You can provide for the long-term needs of the organizations and the people you want to help by establishing, funding, and maintaining your own foundation. The most common is the private grant-making endowed foundation. Two other types of private foundations are the pass-through foundation and the private operating foundation. If you are the owner of a family business or an officer of a corporation, you may want to consider developing a corporate giving program or a corporate foundation. Since the legal and tax ramifications are so complicated, be sure to find an attorney with experience in the specific type of foundation you wish to start. You can ask an estate planning attorney for a referral.

Planned giving

Planned giving makes it possible for you to give to your favorite charity, meet your income needs, and provide for your heirs. Two common vehicles are the charitable remainder trust and the charitable lead trust. Again, be sure to consult your financial adviser or estate planning attorney. In each case, you may designate a particular non-profit organization (or organizations), your own private foundation, your local community foundation or other public foundation, or your own supporting organization to receive the benefits of your planned gifts.

"Mary" is sixty-four years old, has one daughter, and lives next to a famous university. Her house is not large, but because of its location, it is valued at $2 million. Like many of my older clients, she owns significant assets, but does not have enough income. So I said to her, "Why don't I go talk to the university?" I knocked on the door and the development people were extremely hospitable. And an arrangement was made in which the university will pay her a lifetime income based on the value of the house and her life expectancy. It comes out to about $75,000 a year. They will shovel the snow and fix the roof. She can live there as long as she likes, and has agreed to leave it to the university

when she dies. Now what about the daughter? How would you like it if your mother gave away her biggest asset and there was nothing left for you? She purchased a life insurance policy on the life of the mother, so when the mother dies, the daughter will get a check from this life insurance trust of $2-million-plus to replace the house and it is utterly and completely tax-free. And she doesn't have to worry about taking care of her mother's house while the mother is alive. The premium does absorb a fair bit of her new $75,000 yearly income, but she's still $40,000 ahead every year.

GIVE—AND HAVE FUN!

Donating money and time can be very rewarding!

When my kids were small, we often drove to the children's room in the library of another town. We would take a few new dollar bills, maybe five or ten, and slip one into each of our favorite books. We'd then have a great time on the way home and for days afterward, thinking about the delight of the children who found the money, and how maybe they would tell their friends, and then all the kids would get more interested in reading!

When I give clothes to Goodwill or another charity, I usually slip a coin or two into the pocket.

I've always supported Special Olympics, and volunteered several hours a week. But when my daughter became a toddler, it became impossible to bring her. So they found a way for me to volunteer on-line, and I can do the work while she naps or in the evenings.

Instead of a birthday present, I often make a gift in someone's honor. Now, it doesn't have to cost a lot, because the charity doesn't tell the amount of the gift, just that you sent it. And they feel special, and it encourages them to do the same for someone else.

A side effect from a gift like that: I made a gift in the name of my brother to the Juvenile Diabetes Foundation. He is a diabetic, but he had never become involved with them. And then he in turn began to volunteer for them, and made lots of friends. So a gift can have far-reaching effects.

I don't have much money or time to give. But then a friend told me about Dress for Success, a national nonprofit organization that helps low-income women into the workforce by giving them one good donated suit when she has an interview and another when she gets the job. Now, finally, here was something I could do! I now send at least two suits each season. They still are in good shape, and I'm delighted to be able to help. (You can find out more at www.dressforsuccess.org.)

One morning, I was reading the newspaper and saw all the usual depressing stuff. On page 3 was a small article about a library in another part of the state that had been flooded. I thought, "Well, I can't solve the problems of the world, but here is something I can do." So with the help of a couple of friends, I organized a children's book drive. We collected two truckloads of books!

There are many worthy smaller charities that do not have the marketing budget to promote themselves, and consequently often are not known outside their immediate community. Your gift can make a major impact on the work of these excellent organizations.

In Massachusetts, which continually is ranked near the bottom of the "generosity index" (the income-to-charitable-giving ratio), the Ellis Phillips Foundation set about promoting the cause of philanthropy with the mission of raising the total charitable-giving level in that state. In 1997–1999, the foundation conducted a three-year experiment, which is continuing. They compiled and published the *Catalogue for Philanthropy*, mailed to all affluent households, which each year showcased approximately one hundred of the best small charities in the state. Initial results showed a significant increase both in donations and in volunteers to the listed agencies.

Your local community foundation will be happy to sit down with you and find local charities that match your interests. Or you can hire an independent charitable giving adviser to help you think through your giving decisions. Taking into account your emotional, practical, and spiritual needs, an independent charitable giving ad-

---

Consider making a gift to help a woman starting out or starting over. Most women would never dream of asking a friend for help. If you are fortunate enough to be in a position to be able to give $1,000 or $1,500, offer your friend the money, which she can deposit in a bank. She will then be able to get a secured credit card or a secured loan. It is important that you think of this money as a gift, and not as a loan, so you can't be "burned." When she tries to pay you back later, tell her to "pay it forward" instead: that is, use the money to help another woman in a similar circumstance. This keeps the energy flowing!

viser can help you find a charity or charities that match your giving goals. Knowledgeable about a great many large and smaller charities, and skilled in research, she is not affiliated with any particular charities, nor does she get a commission, but generally charges by the hour. After an initial consultation, she will do research sufficient to identify charities that are right for you. You then would meet with your own attorney or financial planner to determine the vehicle for giving that best meets your legal and financial needs.

SUPPORTING PROGRAMS FOR WOMEN AND GIRLS

Of all the charitable dollars given in the United States each year, what percent do you think goes to support programs for women and girls? The answer is: less than 6 percent. The rest goes to general programs or to programs for men and boys. There are several reasons for the discrepancy, which seem to boil down to one: when viewed by foundation program officers, women are seen as a special interest group. "We don't give specifically to women," they may say rightly, "but we do give to arts programs, or health programs, and women are served by them." Yet the "general programs" that are supposed to serve women and girls do so unequally:

In areas such as economic development, health, and violence, many programs are geared toward addressing the needs of men and boys. In a sample of such programs, only 40 of 112 programs actually provided separate time and space for girl participants.[2]

In 1990, the United Way gave the YMCA $39 million more than the YWCA. The Boy Scouts re-

ceived $32 million more than the Girl Scouts from United Way affiliates. Allocations for Boys Clubs (now called Boys and Girls Clubs) and Girls Clubs (now called Girls, Inc.) were seven times greater for boys.[3]

At Big Brother/Big Sister, 75 percent of kids served were boys, in spite of a far greater number of adult female volunteers.[4]

And those in power to make funding decisions overwhelmingly are white males:

Seventy-one percent of foundation board members are male. Ninety-four percent of foundation board members are white. And only 14 percent of foundation CEO's are women, and these women tend to head the smaller foundations.[5]

Twenty-three percent of foundations surveyed had no women or people of color as trustees; only 5 percent of all foundation trustees were women of color.[6]

The *Grants Index*, published by the Foundation Center, tracks allocations made by the largest public foundations. In a typical year, one-third of the foundations make no grants specifically to women or girls. Part of the rationale is that grants often are based on what recipients have been given in the past: because women's programs are underfunded, they continue to be underfunded.

In our community, we have a fast-rising population of "nouveau poor": divorced women and their children.

The lack of support for programs focused on the particular needs of women seems shortsighted, especially since most of the chronic social problems in this country are most severely experienced by women and children. Much new research now is describing this inequity:

The most recent Census Bureau study shows that 45 percent of female-headed households with children are living in poverty. The situation is worse for women of color: 58 percent of Hispanic women who head households and 56 percent of African-American women who head households live in poverty, as do 38 percent of white women.

Nationwide, there are four times more shelters for animals than there are for battered women.

American women spend an average of seventeen years caring for children and eighteen years caring for aging and ill relatives, yet child care and senior programs continue to be woefully inadequate.[7]

WOMEN'S FUNDS: CREATED TO MEET THE NEEDS OF WOMEN AND GIRLS

In the last twenty years or so, there has been a rapidly growing movement in the United States to address the special funding needs of programs serving women and girls. A women's fund combines individual gifts, and gifts from smaller family foundations, as well as corporate gifts, and then disburses grants to programs that help meet the specific needs of women and girls.

Women's funds can be structured in one of several ways: as community foundations, as private foundations, as a federation of member groups, or as designated funds within community or public foundations. Although the funds may differ in structure, and in geographic and programmatic focus, they have much in common with each other. Generally, they involve women in decision making, both in the distribution of funds and in the focus of the organization. They work to increase the number of donors, they seek

to expand opportunities for women and girls, and they tend to support women's empowerment and participation and address discrimination.

A few of the earliest and best-known women's funds are: the Women's Foundation (San Francisco), Women's Way (Philadelphia), the Los Angeles Women's Fund, and the Astraea Foundation (New York).

In addition to making grants for programs and organizations that support women and girls, women's funds may sponsor workshops on a wide variety of topics, operate a "skills bank" available to community women, offer technical assistance, spearhead coalitions among community groups around a common cause, honor women leaders, publish magazines, newsletters, and books, and promote philanthropy among women.

Each foundation has its own focus. Larger foundations make many grants throughout the year to several organizations. Smaller foundations may have a more narrow focus.

The Boston Women's Fund focuses on inner-city women, women of color, differently abled women, long-living women, women who are economically challenged. Not yet fifteen years old, the Boston Women's Fund is relatively small and governed by a multiracial board of women from a range of socioeconomic backgrounds. It makes grants primarily to small grassroot women's organizations, where a grant from the BWF will make a significant difference. Grants from the Boston Women's Fund have started a number of work programs. For example, a grant from the BWF allowed a group of women to buy an oven to start a catering business employing women.

In 1985, some of the existing women's funds joined together to form the National Network of Women's Funds. Network members exchange advice and work together to encourage the creation of new funds. They also work together on special projects. Women's funds have grown from five in 1979 to forty in 1987 to 103 in 2001.

What is the women's fund in your area? What are its priorities? For a list of women's funds in the United States, you can visit the Web site of the Women's Funding Network at www.wfnet.org.

"One of the challenges of women's funds," says former WFN executive director Carol Mollner, "is to educate all women to be donors, to think of themselves as philanthropists, and to plan their giving thoughtfully."[8]

OVERCOMING BARRIERS TO WOMEN'S GIVING

We all are familiar—and fairly comfortable—with the role of women as volunteers. Brownie leaders, den mothers, hospital "pink ladies," Junior League thrift shop managers, library pages, voter registration workers, ESL tutors, phonathon callers, school trip chaperons—and endless bakers of cookies: these are only some of the ways American women have given of themselves throughout the years.

Yet even with countless hours of volunteer work under our belts, we have a hard time thinking of ourselves, and of women, as philanthropists.

In the early part of the twentieth century, "women benefactors such as Anne Morgan, the niece of J. P. Morgan, played an important role during strikes by the International Ladies Garment Workers Union and other women's labor groups." Wealthy women such as Alva Belmont, who purchased the Sewall-Belmont house in Washington, D.C., as headquarters for the National Women's Party, fostered the cause of women's suffrage. Sophia Smith used her resources to create the college for women that bears her name in Northampton, Massachusetts, in 1875. Katherine Dexter McCormick gave "the 2 million dollars necessary for oral contraceptive research when no one else had the courage or vision to do so," making the development of the birth control pill possible.[9] Still, when we think of philanthropists, we do not think of these generous women.

Another barrier to women's giving may be the way we are asked. Women don't necessarily respond well to peer pressure. While men often give because their friend or colleague asked them, or for "one-upmanship," women generally are more interested in building a relationship with an organization. We tend to want more information than most men do.

Women are much more likely to respond to a cause, and not to a person. Tell us why the organization merits our time or our dollars, and if this information resonates with our values and needs, we will give.

Unlike most men, most women will not respond positively to even a close friend who says, "I gave $5,000 to this cause. Why don't you match it?" Instead, most women want to know more about the cause, and about what difference their gift can make to the institution or those it serves.

Many substantial gifts by women are made anonymously. Often, people of means want to support a favorite cause without engendering a lot more requests from other institutions. But women, who rarely put their own names on buildings or programs, tend to want less public recognition than do men.

Although the control of family money is now

shifting toward women, historically many women have felt that since they did not earn the family money, they should have no say in how it was spent or donated. A woman might feel that giving to women's causes could be construed as "unfriendly" to her male partner, rather than as supportive of a cause dear to her heart.

When considering supporting a new charity, women often participate as volunteers before they make a financial contribution to an organization. We often are strongly rooted in our communities, and have both the desire and the influence to help shape them to our satisfaction.

CHARACTERISTICS OF WOMEN'S GIVING

Change

Women give to expedite change rather than to preserve the status quo. Since the nineteenth century, women philanthropists have been creating institutions, such as schools and colleges or galleries and sanitariums, to solve society's problems.

Create

Women donors enjoy setting a creative process in motion with their gifts and watching it unfold. Many of the institutions created by turn-of-the-century women philanthropists have continued to serve long beyond the donors' lifetimes.

Connection

Giving may be just the beginning of a woman donor's relationship with her institution or cause, followed by an increasing commitment to serve and give.

Commitment to volunteerism

For many women, volunteer work precedes a financial gift.

Collaboration

Women generally work effectively with others to solve problems. They enjoy feeling part of a larger effort that helps shape society. In addition, they often form lasting friendships as a result of their involvement.

Celebration

Giving should be fun, with creative giving opportunities and celebrations for campaign kickoffs, wrap-ups, and landmarks in between.[10]

I think we will see a rise in the number of grassroots projects. The future of philanthropy will be in the hands of the mothers who clean up a glass-strewn playground where drug deals now are made so their children can play; in the generosity of those who barely have enough themselves, who drop a dollar in the collection plate to help their church support a needy family; in the dedication of a single mother who loses her home due to divorce and starts an organization to prevent others from losing theirs: these are the women who are making a difference.

THE POTENTIAL POWER OF OUR COLLECTIVE PHILANTHROPY

The world is changing rapidly. The Brownie troops our mothers led have grown up to become wage earners and professional women. Major demographic and economic changes in the lives of women have greatly increased our personal financial status, financial responsibilities, and financial power. With this power comes more responsibility and new leadership.

Consider these facts:

- Eighty-six percent of the wealth in the United States passes through women's hands.[11]

- Because we live an average of seven years longer than men, we also stand to inherit a large portion of the estimated $9 trillion to $10 trillion that will be passed from one generation to the next, during the coming decades.[12]

- In the last decade, women started companies at three times the rate of men. Today, more than 5 million women lead small-to-medium-size growth businesses that will become the top companies of the future. With growth charted at 90 percent in the past decade, women own one-third of all privately held businesses that together employ more people than the *Fortune* 500 companies combined.[13]

- According to *Forbes*, the fifty wealthiest women in America have a combined net worth of $91,875,000,000.

- Women now make up 43 percent of individuals with assets of $500,000 or more. Women make up 35 percent of the country's 51 million shareholders.[14]

Additionally, different sources estimate that between 52 percent and 60 percent of household wealth is now controlled by women. Much of it wasn't earned by women, but it's ours now! This fact has huge implications if we remain relatively uninformed about financial matters. Considering the historical difficulty women have had progressing up through the ranks in corporate America, it would be a shame to waste this opportunity to make our voices heard via financial strength heretofore unavailable.

The "glass ceiling" isn't really a myth to those who are banging their heads on it. As we continue to work for greater opportunities for girls and women in all fields, more women will rise up slowly through the ranks in corporate America and in politics. But there is another route to power to consider. We can continue to work to "crash through" the glass ceiling, or we can go around it—or we can buy the building!

How can we go around the strong invisible barriers that often keep women from adding their voice to the financial and political power structure? When we think carefully about how to give our money away, we can make enormous changes by the collective power of our philanthropy.

> *Don't ever think for a minute that your small gift doesn't matter. It's such a challenge, a mission, to educate ourselves and each other about how powerful we really are when we put our gifts together.*

"Until recently," said Frances K. Moseley, former president and CEO of Boys & Girls Clubs of Boston, "women had not been schooled to view their contribution as an investment. [Now] we women are not fooling around. We've watched how, why, and where the men give and we've learned—money talks—and the more money, the louder the voices and the bigger the impact."[15]

Our advice to you?

Get serious about money. Be determined. Be brave. Keep on learning. Increase your own earning power. Teach your daughters. Remember to turn and give a hand to a woman or girl on her way up.

Women's philanthropy can have far-reaching effects on how our world and the people in it survive and thrive for the next several generations. By taking charge of our own financial lives, by recognizing our responsibility to reach out, to make changes in our lives and in the lives of all women, we can accomplish great things. Remember that the glass ceiling also can be a skylight!

Notes

Tanakh, The Holy Scriptures: The New JPS Translation According to the Traditional Hebrew Text. The Jewish Publication Society, 1985.

CHAPTER 1: CHANGING THE WAY WOMEN THINK ABOUT MONEY

1. Marilyn Waring, *If Women Counted: A New Feminist Economics.* Harper & Row, 1988.
2. Ibid., p. 28.
3. Ibid., p. 27.
4. Nell Giles, *Punch In, Susie!* Harper & Brothers Publishers, 1943.
5. Ibid.
6. Clifford R. Adams, Ph.D., "Making Marriage Work," *Ladies' Home Journal,* June 1950, p. 25.
7. Ibid., p. 26.
8. Marilyn French, *Beyond Power: On Women, Men, and Morals.* Ballantine Books, 1985, p. 16.
9. Anne Wilson Schaef, *Women's Reality: An Emerging Female System in a White Male Society.* Harper & Row, 1981, p. 140.
10. Colette Dowling, *The Cinderella Complex: Women's Hidden Fear of Independence.* Pocket Books, 1990 (reissue).

CHAPTER 4: 'TIL DEATH DO US PART

1. Dee Lee and David Caruso, *Let's Talk Money.* Chandler House Press, 1999.
2. Howard Strong, *What Every Credit Card User Needs to Know.* Henry Holt and Company, 1999.
3. Stacie Zoe Berg, *The Unofficial Guide to Managing Your Personal Finances.* Macmillan, 1999.
4. Strong, op. cit.

CHAPTER 6: INSURANCE

1. Regina Herzlinger, *Market Driven Health Care.* Perseus Books, 1997.
2. Peter J. Strauss and Nancy M. Lederman, *The Elder Law Handbook.* Facts on File, Inc., 1996.
3. Wayne Lacuna, *Health Insurance: Understanding It and Medicare.* Fee Publishing Company, 1992.
4. The Health Insurance Association of America, 1995.
5. Ralph Nader and Wesley Smith, *Winning the Insurance Game.* Knightsbridge Publishing Company, 1990.

CHAPTER 7: MAKING MONEY WORK FOR YOU

1. Source: The National Association of Investors Corporation, 1996.

CHAPTER 9: NEGOTIATION

1. Roger Fisher and William Ury, *Getting to Yes*. Viking Penguin, 1983.
2. Rose Ellen McCaig, *GREAT LIFE! How to Get the Life You REALLY Want*. Publication pending.
3. Pia Mellody, *Facing Codependence*. HarperCollins, 1989.

CHAPTER 10: AROUND THE GLASS CEILING

1. R. P. Hey, "How the Faces of Voluntarism Are Changing in America." *Christian Science Monitor*, December 5, 1988.
2. The Ms. Foundation for Women.
3. The Feminist Majority Foundation.
4. Ibid.
5. The Council on Foundations, 1990.
6. Women and Foundations/Corporate Philanthropy, 1990.
7. The Feminist Majority Foundation.
8. National Council for Research on Women, "Do 'Universal' Dollars Reach Women and Girls? A Special Report," as cited in *Issues Quarterly* 1, no. 2 (1994).
9. The Feminist Majority Foundation.
10. Sondra C. Shaw and Martha A. Taylor, excerpt from "The Six C's of Women's Giving," in *Reinventing Fundraising: Realizing the Potential of Women's Philanthropy*. Jossey-Bass, 1995.
11. Judith Nichols, "Trendwatch, Women Share in the Decision-Making," *Contributions*, March–April 1998.
12. *The Chronicle of Philanthropy*, November 16, 1993.
13. Tamela M. Edwards, "The Power of the Purse," *Time*, May 17, 1999.
14. Nichols, op. cit.
15. Keynote address to Women in Development, December 1996, as cited in *Women in Development of Greater Boston Newsletter*, January 1997.

Resources and Readings

CHAPTER 1: CHANGING THE WAY WOMEN THINK ABOUT MONEY

Books and Other Publications

Simone de Beauvoir, *The Second Sex.* Alfred A. Knopf, 1952, and other writings.

Marilyn French, *Beyond Power: On Women, Men, and Morals.* Ballantine Books, 1985

Betty Friedan, *The Feminine Mystique.* W. W. Norton & Company, 1963, and other writings.

Doris Lessing, *The Golden Notebook.* Ballantine Books, 1962, and other writings.

Adrienne Rich, *Of Woman Born, Motherhood as Experience and Institution.* W. W. Norton, 1995 (reissue).

Anne Wilson Schaef, *Women's Reality: An Emerging Female System in a White Male Society.* Harper & Row, 1981.

Alix Kates Shulman, *Memoirs of an Ex-Prom Queen.* Alfred A. Knopf, 1972, and other writings.

Marilyn Waring, *If Women Counted: A New Feminist Economics.* Harper & Row, 1988.

Virginia Woolf, *A Room of One's Own.* Harcourt Brace, 1990 (reissue), and other writings.

Organizations and Web Sites

www.facstaff.bucknell.edu/jshackel/iaffe/

  "Devoted to all aspects of feminist economics," the International Association for Feminist Economics sponsors conferences and publishes a newsletter.

www.ufenet.org

  United for a Fair Economy: "Inspiring Action to Close the Economic Divide."

CHAPTER 2: WHERE DO YOU WANT TO BE?

Books and Other Publications

Mary Catherine Bateson, *Composing a Life: Life as a Work in Progress.* Penguin, 1990 (reissue).

Richard Nelson Bolles, *What Color Is Your Parachute 2000?* Ten Speed Press, 2000, updated annually.

Julia Cameron, *The Artist's Way: A Spiritual Path to Higher Creativity.* Jeremy P. Tarcher/Putnam, 1992.

Susan Jeffers, *Feel the Fear and Do It Anyway.* Ballantine Books, 1987.

Jennifer Louden, *The Woman's Comfort Book: A Self-Nurturing Guide for Restoring Balance in Your Life.* Harper-SanFrancisco, 1992.

Jennifer Louden, *The Comfort Queen's Guide to Life.* Harmony Books, 2000.

Barbara Sher and Annie Gottlieb, *Wishcraft: How to Get What You Really Want.* Ballantine Books, 1986.

Barbara Sher and Barbara Smith, *I Could Do Anything If I Only Knew What It Was: How to Discover What You Really Want and How to Get It.* Bantam Doubleday Dell, 1995.

Organizations and Web Sites

www.nefe.org/

The National Endowment for Financial Education's mission is to help "all Americans acquire the information and gain the skills necessary to take control of their personal finances." NEFE accomplishes its mission primarily by partnering with other concerned organizations.

www.cfpboard.org

Web site of the Certified Financial Planner Board of Standards. The CFP is a nonprofit organization founded to foster professional standards in the field, and provides information on CFP licensees and the financial planning profession. Consumers can find information on individual planners, and check the status of their license.

www.comfortqueen.com

Web site by Jennifer Louden, author of *The Comfort Queen's Guide to Life* and several other books, offering wonderful tips for women to create balance and explore goals.

www.sba.gov

U.S. Small Business Association's Women's Online Business Center. Personal goal-setting advice offered for women starting businesses, but relevant to all women.

CHAPTER 3: WHERE ARE YOU NOW?

Books and Other Publications

Ronni Eisenberg, *Organize Yourself!* Collier Books, 1986.

Chris Farrell, *Right on the Money: Taking Control of Your Personal Finances.* Villard Books/Random House, 2000.

Julie Morgenstern, *Organization from the Inside Out.* Henry Holt and Company, 1998.

Pipi Campbell Peterson, *Ready, Set, Organize! Get Your Stuff Together: A Workbook for the Organizationally Resistant.* Park Avenue Productions, 1996.

Vicki Robin and Joe Dominguez, *Your Money or Your Life: Transforming Your Relationship with Money and Achieving Financial Independence.* Penguin USA, 1999.

Pam Young and Peggy Jones, *Get Your Act Together: A 7-Day Get-Organized Program for the Overworked, Overbooked, and Overwhelmed.* HarperPerennial, 1993.

Organizations and Web Sites

www.aicpa.org
  American Institute of Certified Public Accountants.

www.ssa.gov
  Social Security Administration, 800-772-1213. You can call to obtain your estimated Social Security benefits.

CHAPTER 4: 'TIL DEATH DO US PART

Books and Other Publications

Stacie Zoe Berg, *The Unofficial Guide to Managing Your Personal Finances.* Macmillan, 1999.
Dee Lee and David Caruso, *Let's Talk Money.* Chandler House Press, 1999.
Rich Mintzer with Kathi Mintzer, *The Everything Money Book.* Adams Media Corp., 1999.
Howard Strong, *What Every Credit Card User Needs to Know.* Henry Holt and Company, 1999.
John Ventura, *The Credit Repair Kit.* Dearborn Financial Publishing, 1993.

Organizations and Web Sites

  The three major credit bureaus are:
  Experian, 800-520-1221, www.experian.com
  Trans Union, 800-916-8800, www.transunion.com
  Equifax, 800-685-1111, www.equifax.com

www.visa.com
www.mastercard.com
  Both credit card companies, Visa and MasterCard, offer much useful information for consumers.

www.cardweb.com
www.myvesta.org
  Web sites with consumer information on credit cards, debt, and related issues.

www.ftc.gov
  The Federal Trade Commission enforces federal statutes and laws and provides consumers with free information. You also can contact your state attorney general and banking commissioner's offices for support and guidance in all credit-related issues.

CHAPTER 5: GETTING THE MOST FOR YOUR MONEY

Buying and Leasing an Automobile

Books and Other Publications

James W. Bragg, *Car Buyer's and Leasor's Negotiating Bible*. Random House, 1999.

Donna Howell, *The Unofficial Guide to Buying or Leasing a Car*. Macmillan, 1998.

Pique Lyle, *How to Buy a Car Without Getting Ripped Off*. Adams Media Corporation, 1999.

Ron Raisglid, *Buying and Leasing Cars on the Internet*. Renaissance Books, 1998.

Editor of Consumer Reports, *Consumer Reports 2001 New Car Buying Guide*. Consumer Reports Books, published annually.

Editor of Consumer Reports, *Consumer Reports 2001 Used Car Buying Guide*. Consumer Reports Books, published annually.

Organizations and Web Sites

www.carbuyer.com

www.autobuyer.com

And a host of other Web sites provide comparative cost information, where to find best buy, etc. Use keywords: "car buying."

Education Planning

Books and Other Publications

Richard Black, *The Complete Family Guide to College Financial Aid*. Perigee, 1995.

Kristin Davis, *Financing College*. Kiplinger Books, 1998.

Guide to Cooperative Education, National Commission of Cooperative Education, 360 Huntington Avenue, Boston, MA 02115 (free), 1997.

Meeting College Costs, The College Board, P.O. Box 886, New York, NY 10101 (free), 2000.

Anne Stockwell, *The Guerrilla Guide to Mastering Student Loan Debt*. HarperCollins, 1997.

Organizations and Web Sites

www.ed.gov

U.S. Department of Education site offers a wealth of information, including the *Student Guide to Financial Aid,* and lists Internet resources for parents and students.

www.octameron.com

Octameron Associates publishes a number of very useful and inexpensive pamphlets and books on student aid and college admissions.

www.collegeboard.org

www.act.org

Creators of college admissions tests offer information on the college admissions process and on aid applications.

www.americanlegion.org

For more information on military/veteran benefits, including booklet, *Need-A-Lift?* American Legion, P.O. Box 1050, Indianapolis, IN 46206.

The telephone number for inquiries on the major federal student aid programs is 800-4-FED-AID.

www.educaid.com

site of Educaid: The Student Loan Specialists.

www.finaid.org

Financial aid information page.

www.nelliemae.com

www.salliemae.com

Student loan problems, offers payment estimator.

www.fastweb.com

A database of more than 400,000 scholarships.

For information on college programs for adult women, use keywords "continuing education for women."

Home Buying

Books and Other Publications

Julie Garton-Good, *All About Mortgages: Insider Tips to Finance the Home.* Dearborn, 1994.
Ilyce Glink, *10 Steps to Home Ownership: A Workbook for First-Time Buyers.* Times Books, 1996.
Eric Tyson and Ray Brown, *Home Buying for Dummies.* IDG Books Worldwide, 1999.

Organizations and Web Sites

www.hud.gov

Federal Housing Authority provides mortgage insurance to those not served by private insurance, including women. Web site has much useful information for first-time home buyers.

www.realtor.com

National Association of Realtors provides useful information for home buyers, and publishes weekly newsletter, *The Voice for Real Estate.*

www.fanniemae.com

Fannie Mae provides "financial products and services that make it possible for low-, moderate- and middle-income families to buy homes." The National Housing Impact Division offers *A Guide to Home Ownership.* Write to: 3900 Wisconsin Avenue, N.W., Washington, D.C. 20016-2899.

www.homeadviser.msn.com

> Site showcasing homes for sale nationwide, including links to find the estimated value of your home, based on comparable home prices in your neighborhood.

Homehold: Single-Parent Resource is a nonprofit organization in Greater Boston that devised Shared Hearth apartments, a housing model that subtly modifies floor plans of apartments in a two-family house where units are thirteen hundred or more square feet, in order to accommodate four single parents or other small families so families can live independently. Families may rent or purchase units. Contact: 781-646-1329.

www.nlihc.org

> National Low Income Housing Coalition, 1012 Fourteenth Street N.W., Suite 1200, Washington, D.C. 20005, 202-662-1530. Established in 1974, the National Low Income Housing Coalition is the only national organization dedicated solely to ending America's affordable housing crisis. It is committed to educating, organizing, and advocating to ensure decent, affordable housing within healthy neighborhoods for everyone. The organization provides up-to-date information, formulates policy, and educates the public on housing needs and the strategies for solutions.

CHAPTER 6: INSURANCE

Books and Other Publications

Janet Bamford, *Smarter Insurance Solutions*. Bamberg Press, 1996.

Harley Gordon, *How to Protect Your Life Savings from Catastrophic Illness and Nursing Homes*. Senior Planning Group Publications, 1995.

Sheryl Lilke, ed., *Understanding Homeowners Insurance*. Dearborn Financial Publishing, 1994.

Ralph Nader and Wesley Smith, *Winning the Insurance Game*. Knightsbridge Publishing Company, 1990.

Peter J. Strauss and Nancy M. Lederman, *The Elder Law Handbook*. Facts on File, Inc., 1996.

Organizations and Web Sites

www.insweb.com

> "A free service that lets you compare insurance quotes from leading insurance companies to find best rates" for auto, home, and other types of insurance.

www.insure.com

> Lists and gives information on all insurance companies.

www.moodys.com

> Web site of Moody's Investors Service, the leading provider of information on "credit ratings, research and financial information to the capital markets."

www.iii.org

> Insurance Information Institute was established by the insurance industry to promote consumer education. 100 William Street, New York, NY 10038, 800-221-4954.

National Insurance Consumer Organization is a nonprofit organization that provides assistance to and is an advocate for insurance customers. 121 North Payne Street, Alexandria, VA 22314, 703-549-8050.

Medical Information Bureau

This bureau keeps information about your health for insurers. (NOTE: They will not release information directly to you but will furnish it to your doctor if you request it. Send your name, Social Security number, your doctor's name and address, and your signed personal request.) P.O. Box 105, Essex Station, Boston, MA 02112.

www.consumerreports.org

Consumer Reports magazine compares and contrasts types of insurance and insurance companies.

Committee for National Health. This national health organization promotes a national health insurance plan that would be a combination of state, federal, and private involvement. 1757 N Street, N.W., Washington, D.C., 20036, 202-223-9685.

www.hhs.gov

Department of Health and Human Services offers government health news, notably on choosing health care, Medicare. Cosponsor with Public Health Service of the National Women's Health Information Center.

CHAPTER 7: MAKING MONEY WORK FOR YOU

Books and Other Publications

Jonathan Clements, *25 Myths You've Got to Avoid—If You Want to Manage Your Money Right.* Simon & Schuster, 1999.

Mary Farrell, *Mary Farrell's Beyond the Basics: How to Invest Your Money, Now That You Know a Thing or Two.* Simon & Schuster, 2000.

David Gardner and Tom Gardner, *The Motley Fool Investment Guide,* completely revised and expanded. Fireside, 2001.

Peter Lynch and John Rothchild, *Learn to Earn: A Beginner's Guide to the Basics of Investing and Business.* Fireside, 1995.

Thomas E. O'Hara and Kenneth S. Janke, Sr., *Starting and Running a Profitable Investment Club.* Times Business/Random House, 1996.

Andrew Tobias, *The Only Investment Guide You'll Ever Need.* Harcourt Brace & Co., 1996.

Organizations and Web Sites

www.micropal.com

Standard and Poor's Micropal is "acknowledged as an international leader in the provision of fund information, monitoring over 38,000 funds across the globe on a daily, weekly and monthly basis."

www.valueline.com

Value Line publishes *The Value Line Investment Survey*, "the world's most widely read investment information service."

www.wsj.com

The Wall Street Journal is a daily newspaper that focuses on business and financial topics.

www.aaii.com

American Association of Individual Investors.

www.vanguard.com

Mutual fund company offers tools to learn about investing, creating a personal financial plan, and retirement planning.

www.berkshirehathaway.com

Website for Warren Buffett's company offers useful information on investments.

www.morningstar.com

Morningstar is "the leading provider of mutual fund, stock and variable-annuity investment information." Morningstar does not own, operate, or hold any interest in mutual funds, stocks, or insurance products, and thus provides unbiased data and analysis.

www.socialinvest.org

The Social Investment Forum site offers "comprehensive information, contacts and resources on socially responsible investing."

www.better-investing.org

Site of the National Association of Investment Clubs. NAIC is a nonprofit organization "whose membership consists of investment clubs and individual investors" to "provide sound investment information, education and support to help create successful, lifetime investors."

www.napfa.org

National association of fee-only financial planners.

CHAPTER 8: PLANNING FOR LONG-LIVING WOMEN

Books and Other Publications

Christine Cassel, ed., *The Practical Guide to Aging: What Everyone Needs to Know.* New York University Press, 1999.

Joseph Cassilli and Paul Winn, *Tax Planning from the Heart: How to Increase Income, Reduce Taxes, and Help Your Favorite Charity.* Ten Speed Press, 1999.

Elmwood Chapman and Marion Haynes, *Comfort Zones: Planning Your Future.* Crisp Publications, 1997.

Denis Clifford and Cora Jordan, *Plan Your Estate: Absolutely Everything You Need to Know to Protect Your Loved Ones,* 4th ed. Nolo Press, 1998.

Guild A. Fetridge, *The Adventure of Retirement: It's About More Than Just Money.* Prometheus Books, 1993.

Keith E. Gregg, *Do Well by Doing Good: The Complete Guide to Charitable Remainder Trusts.* Bonus Books, 1996.

Marion E. Haynes, *From Work to Retirement.* Crisp Publications, 1993.

Sandy F. Kramer, *60 Minute Estate Planner.* Prentice Hall Press, 1999.

Robert K. Otterbourg, *Kiplinger's Retire & Thrive*, 2nd ed. Kiplinger Books, 1999.

Zalman Schachter-Shamomi, *From Age-ing to Sage-ing®: A Profound New Vision of Growing Older.* Warner Books, 1997.

Vickie Schumacher and Jim Schumacher, *Understanding Living Trusts: How You Can Avoid Probate, Save Taxes, and Enjoy Peace of Mind.* Schumacher & Co., 1999.

Diana Laskin Siegal, Paula Brown Doress-Worters, and Wendy Sanford, *The New Ourselves Growing Older.* Touchstone, 1994.

Peter J. Strauss and Nancy M. Lederman, *The Elder Law Handbook: A Legal and Financial Survival Guide for Caregivers and Seniors.* Checkmark Books, 1996.

Ginita Wall and Victoria Collins, *Your Next Fifty Years: A Completely New Way to Look at How, When and If You Should Retire.* Owlet Press, 1997.

Stuart H. Welch, *J. K. Lasser's Estate Planning for Baby Boomers and Retirees: A Comprehensive Guide to Estate Planning.* IDG Books Worldwide, 1998.

Organizations and Web Sites

www.elderweb.com

"Oldest and largest eldercare sourcebook on the Web for professionals, family members." Elderweb has thousands of links to articles, legal, financial, medical, housing policy information, and research on elder care and long-term care.

www.aarp.org

American Association of Retired Persons (AARP) is the nation's "leading voice for addressing the needs of Americans older than 50." 601 E Street N.W., Washington, D.C. 20049, 800-424-3410 or 202-434-2230.

www.ncoa.org

National Council on Aging's Web site provides policy updates on issues such as Medicare and the Older Americans Act, and job opportunities.

www.elderhostel.org

Elderhostel, Inc., is a not-for-profit organization with twenty-five years of experience providing high-quality, affordable, educational adventures for adults who are fifty-five and older. 75 Federal Street, Boston, MA 02110, 877-426-8056.

Older Women's League, 666 Eleventh Street, N.W., Suite 700, Washington, D.C. 20001, 800-825-3695 or 202-783-6686.

www.hfp.heinz.org/initiative/index.html

A project of the Teresa and H. John Heinz III Foundation, The Women's Retirement Initiative's goal is to "raise the profile of critical issues relating to pensions and retirement savings for women."

www.efn.org/~radham/senior.htm

Resources for Active Seniors. Information on senior communities, magazines and articles, chat rooms, and links to hundreds of sites.

CHAPTER 9: NEGOTIATION

Books and Other Publications

Melody Beattie, *Codependent No More: How to Stop Controlling Others and Start Caring for Yourself.* Hazeldon Publishing Group, 1996.

Robert M. Bramson, *Coping with Difficult People.* Bantam Doubleday Dell, 1981.

Patti Breitman and Connie Hatch, *How to Say No Without Feeling Guilty.* Broadway Books, 2000.

Joel Edelman and Mary Beth Crain, *The Tao of Negotiation: How You Can Prevent, Resolve, and Transcend Conflict in Work and Everyday Life.* HarperBusiness, 1994.

Suzette Haden Elgin, *The Gentle Art of Verbal Self-Defense.* Barnes & Noble Books, 1980.

Roger Fisher and William Ury, *Getting to Yes: Negotiating Agreement Without Giving In.* Penguin USA, 1991.

Pia Mellody, *Facing Codependence: What It Is, Where It Comes From, How It Sabotages Our Lives.* HarperSanFrancisco, 1989.

Organizations and Web Sites

www.law.harvard.edu/Programs/PON
   Program on Negotiation at Harvard Law School maintains a clearinghouse of negotiation information and materials.

www.quintcareers.com
   Quintessential Careers offers job seekers helpful tips on job and salary negotiations.

CHAPTER 10: AROUND THE GLASS CEILING

Books and Other Publications

Chuck Collins and Pam Rogers with Joan P. Garner, *Robin Hood Was Right: A Guide to Giving Your Money for Social Change.* W. W. Norton & Company, 2000.

Tracy Gary, Melissa Kohner, and Nancy Adess, *Inspired Philanthropy.* Chardon Press, 1998.

Douglas M. Lawson, *More Give to Live: How Giving Can Change Your Life.* Alti Publishing, 1999.

Renata J. Rafferty and Paul Newman, *Don't Just Give It Away: How to Make the Most of Your Charitable Giving.* Chandler House Press, 1999.

Claude Rosenberg, Jr., *Wealthy and Wise: How You and America Can Get the Most Out of Your Giving.* Little Brown & Company, 1999.

Sondra C. Shaw and Martha Taylor, *Reinventing Fundraising: Realizing the Potential of Women's Philanthropy.* Jossey-Bass Nonprofit Sector, 1995.

Organizations and Web Sites

www.give.org

The National Charities Information Bureau is a nonprofit organization that "promotes informed giving to enable more contributors to make sound giving decisions." Lists information on four hundred charities, and offers *Wise Giving Guide* and *Tips for Giving*.

www.guidestar.org

GuideStar is a database of more than 640,000 nonprofits.

www.efn.org/~impact/

The Impact Project exists "to support people with wealth to significantly contribute their money and talents toward creating a more sustainable and just world." Offers workshops, individual money counseling, literature, journal *More Than Money*.

http://inheritance-project.com/home.html

The Inheritance Project "explores the emotional and social impact of inherited wealth," offers publications and services.

www.ncfp.org

The National Center for Family Philanthropy "encourages individuals and families to create and sustain their philanthropic missions." Offers access to research, small seminars, and other programs and publications.

www.womenphil.org

Women & Philanthropy is a Washington, D.C.– based organization of three-hundred-plus grant makers and others "mobilizing the resources of the philanthropic community to achieve equality for women and girls."

www.wfnet.org

Women's Funding Network is "a growing international association of women's funds, donors and allies around the world committed to social justice, to ensure that women's funds are recognized as the 'investment of choice' for people who value the full participation of women and girls as key to strong, equitable and sustainable communities and societies."

www.women-philanthropy.org

Women's Philanthropy Institute "educates and advances women as major donors and volunteer leaders," and believes that all women should have the knowledge and ability to make individual and collective philanthropic choices wherever they see the need.

GENERAL READINGS

Ginger Applegarth, *Wake Up and Smell the Money: Fresh Starts at Any Age and Any Season of Your Life*. Viking Penguin, 1999.

Chuck Collins, Betsy Leondar-Wright, and Holly Sklar, *Shifting Fortunes: The Perils of the Growing American Wealth Gap*. United for a Fair Economy, 1999.

Annette Lieberman and Vicki Lindner, *The Money Mirror: How Money Reflects Women's Dreams, Fears, and Desires.* Allworth Press, 1996.

Olivia Mellan, *Money Harmony: Resolving Money Conflicts in Your Life and Relationships.* Walker Publishing Company, 1994.

Georgette Mosbacher, *It Takes Money, Honey: A Get-Smart Guide to Total Financial Freedom.* HarperCollins, 1999.

Stephan M. Rosenberg and Ann Z. Peterson, *Every Woman's Guide to Financial Security.* Capital Publishing, 1994.

Barbara Stanny, *Prince Charming Isn't Coming: How Women Get Smart About Money.* Penguin Books, 1999.

Contributing Authors

Jill Zupan Adomaitis brings more than twenty-five years of experience teaching and counseling in the health and fitness field to her position as a representative at Bankers Life and Casualty Company. A strong advocate for seniors, she offers a personally tailored, educational approach to help her clients best meet their insurance needs, specifically in the areas of long-term-care planning and asset preservation. A magna cum laude graduate of the University of South Carolina, Jill lives in Framingham, Massachusetts, with her husband and their two daughters. Contact: Bankers Life and Casualty Company, 125 Newbury Street, Framingham, MA 01701, 508-820-8301, ext. 235; 800-492-0900, ext. 235.

Adelaide Aitken is a certified financial planner and an investment advisory representative of Jefferson Pilot Securities. Her particular interests include educational and retirement planning, charitable giving, and the special financial concerns of women. A former teacher and an alumna of Wellesley College and the London School of Economics, Ms. Aitken is actively involved with her church and has served on the boards of several nonprofit organizations. She lives with her husband and their two sons in Cambridge, Massachusetts. She can be reached at the Hamilton Group, 185 Mount Auburn Street, Cambridge, MA 02138, 617-876-9400.

Rachel Barenblat is editor of *The Women's Times,* a pair of monthly newspapers published in western Massachusetts; her contribution to the retirement chapter of this book originally appeared in *The Women's Times.* She is also associate poetry editor at *Pif Magazine* (www.pifmagazine.com). She has an MFA from the Bennington Writing Seminars, and is at work on a collection of poems; her poetry has appeared in *The Portland Review, Confrontation,* and *The Jewish Women's Literary Annual,* among others. When not writing, she enjoys baking bread, gardening, and playing with her cat. For more information, visit www.rachelbarenblat.com.

Katharine M. Berlin, J.D., is a cum laude graduate of Boston College Law School and is associated with the law office of Leslie S. Madge in Littleton, Massachusetts. Her areas of legal practice include: elder law, estate planning, real estate, and Medicaid eligibility. A member of the Massachusetts Bar Association and the Women's Bar Association, Ms. Berlin serves on the board of directors of Womankind Educational and Resource Center, Inc.

Nancy A. Haverstock, C.F.R.E., has more than twenty years' experience in institutional advancement, and currently is chief development officer at the New England College of Optometry. Ms. Haverstock has been a consultant to numerous nonprofit organizations. She has been a guest lecturer for CASE/NAIS, the National Society of Fund Raising Executives, and has taught "Fundraising and Development" at the graduate-school level. She received her B.S. from Indiana State University and M.S. from Emerson College, and serves on the Womankind board of directors.

Nadine Heaps has been in the insurance industry for sixteen years. Currently, she is an agent for Anderson Insurance, and offers personalized insurance for individuals, families, and small businesses. Guided by a philosophy of "giving back," she participates regularly and enthusiastically in many community and charitable events, and in promoting philanthropy. A regular speaker for Womankind's Financial Literacy Project, Nadine lives with her husband and children in Ashland, Massachusetts. She can be reached at Anderson Insurance, 15 Alden Street, Ashland, MA 01721, 508-881-6680.

Karin Hedberg has twenty years' experience with financial products and services, and is an investment associate for Lantern Investment Services, located at Sovereign Bank New England. She contributed to the development and implementation of the Financial Literacy Project, and is a facilitator as well as a presenter. Formerly a consultant in Silver Spring, Maryland, where her activities included development, marketing, and sales of financial products for several banks and financial institutions, Karin also assisted in the development of presentations for consulting, investment, and venture-capital companies. Contact her at Karin L. Hedberg Company in Watertown, Massachusetts, 617-923-7770.

Barbara Honthumb is an artist who supports herself and her family by providing business development and managed care services for health systems. Prior to entering the health care field, Ms. Honthumb was executive director of WEGO, a nonprofit, micro-enterprise-development project that helped low- and moderate-income women achieve financial self-sufficiency through owning their own businesses. She is a single parent with two young adult children, and remains actively committed to helping women learn the skills they need to be financially independent. Passions include gardening, old home rehab, and sailing.

Jennifer Lane is principal of Compass Planning Associates, a fee-only financial planning firm in Stow, Massachusetts. She founded the company to provide retirement and investment planning to small and medium-size businesses as well as individuals. Ms. Lane, a former pilot and training executive, has taught university classes ranging from aeronautics and flight theory to economics and algebra. She's a certified financial planner and a registered investment adviser. Jennifer cohosts a weekly radio show called *MoneyWise*, which airs Sunday mornings on *Personal Finance Radio* AM1120. She can be reached at 978-897-9993 or by e-mail at jennifer@compassplanning.com. Her company Web site is www.compassplanning.com.

Leslie Sleeper Madge was a managing partner in the family law firm Sleeper & Sleeper Attorneys, and now has her own practice in Littleton, Massachusetts. She is certified as an expert in elder law by the National Elder Law Foundation, and was president of the Massachusetts chapter of the National Academy of Elder Law Attorneys. She regularly speaks to professional organizations and has appeared on cable TV, radio shows, and in the print media, notably through her newspaper column, *Legally Speaking*. She can be reached at her office at 36 Spartan Arrow Road, Littleton, MA 10460, 978-486-9749.

Attorney **Rose Ellen McCaig**'s law offices concentrate in the areas of family and alternate family law, mediation, negotiation, litigation, real estate, contracts, and business transactions. She also created GREAT LIFE!, a result-oriented counseling program to "get the life you REALLY want." Attorney McCaig graduated from Boston College Law School and lives in Newton, Massachusetts, with her husband. Contact: Kohn-McCaig Law Offices at 617-527-4970.

Jill Mirak retired after ten years as general manager and vice president of Mirak Lincoln-Mercury, Nissan, Inc., in Arlington, Massachusetts. She holds a B.A. from Wellesley College, an M.B.A. from Babson College, and currently is vice president of Mirak Properties, a real estate management and development company based in Arlington. She can be reached at 781-641-2495.

Paula Mogan, a certified financial planner with more than eighteen years' experience in the financial services industry, is a vice president, financial consultant with Merrill Lynch. Along with business partner Janet Marcantonio, she formed the high-net-worth team at Merrill's Providence, Rhode Island, office. The team provides comprehensive financial planning and investment management services to corporate executives, business owners, entrepreneurs, and families with multigenerational wealth. They also work with and offer seminars for women in transition. Paula is a speaker for Womankind's Financial Literacy Project and can be reached at: Merrill Lynch, One Citizen's Plaza, Suite 1000, Providence, RI 02903, 800-897-6985, 401-863-8722, or pmogan@pclient.ml.com.

Margery L. Piercey, a C.P.A. with more than sixteen years' experience in public accounting and private industry, brings her assurance and business advisory skills to clients of PricewaterhouseCoopers' Middle Market Advisory Services practice. She is a member of the American Institute of CPAs, has been an active member of the Massachusetts Society of CPAs, where she served as an officer of the board of directors and on various committees, and also long has been with the United Way of Tri-County, where she has chaired the finance and executive committees of the board of directors. Margery has been a regular speaker for Womankind's Financial Literacy Project since the pilot class.

Nanci Pisani has been involved in consumer and business solutions for more than eighteen years. For most of her tenure at Community National Bank, she headed the Consumer Loan Division, which included the originations, collections, and asset management of a $72 million loan portfolio. She recently left the banking industry and is an executive consultant working in business development at CGI Information Systems and Management Consultants, Inc., for the financial services industry. Nanci has been a regular Financial Literacy Project speaker since the pilot class. She can be reached at CGI-USA, 600 Federal Street, Andover, MA 01810, 978-946-3234.

Maureen Reilly, based in Wellesley, Massachusetts, has been a mortgage originator for more than eleven years. She works closely with both real estate agents and home buyers. She gives First Time Home Buyers Seminars and workshops for real estate agents to keep them up to date on mortgages and mortgage products. Maureen has been a regular speaker for the Financial Literacy Project since the pilot class, and can be contacted at: Mortgage Network, 44 Washington Street, Wellesley, MA 02481, 781-239-0090.

Gail R. Shapiro is a principal of Cataldo & Shapiro, a consulting firm specializing in grant writing and consulting to nonprofit organizations. She is the founder and executive director of Womankind Educational and Resource Center, Inc., and cocreator of Womankind's Financial Literacy Project. Ms. Shapiro teaches and lectures on grant writing, strategic planning, philanthropy, women's economic empowerment, home-based businesses, meeting planning, and organizational skills. She holds a B.A. from Framingham State College and an Ed.M. from Harvard University. She can be reached via e-mail at Womankind wkerc@ziplink.net.

Maxine Wolin, A.B.R., C.R.S., G.R.I., has been a Realtor in Tucson for more than twenty years and is an associate broker with Long Realty Company, Foothills Office. She has moved from coast to coast and sold real estate in five different states while raising a son, a daughter, and two dogs! A President's Club member, she has sold and listed properties in all price ranges. Her interests in community arts, sports, and golf facilities are an advantage when helping someone transfer to Tucson. Contact her at: Long Realty Company, 5683 North Swan Road, Tucson, AZ 85718, 520-299-2201 or 800-843-4291, or at maxlin@longrealty.com.

INDEX